CLEP® SPANISH LANGUAGE

Viviana Gyori, M.A.

AP Spanish Teacher
Waubonsie Valley High School
Aurora, IL

April Schneider, M.E.

Spanish Teacher
Elkhart Central High School
Elkhart, IN

 Research & Education Association
www.rea.com

Research & Education Association
258 Prospect Plains Road
Cranbury, New Jersey 08512
Email: info@rea.com

CLEP® Spanish Language with Online Practice Exams

Published 2021
Copyright © 2013 by Research & Education Association.
Prior editions copyright © 2007, 2003, 2002, 1999 by Research &
Education Association. All rights reserved. No part of this book may
be reproduced in any form without permission of the publisher.

Printed in the United States of America

Library of Congress Control Number 2012953515

ISBN-13: 978-0-7386-1089-4
ISBN-10: 0-7386-1089-5

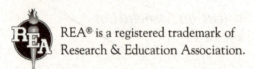

CONTENTS

About the Authors vi
About REA vi

CHAPTER 1
Passing the CLEP Spanish Language Exam 1

Getting Started 3
The REA Study Center 4
An Overview of the Exam 5
All About the CLEP Program 6
Options for Military Personnel and Veterans 8
SSD Accommodations for Candidates with Disabilities 8
6-Week Study Plan 9
Test-Taking Tips 9
The Day of the Exam 10

CHAPTER 2
CLEP Spanish Review 11

The Alphabet 13
Rules for Stress in Spanish 15
Syllabic Division 17
Articles 17
Gender 22
Number 25
Adjectives 26
Comparison of Adjectives and Adverbs 29
Present Indicative 40
Preterite and Imperfect 43
Future and Conditional 51
Formation of Compound Tenses 63
The Present Participle 67
Reflexive Pronouns 69
The Infinitive 78

Formation of the Subjunctive 82

Commands: Formal and Familiar 85

The Subjunctive–Uses 91

Conjugation of *Ser* 109

Conjugation of *Estar* 110

Pronouns 117

Subject Pronouns 117

Object Pronouns 118

Idioms with *A, De, En, Sin* 127

Verbs with Prepositions 130

Conjunctions 134

Gustar 145

Demonstratives: Adjectives/Pronouns 150

Neuter Forms 150

Relative Pronouns 155

Affirmatives and Negatives 161

Interrogatives 168

The Personal *A* 175

Possessives: Adjectives/Pronouns 176

The Passive Voice 182

Measures of Time 188

Telling Time 189

Hacer with Expressions of Time 191

Age 192

Weather Expressions 192

Cardinal and Ordinal Forms of Numerals 193

Dates 196

Arithmetic Signs 197

Collective Numerals 197

Fractions 198

Vocabulary/Idioms 202

Practice Test 1 (also available online at *www.rea.com/studycenter*) **221**

Answer Key 255

Detailed Explanations of Answers 256

Practice Test 2 (also available online at *www.rea.com/studycenter*) **279**
  Answer Key 315
  Detailed Explanations of Answers....................................... 316

CLEP Transcripts: Test 1
  Listening Section I.. 339
  Listening Section II 343

CLEP Transcripts: Test 2
  Listening Section I.. 349
  Listening Section II 353

Answer Sheets.. **359**

ABOUT THE AUTHORS

Viviana Gyori, **M.A.**, teaches AP Spanish at Waubonsie Valley High School, Aurora, Illinois, and is an AP Spanish Language exam grader. She has been nominated for the most influential teacher in the Indian Prairie Awards for three years.

April Schneider, **M.Ed.**, teaches Spanish and is the World Language Department Chair at Elkhart Central High School, Elkhart, Indiana. She is also editor of *Forever My Lady*, a novel by Jeff Rivera.

ABOUT REA

Founded in 1959, Research & Education Association (REA) is dedicated to publishing the finest and most effective educational materials—including study guides and test preps—for students of all ages.

Today, REA's wide-ranging catalog is a leading resource for students, teachers, and other professionals. Visit *www.rea.com* to see a complete list of all our titles.

ACKNOWLEDGMENTS

We would like to thank Pam Weston, Publisher, for setting the quality standards for production integrity and managing the publication to completion; John Paul Cording, Technology Director, for coordinating the design and development of the REA Study Center; Larry B. Kling, Editorial Director, for overall direction; Diane Goldschmidt, Managing Editor, for coordinating development of this edition; Transcend Creative Services for typesetting this edition; and Jennifer Calhoun for file prep.

CHAPTER 1

Passing the CLEP Spanish Language Exam

PASSING THE CLEP SPANISH LANGUAGE EXAM

Congratulations! You're joining the millions of people who have discovered the value and educational advantage offered by the College Board's College-Level Examination Program, or CLEP. This test prep focuses on what you need to know to succeed on the CLEP Spanish Language exam, and will help you earn the college credit you deserve while reducing your tuition costs.

GETTING STARTED

There are many different ways to prepare for a CLEP exam. What's best for you depends on how much time you have to study and how comfortable you are with the subject matter. To score your highest, you need a system that can be customized to fit you: your schedule, your learning style, and your current level of knowledge.

This book, and the online tools that come with it, allow you to create a personalized study plan through three simple steps: assessment of your knowledge, targeted review of exam content, and reinforcement in the areas where you need the most help.

Let's get started and see how this system works.

Test Yourself and Get Feedback	Assess your strengths and weaknesses. Take Practice Test 1 as a diagnostic exam. Your score report gives you a fast way to pinpoint what you already know and where you need to spend more time studying.
Review with the Book	Armed with your diagnostic score report, review the parts of the book where you're weak and study the answer explanations for the test questions you answered incorrectly.
Ensure You're Ready for Test Day	After you've finished reviewing with the book, take Practice Test 2. Review your score report and re-study any topics you missed. We give you two full-length practice tests to ensure you're confident and ready for test day.

THE REA STUDY CENTER

The best way to personalize your study plan is to get feedback on what you know and what you don't know. At the online REA Study Center (*www.rea.com/studycenter*), you can access two full-length practice exams. These tests provide true-to-format questions and deliver a detailed score report that follows the topics set by the College Board.

Diagnostic Exam

Before you begin your review with the book, take the online diagnostic exam. Use your score report to help evaluate your overall understanding of the subject, so you can focus your study on the topics where you need the most review.

Full-Length Practice Exams

Our full-length practice tests give you the most complete picture of your strengths and weaknesses. After you've finished reviewing with the book, test what you've learned by taking the first of the two online practice exams. Review your score report, then go back and study any topics you missed. Take the second practice test to ensure you have mastered the material and are ready for test day.

If you're studying and don't have internet access, you can take the printed tests in the book. These are the same practice tests offered at the REA Study

Center, but without the added benefits of timed testing conditions and diagnostic score reports. Because the actual exam is internet-based, we recommend you take at least one practice test online to simulate test-day conditions.

Both practice tests are accompanied with audio for the listening portions of the exam. When you take our online practice tests, the audio is conveniently integrated for you. If, however, you take the printed tests, the audio files are available for download at the REA Study Center. Register at *www.rea.com/studycenter*, and enter your access code found on the inside front cover of this book for the online practice tests and downloadable audio files.

AN OVERVIEW OF THE EXAM

The CLEP Spanish Language exam consists of approximately 120 multiple-choice questions, each with four possible answer choices, to be answered in three separately timed sections. You will be allotted a total of approximately 30 minutes for the Listening portion of the test (which comprises Sections I and II) and 60 minutes for the Reading portion of the test (which comprises Section III).

The exam assumes you'll have a level of mastery that would equate to skills normally achieved during two to four semesters of college-level work. The exam tests basic vocabulary and word usage, as well as the ability to understand oral and written Spanish.

The approximate breakdown of the exam is as follows:

Section I (15%)—Listening: Rejoinders

Section II (25%)—Listening: Dialogues and narratives

Section III (60%)—Reading

    Part A (16%): Discrete sentences (vocabulary and structure)

    Part B (20%): Short cloze passages (vocabulary and structure)

    Part C (24%): Reading passages and authentic stimulus materials (reading comprehension)

CLEP and technology-enhanced questions

While most of the questions you will find on your CLEP exam will be standard multiple-choice questions, the College Board is now incorporating some technology-enhanced questions. These new question types include: filling in a numeric answer; shading areas of an object; or putting items in the correct order. In addition, several exams now have an optional essay section.

If you're familiar with basic computer skills, you'll have no trouble handling these question types if you encounter them on your exam.

ALL ABOUT THE CLEP PROGRAM

What is CLEP?

More adult learners use CLEP than any other credit-by-examination program in the United States. The CLEP program's 34 exams span five subject areas. The exams assess the material commonly required in an introductory-level college course. Based on recommendations from the American Council on Education, a passing score can earn you at least three credits per exam at more than 2,900 colleges and universities in the U.S. and abroad. Policies vary, so check with your school on the exams it accepts and the scores it requires. For a complete list of the CLEP subject examinations offered, visit the College Board website: *clep.org*.

Who takes CLEP exams?

CLEP exams are typically taken by people who have acquired knowledge outside the classroom and wish to bypass certain college courses and earn college credit. The CLEP program is designed to reward examinees for prior learning—no matter where or how that knowledge was acquired.

CLEP appeals to a wide spectrum of candidates, including home-schooled and high school students, adults returning to college, traditional-age college students, military personnel, veterans, and international students. There are no prerequisites, such as age or educational status, for taking CLEP examinations. However, because policies on granting credits vary among colleges, you should contact the particular institution from which you wish to receive CLEP credit.

How is my CLEP score determined?

Your CLEP score is based on two calculations. First, your CLEP raw score is figured; this is just the total number of test items you answer correctly. After the test is administered, your raw score is converted to a scaled score through a process called *equating*. Equating adjusts for minor variations in difficulty across test forms and among test items, and ensures that your score accurately represents your performance on the exam regardless of when or where you take it, or on how well others perform on the same test form.

Your scaled score is the number your college will use to determine if you've performed well enough to earn college credit. Scaled scores for the CLEP exams are delivered on a 20–80 scale. Institutions can set their own scores for granting college credit, but a good passing estimate (based on recommendations from the American Council on Education) is generally a scaled score of 50, which usually requires getting roughly 66% of the questions correct.

For more information on scoring, contact the institution where you wish to be awarded the credit.

Who administers the exam?

CLEP exams are developed by the College Board, administered by Educational Testing Service (ETS), and involve the assistance of educators from throughout the United States. The test development process is designed and implemented to ensure that the content and difficulty level of the test are appropriate.

When and where is the exam given?

CLEP exams are administered year-round at more than 2,000 test centers in the United States and abroad. To find the test center nearest you and to register for the exam, contact the CLEP Program:

CLEP Services
P.O. Box 6600
Princeton, NJ 08541-6600
Phone: (800) 257-9558 (8 a.m. to 6 p.m. ET)
Fax: (610) 628-3726
Website: *clep.org*

The CLEP iBT Platform

To improve the testing experience for both institutions and test-takers, the College Board's CLEP Program has transitioned its 34 exams from the eCBT platform to an internet-based testing (iBT) platform. All CLEP test-takers may now register for exams and manage their personal account information through the "My Account" feature on the CLEP website. This new feature simplifies the registration process and automatically downloads all pertinent information about the test session, making for a more streamlined check-in.

OPTIONS FOR MILITARY PERSONNEL AND VETERANS

CLEP exams are available free of charge to eligible military personnel as well as eligible civilian employees. All the CLEP exams are available at test centers on college campuses and military bases. Contact your Educational Services Officer or Navy College Education Specialist for more information. Visit the DANTES or College Board websites for details about CLEP opportunities for military personnel.

Eligible U.S. veterans may apply for reimbursement of CLEP exam fees pursuant to provisions of the Harry W. Colmery Veterans Educational Assistance Act of 2017, commonly called the "Forever GI Bill." For details on eligibility and submitting a claim for reimbursement, visit the U.S. Department of Veterans Affairs website at *www.gibill.va.gov.*

SSD ACCOMMODATIONS FOR CANDIDATES WITH DISABILITIES

Many test candidates qualify for special accommodations when taking CLEP exams. Accommodations include, among other things, extra time, screen magnification, modifiable screen colors, and untimed rest breaks that don't cut into test time. You must make arrangements for these accommodations in advance. For information, contact:

College Board SSD Program
P.O. Box 7504
London, KY 40742-7504
Phone: (844) 255-7728 (Monday through Friday, 8 a.m. to 6 p.m. ET)
SSD Coordinators' Help Line: (844) 255-7728
TTY: (609) 882-4118
Fax: (866) 360-0114
Email: ssd@info.collegeboard.org
Website: *www.collegeboard.org/students-with-disabilities*

6-WEEK STUDY PLAN

Be sure to set aside enough time—at least two hours each day—to study. The more time you spend studying, the more prepared and relaxed you will feel on the day of the exam.

Week	Activity
1	Take the Diagnostic Exam at the online REA Study Center. The score report will identify topics where you need the most review.
2—4	Study the review focusing on the topics you missed (or were unsure of) on the Diagnostic Exam.
5	Take Practice Test 1 at the REA Study Center. Review your score report and re-study any topics you missed.
6	Take Practice Test 2 at the REA Study Center to see how much your score has improved. If you still got a few questions wrong, go back to the review and study any topics you may have missed.

TEST-TAKING TIPS

Know the format of the test. Familiarize yourself with the CLEP computer screen beforehand by logging on to the College Board website. Waiting until test day to see what it looks like in the pretest tutorial risks injecting needless anxiety into your testing experience. Also, familiarizing yourself with the directions and format of the exam will save you valuable time on the day of the actual test.

Read all the questions—completely. Make sure you understand each question before looking for the right answer. Reread the question if it doesn't make sense.

Read all of the answers to a question. Just because you think you found the correct response right away, do not assume that it's the best answer. The last answer choice might be the correct answer.

Use the process of elimination. Stumped by a question? Don't make a random guess. Eliminate as many of the answer choices as possible. By eliminating just one answer choice, you give yourself a better chance of getting the item correct, since there will only be three choices left from which to make your guess. Remember, your score is based only on the number of questions you answer correctly.

Don't waste time! Don't spend too much time on any one question. Your time is limited so pacing yourself is very important. Work on the easier questions first. Skip the difficult questions and go back to them if you have the time. Taking the timed practice tests online will help you learn how to budget your time.

Look for clues to answers in other questions. If you skip a question you don't know the answer to, you might find a clue to the answer elsewhere on the test.

Be sure that your answer registers before you go to the next item. Look at the screen to see that your mouse-click causes the pointer to darken the proper oval. If your answer doesn't register, you won't get credit for that question.

THE DAY OF THE EXAM

On test day, you should wake up early (after a good night's rest, of course) and have breakfast. Dress comfortably, so you are not distracted by being too hot or too cold while taking the test. (Note that "hoodies" are not allowed.) Arrive at the test center early. This will allow you to collect your thoughts and relax before the test, and it will also spare you the anxiety that comes with being late.

Before you leave for the test center, make sure you have your admission form and another form of identification, which must contain a recent photograph, your name, and signature (i.e., driver's license, student identification card, or current alien registration card). You may not wear a digital watch (wrist or pocket), alarm watch, or wristwatch camera. In addition, no cell phones, dictionaries, textbooks, notebooks, briefcases, or packages will be permitted, and drinking, smoking, and eating are prohibited.

Good luck on the CLEP Spanish Language exam!

CHAPTER 2

CLEP Spanish Review

CHAPTER 2

CLEP SPANISH REVIEW

THE ALPHABET

Spanish uses the same Latin alphabet as English except for the addition of three letters:

ch   pronounced like "ch" in "chief"

ll   pronounced like the "y" in "beyond"

ñ   pronounced like "ni" in "opinion" or "ny" in "canyon"

Some consonants have different pronunciation*:

c   sounds like "s" before "e" and "i," and like "k" in all other cases.

g   sounds like the "h" in "humid" before "e" and "i," and like the "g" in "go" or "get" in front of "a," "o," and "u." In order to obtain the hard sound before "e" and "i," Spanish interpolates the vowel "u": *guerra, guión.* In these cases the "u" is silent; a dieresis indicates that it must be pronounced: *vergüenza, güero.*

h   is always silent: *ahora, húmedo, horrible.*

v   is pronounced like "b" in all cases.

y   sounds like "ll" at the beginning of a word or syllable. When it stands alone or comes at the end of a word, it is equivalent to the vowel "i."

z   is pronounced like "s."

---

*This pronunciation guide follows Latin American usage. In Castilian Spanish the soft "c" and the "z" are pronounced like "th" in "thin."

Letter		Spanish Example	English Example
b	[b]	*bomba*	boy
c	[k]	*calco*	keep
	[T]	*cero*	same
ch	[+S]	*mucho*	chocolate
d	[d]	*andar*	dog
f	[f]	*fama*	fake
g	[x]	*general*	humid
	[g]	*rango*	get
h	always silent	*hombre*	honor
j	[x]	*justo*	humid
k	[k]	*kilogramo*	kite
l	[l]	*letra*	light
ll	[¥]	*ella*	beyond
m	[m]	*mano*	mad
n	[n]	*pan*	no
ñ	[ñ]	*uña*	onion
p	[p]	*padre*	poke
q	[k]	*que*	kite
r	[r]	*rápido*	(this is a trilled sound with no English equivalent)
s	[s]	*casa*	some
	[z]	*mismo*	rose
t	[t]	*patata*	tame
v	[b]	*vamos*	boy
x	[ks]	*máximo*	fox
y	[j]	*yo*	yes
z	[T]	*zapato*	same

The sounds of the Spanish vowels are invariable.

a sounds approximately like "a" in "ah."
e sounds approximately like "e" in "men."
i sounds approximately like "ee" in "eel."
o sounds approximately like "o" in "or."
u sounds approximately like "oo" in "moon."

Letter		Spanish Example	English Example
a	[a]	*pata*	father
e	[e]	*pelo*	men
i	[i]	*filo*	eel
o	[o]	*poco*	or
u	[u]	*luna*	moon

A combination of one strong (a, e, o) and one weak vowel (i, u) or of two weak ones is a diphthong and counts as one syllable:

ai, ay	*aire, hay*	pronounce like "eye"
ei, ey	*reino, ley*	pronounce like "may"
oi, oy	*oigo, hoy*	pronounce like "toy"
iu	*triunfo*	pronounce like "you"
ui, uy	*cuidar, muy*	pronounce like "Louie"
ue	*hueso, muerde*	pronounce like "west"

RULES FOR STRESS IN SPANISH

There are two rules that indicate stress in Spanish. If either of these two rules is broken, a written accent mark will appear on the word.

1. If a word ends in a vowel, *–n,* or *–s,* the **normal** stress is on the penultimate (next to last) syllable.

   mano (over the *–a*) *tribu* (over the *–i*)
   esposa (over the *–o*) *hablan* (over first *–a*)
   clase (over the *–a*) *tomaban* (over first *–a*)

2. If the word ends in any other letter (than those mentioned above), the **normal** stress will fall on the last syllable.

   hablar (over the *–a*) *papel* (over the *–e*)
   comer (over the *–e*) *ejemplar* (over the *–a*)
   vivir (over the *–i*) *nivel* (over the *–e*)

3. Spanish words will have an accent for the following specific reasons:

   a. There is another identical word and the accent distinguishes the one from the other.

de (of, from)	vs.	*dé* (give—formal command)
se (reflexive pronoun)	vs.	*sé* (I know, verb)
el (article)	vs.	*él* (he, pronoun)
tu (yours possessive adj.)	vs.	*tú* (you, pronoun)
mas (but, conjunction)	vs.	*más* (more, adverb)
si (if)	vs.	*sí* (yes)

   b. A pronoun has been added to a verb form.

diciéndolo	saying it
diciéndomelo	saying it to me
explíquelo	explain it
explíquemelo	explain it to me

   Note: *decírselo* (to say it to him). Infinitives require two pronouns before an accent is necessary.

   c. The accent is the result of a stem change.

   reunir (ú) — The *ú* will appear in the first, second, and third person singular and third person plural of the present indicative/subjunctive.

   Other examples:

   continuar (ú),   *enviar (i)*
   graduarse (ú)

   d. There may be a diphthong (two weak vowels or a weak with a strong) where the weak vowel (*u* or *i*) needs to be stressed.

   Examples:

divertíos	Enjoy yourselves!
creíste	you believed

SYLLABIC DIVISION

A consonant between two vowels joins the second vowel to form a syllable: *li-te-ra-tu-ra, e-ne-mi-go, a-ho-ra.*

- Two consonants together must be separated: *cuer-no, pac-to.*
- "ch," "ll," and "rr" are considered one letter and are not separated.
- "l" or "r" preceded by "b," "c," "d," "f," "g," "p," and "t" are not separated: *ha-blar, a-brup-to, te-cla, pul-cri-tud, me-lo-dra-ma, in-flu-jo, a-gra-de-cer.*
- "ns" and "bs" are not separated in groups of three or four consonants: *ins-cri-bir, obs-tá-cu-lo.*
- In words formed with prefixes, the prefix stands alone as one syllable: *sub-ra-yar, in-ú-til, des-a-gra-dar.*

ARTICLES

The forms of the definite article are:

	Masculine	Feminine
Singular	*el*	*la*
Plural	*los*	*las*

El is used instead of *la* before feminine nouns beginning with stressed "a" or "ha": *el agua, el hacha, el alma, el hambre.*

El contracts to *al* when the article follows the preposition *a* (*a + el*) and to *del* when the article follows the preposition *de* (*de + el*).

Uses of the Definite Article

The definite article is used in Spanish (but not in English):

- when the noun represents an abstraction: **life** is short; **time** is money; **freedom** is worth fighting for; **politics** is a practical art. (In Spanish: *la vida, el tiempo, la libertad, la política.*);

- when the noun includes the totality of a category: **books** are good; **man** is mortal; the Incas were acquainted with **gold**; **bread** is a staple. (In Spanish: *los libros, el hombre, el oro, el pan.*);

- with the days of the week (except after a form of the verb *ser*) and the seasons of the year: *el lunes* (but *hoy es lunes*), *la primavera, el otoño;*

- with the hours of the day: *son las tres de la tarde; a las doce del día* (or *al mediodía*);

- with personal or professional forms of address in the third person: *el señor Jiménez, la señorita Méndez, el doctor Márquez, el licenciado Vidriera.* (It is omitted when the individual is directly addressed and in front of titles such as *Don, Doña, San,* or *Santo[a]: venga, señor Jiménez; no se preocupe, señorita Méndez*);

- with the parts of the body or articles of clothing instead of the possessive adjective: I brushed **my** teeth. *Me cepillé los dientes.* I put on **my** shirt. *Me puse la camisa;*

- with the names of languages except after the prepositions *en* and *de* and the verb *hablar: el francés es difícil* (but *no hablo francés; ese texto está en francés*);

- with weights and measures: *un dólar la libra,* one dollar per pound; *diez pesos la docena,* ten pesos per dozen;

- with infinitives used as nouns (gerunds): Lying is a vice. *El mentir es un vicio.* (This use is optional, especially in proverbs.) Seeing is believing. *Ver es creer;*

- with names of "generic" places: jail, *la cárcel;* class, *la clase;* church, *la iglesia;* market, *el mercado;*

- with family names: The García's, *los García;*

- with adjectives to make them nouns: the pretty one, *la bonita;* the poor, *los pobres;* the old man, *el viejo;*

- with nouns in apposition with a pronoun: We Americans… *Nosotros los americanos…*

Omission of the Definite Article in Spanish

The definite article in Spanish is omitted in the following cases:

1. With fields of knowledge, in general, one needs an article unless one...

   a. gives a **definition**   *¿Qué es astronomía?*

                                           Astronomía es una ciencia.

   b. uses *estudiar* or *examinar*   *Estudiamos química.*

2. With the expressions *de...a*

   En casa comemos *de seis a ocho*.
   At home we eat from 6:00 to 8:00.

3. With expressions such as

por primera vez	for the first time
por segunda vez	for the second time
en primer lugar	in the first place

4. With *con* and *sin* before an unmodified abstract noun.

   *No puedo vivir **sin libertad.***
   I cannot live without liberty.

   ***Con amor** la vida tiene sentido.*
   With love, life has meaning.

5. With a numeral that denotes the order of a monarch.

   Carlos Quinto   Charles the Fifth

The Neuter Article *Lo*

This article is used exclusively in the singular as follows:

1. *Lo* + adjective = **part/thing**

Examples:	*lo importante*	the important thing/part
	lo mejor	the best thing/part

2. *Lo* + adj/adv + *que* = **how**

    Examples: *Tú no sabes lo importante que es.*
    You don't know **how** important it is.

    Él no entiende lo despacio que va.
    He doesn't know **how** slowly it goes.

3. *Lo de* = All that or everything that (happened)

    Example: *Vamos a cubrir lo de ayer.*
    We'll cover everything we did yesterday.

4. *Lo* is used in sentences with the pronoun *todo* as the direct object.

    Example: *Lo entiendo todo.*
    I understand everything.

5. *Todo lo que* = All that

    Example: *Todo lo que oí no es verdad.*
    All that I heard isn't true.

6. *Lo* is used as a complement to replace adjectives, pronouns, or nouns with *ser, estar,* and *parecer.*

    Examples: *Pareces enojada.* [adj-*enojada*]
    You seem angry.

    —Quizás **lo** parezca, pero no **lo** estoy.
    Perhaps I seem it, but I'm not.

    ¿Estas llaves son tuyas? [noun-*llaves*]
    Are these keys yours?

    —*No, no* **lo** *son.*
    No, they're not.

Forms of the Indefinite Article

The indefinite article must agree in gender and number with the noun it modifies. Its forms are the following:

	Masculine	Feminine
Singular	*un*	*una*
Plural	*unos*	*unas*

Examples: *un perro* – a dog
unos perros – some dogs

Note: feminine nouns beginning with a stressed "a" or "ha" take *un* instead of *una*: **un** *alma,* **un** *hacha,* **un** *hada madrina.* This rule only applies if the noun is singular.

Uses of the Indefinite Article

Spanish *omits* the indefinite article (but not English) as follows:

- after the verb *ser* with nouns denoting profession, religion, or nationality: *soy professor, son católicos, es española.* (This rule does not apply when the noun is followed by an adjective or some other modifier: *soy* **un** *profesor exigente* (I'm a demanding teacher)).

- with words such as *otro* (other), *medio* (half), *cien* (one hundred or a hundred), *mil* (one thousand or a thousand), *tal* (such a), *cierto* (a certain), and *qué* (what a): *cierta mujer* (a certain woman), *¡qué día! (What a day!),* cien libros (a hundred books), *mide un metro y medio* (it measures one and one-half meters), *otra respuesta* (another answer), *tal hombre* (such a man).

- after **sin***:*
  Salío sin abrigo.   He left without a coat.

- after **haber** used impersonally, **buscar,** and **tener** (otherwise it means **one**)*:*
  No hay respuesta.   There isn't **an** answer.
  Estoy buscando trabajo.   I'm looking for **a** job.
  No tiene coche.   He doesn't have **a** car.

GENDER

In Spanish most nouns are either masculine or feminine. Most nouns ending in *-o* or *-or* are masculine and most of those ending in *-a ,-d, -ión, -umbre, -ie, -sis, -itis* are feminine.

Masculine	Feminine
el dinero – money	*la muchedumbre* – crowd
el otoño – autumn	*la serie* – series
el amor – love	*la crisis* – crisis
	la presencia – presence
	la bronquitis – bronchitis
	la acción – action

Note: Drop the accent on *–ión* words when made plural: *nación, naciones*

Many masculine nouns become feminine by changing the *-o* ending to *-a* or by adding an *-a* if the word ends in a consonant:

Masculine	Feminine
el escritor – the writer	*la escritora* – the woman writer
el doctor – the doctor	*la doctora* – the woman doctor
el hijo – the son	*la hija* – the daughter
el muchacho – the young man	*la muchacha* – the young woman

Exceptions

A few common words ending in *-o* are feminine:

la mano – the hand
la foto (la fotografía) – the photo, picture
la moto (la motocicleta) – the motorcycle

There is a large number of words ending in *-ma*, *-pa*, and *-ta* that are masculine. For the most part, if these are easily identifiable in English, they are probably masculine.

el clima – climate	*el problema* – problem
el diploma – diploma	*el sistema* – system
el drama – drama	*el mapa* – map
el poema – poem	*el profeta* – prophet
el tema – theme	*el aroma* – aroma

There are also other ways of forming the feminine than by adding an -*a* ending:

Masculine	Feminine
el rey – the king	*la reina* – the queen
el poeta – the poet	*la poetisa* – the woman poet
el gallo – the rooster	*la gallina* – the hen

Sometimes the masculine and feminine words corresponding to a matched pair of concepts are different:

Masculine	Feminine
el yerno – the son-in-law	*la nuera* – the daughter-in-law
el macho – the male	*la hembra* – the female
el toro – the bull	*la vaca* – the cow

Masculine words that appear to be feminine:

el día – day	*el césped* – turf
el sofá – sofa	*el colega* – colleague
el ataúd – coffin	*el tranvía* – trolley

Nouns of Invariable Gender

Some nouns can be either masculine or feminine depending on their content or reference, without undergoing any formal alterations.

Masculine	Feminine
el artista – the male artist	*la artista* – the woman artist
el estudiante – the student	*la estudiante* – the female student
el joven – the young man	*la joven* – the young woman

Gender and Meaning Change

There are nouns that have different meanings depending on whether they are used as masculine or feminine:

el *policía* – the policeman	la *policía* – the police (force)
el *Papa* – the Pope	la *papa* – the potato
el *cometa* – the comet	la *cometa* – the kite
el *orden* – order	la *orden* – the order
(as in public order)	(to do something)
el *cura* – the priest	la *cura* – the cure
el *guía* – the guide (person)	la *guía* – the guide
	(book, as in *guía de teléfonos*)
el *frente* – the front	la *frente* – the forehead

Use of *El* Before a Feminine Noun

If the feminine noun begins with a stressed **a** or **ha**, the singular forms of the article used are **el** or **un**. If anything intercedes between these two items, use the normal **la** or **una**.

el *águila* (eagle)	las *águilas*	la gran *águila*
un *hacha* (hatchet)	unas *hachas*	una gran *hacha*

Other examples: *el alma* – soul, *el aula* – classroom. *el agua* – water, *el ala* – wing, *el alba* – dawn, *el hada* – fairy, *el hambre* – hunger.

Note: On some standardized exams, this concept is tested by asking students to write the correct form of an adjective that follows, as in these examples. Observe that the adjective is feminine because the noun is, despite the masculine article.

el *agua tibia*	the warm water
el *alba bonita*	the pretty dawn
el *águila maravillosa*	the marvelous eagle

Other Feminine Words (Often Used on Exams)

la *pirámide* – pyramid	la *vez* – time
la *torre* – tower	la *razón* – reason
la *leche* – milk	la *imagen* – image
la *carne* – meat	la *luz* – light
la *gente* – people	la *catedral* – cathedral
la *frase* – sentence	la *suerte* – luck

NUMBER

In Spanish, as in English, nouns can be singular or plural. The most common way to form the plural is by adding the *-s* ending to the singular form of the word. (Note that the following examples are of words ending in an unstressed vowel.)

Singular	Plural
hombre – man	*hombres* – men
niño – boy	*niños* – boys
perro – dog	*perros* – dogs

Formation of the Plural by Addition of *-es*

In other cases (words ending in a consonant or in a stressed vowel other than *-é*), the plural is formed by adding an *-es* ending to the singular form of the word:

Singular	Plural
mujer – woman	*mujeres* – women
razón – reason	*razones* – reasons
jabalí – boar	*jabalíes* – boars

Exceptions: *mamá* (mother), pl. *mamás; ley* (law), pl. *leyes.*

Nouns of Invariable Number

Nouns ending in *-s* are the same in the singular and the plural if the final syllable is unstressed:

el (los) rascacielos – the skyscraper(s)
el (los) paraguas – the umbrella(s)
el (los) lunes – Monday(s)

Diminutives

The Spanish endings *-ito, -cito,* and their feminine forms are used to indicate affection or to emphasize smallness of size:

*Tú eres mi **amor.***
You are my **love.**

*Tú eres mi **amorcito.***
You are my **sweetheart.**

*Quiero chocolate. Dame un **poco.***
I want chocolate. Give me **some.**

*Quiero chocolate. Dame un **poquito.***
I want chocolate. Give me **a little.**

*Ese **hombre** tiene buen aspecto.*
That **man** is good looking.

*Ese **hombrecito** debe ser muy desgraciado.*
That **poor man** must be very unfortunate.

Augmentatives

The endings *-ote, -ón,* and *-ona* are added to express increased size:

hombre – man   *hombrón* – big man
mujer – woman   *mujerona* – big woman
casa – house   *casona* – big house

ADJECTIVES

Adjectives agree in gender and number with the noun they modify.

a) Adjectives ending in *-o* change their ending to *-a* when they modify a feminine noun:

bueno, buena – good; *malo, mala* – bad; *bello, bella* – beautiful

b) Adjectives ending in *-or* (or *-ón* or *-án*) add an *-a* to become feminine:

hablador, habladora – talkative

Exceptions:

mejor – better   *peor* – worse
superior – upper, superior   *inferior* – lower, inferior
exterior – outer, external   *interior* – inner, internal
anterior – earlier, anterior   *posterior* – later, posterior

c) Most other adjectives have the same ending for both genders:

verde – green   *grande* – big, great
azul – blue   *soez* – mean, vile
cortés – courteous

d) Adjectives of nationality have four forms. If they end in *-o,* they follow the normal pattern of change. All others may be changed by adding *-a* to make them feminine and *-as* to make them feminine plural.

inglés, inglesa, ingleses, inglesas
alemán, alemana, alemanes, alemanas
español, española, españoles, españolas

Number

a) Adjectives ending in a vowel add an *-s* to form the plural:

bello, bellos – beautiful; *grande, grandes* – big, great

b) Adjectives ending in a consonant add *-es* to form the plural:

azul, azules – blue; *débil, débiles* – weak; *vulgar, vulgares* – vulgar

c) If an adjective modifies more than one noun and one of those nouns is masculine, the adjective must be **masculine** and **plural:**

Mis tíos y tías eran **ricos.** My uncles and aunts were **rich.**

Los hombres y las mujeres son **viejos.** **The** men and women are old.

Shortening of Adjectives

Some adjectives that directly precede the noun lose their final vowel or syllable:

ciento → cien   *grande → gran**
*bueno → buen***   *malo → mal***
*Santo → San***   *primero → primer***
*tercero → tercer***   *alguno → algún***
*ninguno → ningún***   *cualquiera → cualquier**

* The shortening of this adjective only happens in front of singular nouns, either masculine or feminine. Compare:

*El acontecimiento fue **grande**.*
The event was **big.**

*el **gran** acontecimiento* – the **big** event

** These adjectives only shorten in front of masculine singular nouns. Compare:

*El hombre es **bueno**.*
The man is **good.**

*el **buen** hombre* – the **good** man

Qualifying Adjectives

Qualifying adjectives usually follow the noun:

*un día **frío*** – a **cold** day
*unas sábanas **limpias*** – some **clean** sheets

Change of Meaning with Location

Some common adjectives change their meaning with their location:

*el hombre **pobre*** – the poor man (impecunious)
*el **pobre** hombre* – the poor man (pitiable)

*un cuadro **grande*** – a large painting
*un **gran** cuadro* – a great painting

*el policía **mismo*** – the policeman himself
*el **mismo** policía* – the same policeman

__ciertas__ palabras – certain words (specific words from among many)
*palabras **ciertas*** – certain (sure)

__nueva__ casa – new house (different)
*casa **nueva*** – new house (brand new)

*un **simple** empleado* – a mere employee
*un empleado **simple*** – a simple-minded employee

COMPARISON OF ADJECTIVES AND ADVERBS

Adverbs modify verbs, adjectives, and other adverbs and are invariable.

The following is a list of frequently used adverbs:

bien – well	*mal* – badly
más – more	*menos* – less
siempre – always	*nunca* – never
cerca – near	*lejos* – far
antes – before	*después* – afterwards
bastante – enough	*demasiado* – too much
temprano – early	*tarde* – late
así – thus, so	*casi* – almost
entonces – then	*luego* – later, afterward
todavía – still	

Aún is a common adverb whose meaning depends on whether the sentence is affirmative or negative:

Aún *quiere trabajar.*
He **still** wants to work.

Aún *no está despierta.*
She's not **yet** awake.

Aun (no accent) normally has the meaning **even** and commonly precedes the word it modifies.

¿Aun no ha llegado Juan?
Juan hasn't **even** arrived?

Adverbs Ending in *-mente*

Many adverbs are derived from the **feminine** form of the adjective (when such a form is available) by the addition of *-mente:*

claro/claramente – clearly
rápido/rápidamente – quickly
feliz/felizmente – happily

hábil/hábilmente – skillfully
dulce/dulcemente – sweetly

When two or more adverbs are used in a sequence, only the last adverb ends in –*mente*. All others are written as feminine adjectives (if they have a feminine form).

*Habla lenta y elocuente**mente**.*
He speaks slowly and eloquently.

*Juan corre rápida y hábil**mente**.*
Juan runs rapidly and skillfully.

Con, *Sin* + Noun

At times an adverb can be formed by using the preposition *con* (with) or *sin* (without) + a noun.

con cuidado – carefully
sin cuidado – carelessly
con rapidez – rapidly

Recientemente vs. *Recién*

Recientemente becomes *recién* before a past participle.

los recién llegados – the recent arrivals
los recién casados – the newlyweds

Adverbs Replaced by Adjectives

Adverbs may be replaced by adjectives with verbs of motion.

Ellos van y vienen silenciosos.
They come and go silently.

Comparison of Equality

This is constructed in the following ways:

Tanto, a, os, as + (noun) + ***como***
Tan + (adverb or adjective) + ***como***

*Tuve **tantas** deudas **como** el mes pasado.* I had **as many** debts **as** last month.

*Su música es **tan** clara **como** el agua.*
Her music is **as** clear **as** water.

*Llegué **tan** tarde **como** ayer.*
I arrived **as** late **as** yesterday.

***Tanto com**o* (without intervening expressions) means "as much as."

*Tu amigo estudia **tanto como** yo.*
Your friend studies **as much as** I [do].

Comparison of Inequality

The formula for describing levels of superiority is:

más + (noun, adjective, or adverb) + ***que***

*Tengo **más** dinero **que** tú.*
I have **more** money **than** you.

*Su auto es **más** caro **que** el mío.*
His car is **more** expensive **than** mine.

*Me levanto **más** temprano **que** ella.*
I get up earli**er than** she does.

The above formula changes to ***más de*** if a numerical expression is involved and the sentence is in the affirmative:

*Vimos **más de** mil estrellas en el cielo.*
We saw **more than** a thousand stars in the sky.

But:

***No** tengo **más que** cinco dólares en el bolsillo.*
I don't have **more than** five dollars in my pocket.

The formula for describing levels of inferiority is:
menos + (noun, adjective, or adverb) + ***que***

*Nos dieron **menos** tiempo **que** a ustedes para completar el examen.*
They gave us **less** time **than** they gave you to finish the exam.

*Eres **menos** pobre **que** ella.*
You are **less** poor **than** she is.

*Tiene **menos** problemas **que** su madre.*
She has **fewer** problems **than** her mother.

The same change applies to the comparison of inferiority **except** that even in negative sentences *de* is used instead of *que:*

*No eran **menos** de cinco los asaltantes.*
The assailants were no **fewer than** five.

If the second part of the comparison has a different verb from the first, **than** is expressed in one of five ways: *del que, de la que, de los que, de las que* (which all have gender and refer to nouns that are objects of both verbs), and *de lo que* (which is used when adjectives or adverbs are being compared).

*Ella gasta más dinero **del que** gana su esposo.* [*dinero*]
She spends more money **than** her husband earns.

*Tengo más coches **de los que** puedo contar.* [*coches*]
I have more cars **than** I can count.

*Es más fácil **de lo que** crees.* [*fácil*]
It is easier **than** you believe.

*Anda más despacio **de lo que** corre.* [*despacio*]
He walks more slowly **than** he runs.

Special Comparatives

Adjective (Adverb)	Comparative
bueno (bien) – good, well	*mejor* – better
malo (mal) – bad, badly	*peor* – worse
grande – big	*mayor** – older
pequeño – small	*menor** – younger

> * *Mayor* and *menor* only refer to age; otherwise, *más (menos) grande (pequeño) que* is used.

*Mi padre es **mayor** que yo; mi hijo es **menor**.*
My father is **older** than I; my son is **younger.**

*Esta ciudad es **más grande que** la capital.*
This city is **bigger than** the capital.

Superlatives

In English the true or relative superlative is rendered by **the most (least) of** a category:

El, la, los, las + más (menos) + (adjective) + de

Lo + más (menos) + (adverb) + de

*Estos anillos son **los más** caros **de** la tienda.*
These rings are **the most** expensive **in** the store.

*Tienes **los** ojos **más** lindos **del** mundo.*
You have **the prettiest** eyes **in** the world.

*Corre **lo más** rápidamente **de** todos.*
He runs **the most** quickly **of** all.

The special comparatives previously noted have a superlative form:

El, la, los, las + (special comparatives) + de
*Mi hijo es **el mayor de** la clase.* My son is **the oldest in** the class.

Absolute Superlative

Superlatives can also be formed by adding the *-ísimo(a)* ending to adjectives and adverbs. (Some spelling adjustments may be necessary.)

The absolute superlative is usually rendered in English as "very pretty," "very ugly," etc.

lindo/lindísimo – very pretty
feo/feísimo – very ugly
tarde/tardísimo – very late
cerca/cerquísimo – very near
rico/riquísimo – very rich
fácil/facilísimo(a) – very easy

The adjective *malo* has the special superlative *pésimo* in addition to the more informal *malísimo*. The adjective *bueno* has the special superlative *óptimo* in addition to *buenísimo*.

➲ DRILL 1

1. Ramiro es más guapo_____ Felipe.

    (A) que   (C) de

    (B) como   (D) tan

2. _____ arma de fuego es peligrosa.

    (A) El   (C) Los

    (B) La   (D) Las

3. Mercedes lavó los platos _____.

    (A) rápidamente y   (C) rápida y cuidadosamente
        cuidadosamente

    (B) rápida y cuidadosa   (D) rápidamente y cuidadosa

4. Los explicaron_____ nosotros.

    (A) menor que   (C) mayor que

    (B) tanto   (D) mejor que

5. Elena tiene más amigas_____ puede contar.

    (A) de los que   (C) de las que

    (B) que   (D) de lo que

6. Pablo trabaja mejor_____ usted cree.

    (A) que   (C) del que

    (B) de lo que   (D) de la que

7. Anita es menos alta_____ Elena

    (A) tan   (C) como

    (B) de   (D) que

8. Estas películas son _____ interesantes como ésas.

    (A) tan   (C) tantas

    (B) tantos   (D) como

9. Roberto y Ana son _____ inteligentes de la clase.

    (A) las más   (C) más

    (B) los más   (D) menos

10. Ellos corren _____ y hábilmente.

    (A) rápida   (C) rápidamente

    (B) rápido   (D) rápidos

11. Las chicas hablan _____ lentamente de todos.

    (A) el más   (C) lo más

    (B) las más   (D) más

12. Hay _____ torres como palacios en aquel país.

    (A) tan   (C) tan muchos

    (B) tantos   (D) tantas

13. _____ persona puede estudiar este curso.

    (A) Algún   (C) Ningún

    (B) Cualquier   (D) Cualquiera

14. Juan y María son chicos _____.

    (A) alemanas   (C) alemanes

    (B) de alemanes   (D) alemanos

15. Isabela I fue _____.

    (A) una gran mujer   (C) una mujer gran

    (B) una grande mujer   (D) mujer grande

16. Mis notas son _____ las de Juan.

    (A) mayor que   (C) mejores que

    (B) mayores de   (D) mejores de

17. Tú no sabes_____ importante_____ son las tareas.

    (A) los...que   (C) lo...que

    (B) las...que   (D) lo...de

18. ¿Estas llaves son tuyas? –No, no_____ son.

    (A) las   (C) ellas

    (B) lo   (D) nothing needed

19. Juan lo hizo_____ ayer.

    (A) para primera vez   (C) por primera vez

    (B) por primer vez   (D) por la primera vez

20. Todo_____ oí ayer no es verdad.

    (A) que   (C) la que

    (B) lo que   (D) de

Drill 1—Detailed Explanations of Answers

1.　**(A)**　The most common pattern to express a **comparison** of superiority (i.e., to show that one thing or person is superior to another in some respect) is "más...que" (more than); for example, "Yo soy más delgado que tú" (I am thin**ner than** you); "Hablas español más fácilmente que yo" (You speak Spanish more easily than I); "Tengo más años que ella" (I am older than she). Notice from these three examples that we may use either adjectives, adverbs, or nouns between the words "más" and "que." The only time we use "de," as in (C), after "más" is when there is a number immediately afterwards: "Tenemos más de tres pesos" (We have more than three pesos).

2.　**(A)**　"Arma de fuego" means "firearm." Of the possible choices, we can immediately eliminate (C) and (D) because they are plural definite articles and cannot be placed before a singular noun such as "arma." This reduces our choices to "El" or "La." We know that most nouns that end in -*a* are feminine. By looking at the sentence carefully, we also see that the adjective "peligrosa" (dangerous) is feminine and most certainly modifies "arma." Therefore, you might have been tempted to choose (B), "La." This is not correct, however. Feminine singular nouns which end in -*a* but begin with "a" or "ha" and have their **stress** on the **first syllable**, as in "arma," require that we use the masculine singular definite article in front of them. This does not change the gender of the noun, however. It still stays feminine. We can see this in our sentence because we used the feminine adjective "peligrosa" to describe "arma." Remember that this rule applies only to feminine **singular** nouns. In the plural, we use the feminine plural definite article: "Las armas de fuego son peligrosas."

3.   **(C)**   When two or more adverbs are used together to refer to the same verb, the last one is the only one with the *–mente* ending.

4.   **(D)**   The verb "explicaron" in our sentence means "they explained." Comparisons of superiority, i.e., comparisons which show that in some respect someone or something is superior to someone or something else, are usually formed according to the following pattern: "más" + adjective or adverb or noun + "que." Example: "Enrique es **más rico que** yo." (Enrique is richer than I). There are some adjectives and adverbs which have irregular comparatives. For example, "menor," which appears in (A), is the comparative form of "pequeño." "Mayor," in (C), is the comparative for "grande." Neither of these could be used in the blank because we are not talking about size. On the other hand, "mejor que" would mean "better than" and makes sense in our sentence. The word "tanto," in (B), means "as much" or sometimes "so much." It is usually followed by "como" to form comparisons of equality, i.e., to show that two persons or things are equal in some respect: "Tengo **tanto dinero como** tú" (I have as much money as you). In (B), however, we have omitted the word "como," which is obligatory in comparisons of equality.

5.   **(C)**   When the verbs in each half of the comparison are both referring to the same noun ("amigas"), the longer form of **than** is required. Because "amigas" is a feminine noun, "de las que" is used. For this reason (A) would be incorrect because it is masculine plural, and (D) is also incorrect because it is neuter. Answer (B) would be used in a simple comparison where the verb is not repeated in the second half.

6.   **(B)**   Because an adjective is the point of comparison for each verb ("trabaja" and "cree"), the neuter form of **than** is used. Therefore, (C), the masculine form, and (D), the feminine form, are not correct. Answer (A) would be used in a simple comparison where the verb is not repeated in the second half.

7.   **(D)**   This is a simple comparison where the verb in the second half of the comparison is not stated but understood to be from the same infinitive (**ser** in this case). Choice (A) is used in the first half of an equal comparison and means **as**. Choice (C) is used in the second half of an equal comparison to mean **as**. Choice (B) is used in an unequal comparison when followed by a number.

8. **(A)** When there is an equal comparison that involves using an adjective or adverb, the word preceding this adjective or adverb is **tan**, meaning **as**. The second half of this comparison requires using **como**, which is already in the sample. Therefore, choice (D) cannot be used to precede the adjective. Choices (B) and (C) each have gender and would precede nouns.

9. **(B)** Superlative statements require the use of the definite article and are followed by **de**. In this sample, because Roberto is masculine and Ana is feminine, the masculine plural "los" is required. Therefore, choice (A), the feminine plural, is incorrect. In order to use either choice (C) or (D), the sentence would need to be in the comparative form (not the superlative) and **que** would then need to follow the adjective.

10. **(A)** Whenever there are two or more adverbs modifying a verb, only the last adverb ends in -*mente*. The other must be written in the feminine form of the adjective (if there is one). This would eliminate choice (B), which is a masculine adjective, and (D), which is a masculine plural adjective. Choice (C) is incorrect because it ends in -*mente*.

11. **(C)** When dealing with the superlative forms of adverbs, instead of using the definite article, which has gender, **lo** is used with **más** or **menos**. Therefore, (A), which is masculine, and (B), which is feminine plural, are incorrect. Choice (D) is incomplete because **lo** is needed.

12. **(D)** Because "torres" is a feminine plural noun, the feminine plural form of **tanto** is required. Choice (A) means **as** and does not translate correctly with a noun after it. Choice (C) is a completely incorrect form since forms of **tanto** mean **as much** or **as many**.

13. **(B)** Before any singular noun, "cualquiera" apocopates (drops the -a). Therefore, (D) is incorrect. Choices (A) and (C), although apocopated, are used with masculine singular nouns. To be correct, each would need to end in -a.

14. **(C)** Adjectives of nationality have four forms. The masculine plural form is required here because the adjective is modifying both a masculine and feminine subject. Because the masculine singular form is **alemán**, the plural adds -**es** to that form. (Note that the accent is dropped to form the plural.) This would eliminate (A), which is feminine plural, and (D), which is nonexistent. Choice (B) is incorrect because adjectives of this sort are not preceded by **de**.

15. **(A)** There are two grammatical points here: "grande" becomes "gran" before any singular noun and means **great**; the indefinite article ("una") is required before predicate nouns of occupation that are modified (have adjectives). Choice (B) is incorrect because "grande" is not apocopated, and (C) is incorrect because the apocopated form precedes, not follows, the noun. Choice (D) requires an indefinite article.

16. **(C)** This answer requires knowing the meaning of "mejor" (better) and "mayor" (older). Also, a comparison is followed by **que** not **de**. "Mejor" must be plural in this sample to match "notas." Although choices (B) and (D) are plural, they are followed by **de**. Choices (A) and (B) also mean "older," which doesn't make sense in this context. Although (D) is plural, it is also followed by **de** and is, therefore, incorrect.

17. **(C)** To express **how** followed by an adjective or adverb, use **lo** before that adjective/adverb and follow it with **que**. This would eliminate (A), (B), and (D) as correct choices.

18. **(B)** **Lo** is used as a complement to replace adjectives, pronouns, or nouns used with **ser, estar,** and **parecer**. In this sample, the noun "llaves" (keys) is being replaced in the answer with **lo**. *Lo* used in this sense is invariable and will not, therefore, have the same gender and number as the noun it replaces.

19. **(C)** The definite article is omitted with expressions such as this one (por primera vez, en primer lugar, etc.) Also, "vez" is feminine.

20. **(B)** "Todo lo que" is an expression meaning "all that."

PRESENT INDICATIVE

	amar to love	*comer* to eat	*vivir* to live
yo	*amo*	*como*	*vivo*
tú	*amas*	*comes*	*vives*
él/ella/Ud.	*ama*	*come*	*vive*
nosotros, –as	*amamos*	*comemos*	*vivimos*
vosotros, –as*	*amáis*	*coméis*	*vivís*
ellos/ellas/Uds.	*aman*	*comen*	*viven*

* This pronoun and corresponding forms of the verb are used in Spain only.

Verbs irregular in **yo** form only:

caber	to fit	*quepo*	*saber*	to know	*sé*
caer	to fall	*caigo*	*salir*	to leave	*salgo*
dar	to give	*doy*	*traer*	to bring	*traigo*
hacer	to make/do	*hago*	*valer*	to be worth	*valgo*
poner	to put	*pongo*	*ver*	to see	*veo*

Verbs irregular in more than one form:

decir to tell or say	*estar* to be	*haber* to have (auxiliary)	*ir* to go
digo	*estoy*	*he*	*voy*
dices	*estás*	*has*	*vas*
dice	*está*	*ha*	*va*
decimos	*estamos*	*hemos*	*vamos*
decís	*estáis*	*habéis*	*vais*
dicen	*están*	*han*	*van*

oír to hear	*ser* to be	*tener* to have	*venir* to come
oigo	*soy*	*tengo*	*vengo*
oyes	*eres*	*tienes*	*vienes*
oye	*es*	*tiene*	*viene*
oímos	*somos*	*tenemos*	*venimos*
oís	*sois*	*tenéis*	*venís*
oyen	*son*	*tienen*	*vienen*

Verbs Ending in *-cer, -cir*

The *yo* form ends in *–zco* if preceded by a vowel. If the ending is preceded by a consonant, the form ends in *–zo*.

conocer	to know	*conozco*
traducir	to translate	*traduzco*
vencer	to conquer	*venzo*

Others:

merecer – to deserve	*crecer* – to grow
carecer – to lack	*convencer* – to convince
aparecer – to appear	*nacer* – to be born
parecer – to seem	

Verbs that Have Stem Changes

There are five types of stem changes that may occur in the present tense: (*ie*), (*ue*), (*i*), (*ú*), (*í*). This will occur in all forms except nosotros/vosotros and appears in the stressed syllable.

ie *pensar* to think	ue *dormir* to sleep	i *pedir* to ask for	ú *actuar* to act	í *enviar* to send
pienso	*duermo*	*pido*	*actúo*	*envío*
piensas	*duermes*	*pides*	*actúas*	*envías*
piensa	*duerme*	*pide*	*actúa*	*envía*
pensamos	*dormimos*	*pedimos*	*actuamos*	*enviamos*
pensáis	*dormís*	*pedís*	*actuáis*	*enviáis*
piensan	*duermen*	*piden*	*actúan*	*envían*

Other examples:

ie: *comenzar/empezar* – to begin, *nevar* – to snow, *cerrar* – to close, *apretar* – to tighten, *perder* – to lose, *querer* – to want, *mentir* – to lie, *sentir* – to feel, *herir* – to wound

ue: *morir* – to die, *dormir* – to sleep, *volar* – to fly, *poder* – to be able, *volver* – to return, *rogar* – to beg, *jugar* – to play

í: *elegir* – to elect, *repetir* – to repeat, *servir* – to serve, *corregir* – to correct

ú: *graduarse* – to graduate, *continuar* – to continue

í: *confiar* – to confide, *guiar* – to guide, *variar* – to vary

Verbs Ending in *-ger, -gir*

In the **yo** form there will be a spelling change because the **-go** combination will produce a **g** sound and the infinitive has an **h** sound.

coger	to catch	**cojo**
elegir	to elect	**elijo**

Others:

escoger	to choose	*recoger*	to gather
corregir	to correct		

Verbs Ending in *-uir*

All forms except *nosotros/vosotros* have a **y**.

huir	**construir**
to flee	**to build**
huyo	*construyo*
huyes	*construyes*
huye	*construye*
huimos	*construimos*
huís	*construís*
huyen	*construyen*

Verbs Ending in *-guir*

The **yo** form drops the **u**.

seguir (i) – to follow   **sigo**

perseguir (i) – to pursue   **persigo**

Uses of the Present Indicative

There are three possible translations for the present tense as expressed below with the verb "to eat" (*comer*).

I eat./I do eat./I am eating. = *Como*.

Immediate Future

The present tense is commonly used to express the immediate future.

Mañana voy a ir a la casa.
Tomorrow I will go home.

The "*Hace*" Sentence

When an action began in the past and is still continuing in the present, the Spanish sentence is rendered with the following formula:

hace + time + *que* + Present/Present Progressive

Hace dos horas que comemos/estamos comiendo.
We have been eating for two hours.

¿Cuánto tiempo hace que ella canta/está cantando?
How long has she been singing?

PRETERITE AND IMPERFECT

Preterite Indicative–Regular: *-ar, -er, -ir*

	amar **to love**	**comer** **to eat**	**vivir** **to live**
yo	*amé*	*comí*	*viví*
tú	*amaste*	*comiste*	*viviste*
él/ella/Ud.	*amó*	*comió*	*vivió*
nosotros, –as	*amamos*	*comimos*	*vivimos*
vosotros, –as	*amasteis*	*comisteis*	*vivisteis*
ellos/ellas/Uds.	*amaron*	*comieron*	*vivieron*

Preterite Indicative–Irregular

The following group of preterites shares the same set of irregular endings: *–e, –iste, –o, –imos, –isteis, –ieron.*

andar to walk	*caber* to fit	*estar* to be	*haber* to have	*hacer* to make/do
anduve	cupe	estuve	hube	hice
anduviste	cupiste	estuviste	hubiste	hiciste
anduvo	cupo	estuvo	hubo	hizo
anduvimos	cupimos	estuvimos	hubimos	hicimos
anduvisteis	cupisteis	estuvisteis	hubisteis	hicisteis
anduvieron	cupieron	estuvieron	hubieron	hicieron

*poder** to be able		*poner* to put		*querer** to want
pude		puse		quise
pudiste		pusiste		quisiste
pudo		puso		quiso
pudimos		pusimos		quisimos
pudisteis		pusisteis		quisisteis
pudieron		pusieron		quisieron

venir to come		*saber** to know		*tener** to have
vine		supe		tuve
viniste		supiste		tuviste
vino		supo		tuvo
vinimos		supimos		tuvimos
vinisteis		supisteis		tuvisteis
vinieron		supieron		tuvieron

* These verbs have an altered translation in the preterite and will be discussed later in this chapter.

Irregular Preterites with a –j

decir to say/tell	traer to bring	–ducir types conducir to drive
dije	traje	conduje
dijiste	trajiste	condujiste
dijo	trajo	condujo
dijimos	trajimos	condujimos
dijisteis	trajisteis	condujisteis
dijeron	trajeron	condujeron

Note: The third plural does not have an *i* after the *j*.

Irregulars of *Dar, Ir, Ser*

Dar is irregular in that it takes the endings of the *-er/-ir* verbs (without accents). *Ser* and *ir* are identical in this tense.

dar to give	ir/ser to go/to be
di	fui
diste	fuiste
dió	fue
dimos	fuimos
disteis	fuisteis
dieron	fueron

Stem-Changing Verbs

Stem changes commonly occur in the preterite for *–ir* verbs that have a stem change in the present. These changes have a pattern (*ue/u*), (*ie/i*), and (*i/i*). The second vowel in parenthesis will surface in the preterite third person singular and plural.

dormir (ue, u) to sleep	*sentir* (ie, i) to regret or feel	*pedir* (i, i) to ask for
dormí	sentí	pedí
dormiste	sentiste	pediste
durmió	sintió	pidió
dormimos	sentimos	pedimos
dormisteis	sentisteis	pedisteis
durmieron	sintieron	pidieron

Others:

morir — to die	*divertirse* — to enjoy oneself	*servir* — to serve
	herir — to wound	*repetir* — to repeat
	mentir — to lie	*seguir* — to follow

Verbs ending in *–car*, *–gar*, *–zar*

Verbs ending in *–car*, *–gar*, and *–zar* are affected in the *yo* form of the preterite by the final *–é*. This vowel will cause the consonants before it (*c, g, z*) to change in sound. To maintain the original sound of the infinitive, these verbs will require a spelling change in that form as follows.

–car = qué	*–gar = gué*	*–zar = cé*

Examples:	atacar = ataqué	I attacked.
	entregar = entregué	I delivered.
	rezar = recé	I prayed.

Verbs that Change I to Y

All *–er* and *–ir* verbs with double vowels in the infinitive (with the exception of *traer/atraer*) will require this change in the third person singular and plural.

oír to hear	*creer* to believe	*leer* to read
oí	creí	leí
oíste	creíste	leíste
oyó	creyó	leyó
oímos	creímos	leímos
oísteis	creísteis	leísteis
oyeron	creyeron	leyeron

An added requirement for these verbs is the accent mark over the *i* in the *tú, nosotros*, and *vosotros* forms to split the diphthong.

Verbs Ending in *–ller, –llir, –ñir, –ñer*

Although these verbs are used with less frequency, they can surface on an exam. Because of the double *l* and the tilde over the *n,* these verbs in the third person singular and plural do not need the *i* of those endings.

bruñir to polish	*bullir* to boil
bruñí	*bullí*
bruñiste	*bulliste*
bruñó	*bulló*
bruñimos	*bullimos*
bruñisteis	*bullisteis*
bruñeron	*bulleron*

Verbs Ending in *–uir*

Just like the present tense of these verbs, the preterite also needs a *y*. It will occur in the third person singular and plural only.

huir to flee	*construir* to build
huí	*construí*
huiste	*construiste*
huyó	*construyó*
huimos	*construimos*
huisteis	*construisteis*
huyeron	*construyeron*

Verbs Ending in *–guar*

In this particular combination of letters, the *u* is heard as a separate letter, not treated as a diphthong with the *a* that follows. This sound will be altered in the *yo* form because of the final *–é*. To maintain the sound of the *u*, a dieresis mark is placed over it.

averiguar (to verify) = *averigüé*

Note: This also occurs in other Spanish words:

la vergüenza (shame), *el agüero* (omen)

Imperfect Indicative–Regular: *-ar, -er, -ir*

This tense may be translated as "used to + verb," "was" or "were + ing," or the normal past tense ending "–ed."

	amar	**comer**	**vivir**
	to love	*to eat*	*to live*
yo	*amaba*	*comía*	*vivía*
tú	*amabas*	*comías*	*vivías*
él/ella/Ud.	*amaba*	*comía*	*vivía*
nosotros, –as	*amábamos*	*comíamos*	*vivíamos*
vosotros, –as	*amabais*	*comíais*	*vivíais*
ellos/ellas/Uds.	*amaban*	*comían*	*vivían*

Imperfect Indicative–Irregulars

There are only three irregular verbs in this tense.

ser	*ir*	*ver*
to be	**to go**	**to see**
era	*iba*	*veía*
eras	*ibas*	*veías*
era	*iba*	*veía*
éramos	*íbamos*	*veíamos*
erais	*ibais*	*veíais*
eran	*iban*	*veían*

Continuation vs. Completion of an Action

The imperfect is used for an action **continuing** in the past; the preterite designates a **finished** action or an action whose beginning, duration, or end is emphasized by the speaker.

Estaba nublado. (Imperfect)
It was cloudy. (No indication of when it got that way.)

Estuvo nublado. (Preterite)
It was cloudy. (But now it has changed.)

Ella quería a su marido. (Imperfect)
She loved her husband. (Indefinitely in the past.)

Ella quiso a su marido. (Preterite)
She loved her husband. (While he was alive, while she was married to him, etc.)

Description vs. Narration

The imperfect is used to **describe** a quality or a state in the past; the preterite is used to **narrate** an action.

> *Los soldados **marcharon** (pret.) toda una mañana y **llegaron** (pret.) al fuerte enemigo al mediodía cuando **hacía** (imp.) mucho calor. Se **sentían** (imp.) cansados y **necesitaban** (imp.) descansar. Se **sentaron** (pret.) a la sombra de un árbol.*
>
> The soldiers marched one full morning and arrived at the enemy fort at noon when it was very hot. They were tired and needed to rest. They sat down in the shade of a tree.

"Used to" Followed by Infinitive

The English expression **used to** followed by an infinitive is rendered by the imperfect, as this is the tense that designates a habitual action in the past.

> ***Pasábamos** las vacaciones en la costa.*
> We **used to spend** the holidays on the shore.

> ***Eran** amigos.*
> They **used to be** friends.

Alternatively, the verb *soler* (to be in the habit of) may be used in the imperfect to render the sense of "used to." *Soler* must be accompanied by an infinitive: *solíamos pasar las vacaciones en la costa; solían ser amigos,* etc.

"Was" or "Were" plus Present Participle

Expressions formed with the past tense of "to be" followed by the present participle of another verb (**was** or **were** doing, singing, studying, etc.) are rendered by the imperfect.

*El **conducía** cuando ocurrió el accidente.*
He **was driving** when the accident occurred.

Pensaban visitarnos ese verano.
They **were thinking** of visiting us that summer.

Telling Time in the Past

The imperfect (of *ser*) is used to tell time in the past.

Eran las tres.
It was 3 o'clock.

Era tarde cuando se fueron los invitados.
It was late when the guests left.

Special Preterites

The preterite of some verbs (such as *conocer, saber, poder, poner, tener,* and *querer*) has a special meaning:

*Yo la **conocí** el año pasado.*
I **met** her last year.

*Cuando **supimos** la noticia nos pusimos tristes.*
When we **learned/found out** the news we felt sad.

*El fugitivo **pudo** abandonar el país a última hora.*
The fugitive **managed to** abandon the country at the last minute.

*Jamás **tuvo** noticias de su familia.*
She never **received** news of her family.

*El ladrón **quiso** abrir la puerta con una barra.*
The thief **tried to** open the door with a bar.

*Juan no **quiso** pagar la cuenta.*
Juan **refused** to pay the bill.

States of Mind

Normally verbs indicating state of mind (*saber, creer, pensar, comprender, convencerse,* etc.) are expressed using the imperfect unless there is an indication of change in that state. Look for words to indicate this change like *de pronto* (soon), *de repente* (suddenly), *luego que* (as soon as), *cuando* (when), *al + infinitive* (upon + ing).

Juan creía la verdad.
Juan believed the truth.

But:

De pronto Juan la creyó.
Suddenly Juan believed it.

"Ago" Statements

Ago statements are normally expressed with this formula:

Hace + time + *que* + preterite

Hace dos años que fuimos allí.
We went there two years ago.

"Hacía" Statements

To express "had been + ing," use the formula:

hacía + time + *que* + imperfect past progressive

Hacía dos horas que cantaba/estaba cantando.
He had been singing for two hours.

FUTURE AND CONDITIONAL

Future/Conditional Indicative–Regular: *–ar, –er, –ir*

Since these two tenses use the entire infinitive as their stem, only two examples are given here.

	amar to love	*comer* to eat
yo	*amaré/ía*	*comeré/ía*
tú	*amarás/ías*	*comerás/ías*
él/ella/Ud.	*amará/ía*	*comerá/ía*
nosotros, –as	*amaremos/íamos*	*comeremos/íamos*
vosotros, –as	*amaréis/íais*	*comeréis/íais*
ellos/ellas/Uds.	*amarán/ían*	*comerán/ían*

Future/Conditional Indicative–Irregulars

Verbs that drop the –*e* of the infinitive.

caber to fit	*haber* to have– auxiliary	*poder* to be able
cabré/ía	*habré/ía*	*podré/ía*
cabrás/ías	*habrás/ías*	*podrás/ías*
cabrá/ía	*habrá/ía*	*podrá/ía*
cabremos/íamos	*habremos/íamos*	*podremos/íamos*
cabréis/íais	*habréis/íais*	*podréis/íais*
cabrán/ían	*habrán/ían*	*podrán/ían*

querer to want	*saber* to know
querré/ía	*sabré/ía*
querrás/ías	*sabrás/ías*
querrá/ía	*sabrá/ía*
querremos/íamos	*sabremos/íamos*
querréis/íais	*sabréis/íais*
querrán/ían	*sabrán/ían*

Verbs that change the vowel (*e* or *i*) to a *d*.

poner to put	*salir* to leave	*tener* to have
pondré/ía	*saldré/ía*	*tendré/ía*
pondrás/ías	*saldrás/ías*	*tendrás/ías*
pondrá/ía	*saldrá/ía*	*tendrá/ía*
pondremos/íamos	*saldremos/íamos*	*tendremos/íamos*
pondréis/íais	*saldréis/íais*	*tendréis/íais*
pondrán/ían	*saldrán/ían*	*tendrán/ían*

valer **to be worth**	*venir* **to come**
valdré/ía	*vendré/ía*
valdrás/ías	*vendrás/ías*
valdrá/ía	*vendrá/ía*
valdremos/íamos	*vendremos/íamos*
valdréis/íais	*vendréis/íais*
valdrán/ían	*vendrán/ían*

Verbs that drop the *e* and *c* of the infinitive.

decir **to tell/say**	*hacer* **to make/do**
diré/ía	*haré/ía*
dirás/ías	*harás/ías*
dirá/ía	*hará/ía*
diremos/íamos	*haremos/íamos*
diréis/íais	*haréis/íais*
dirán/ían	*harán/ían*

Note: Compounds of the above words are conjugated in the same manner (*proponer, detener, contener*). However, **maldecir** and **bendecir** are conjugated as regular verbs in these two tenses and do not follow the pattern for **decir**.

Uses of Future/Conditional

Common translations include **will/shall** for the future and **would** for the conditional.

Saldré en seguida.	I shall leave immediately.
Me gustaría saberlo.	I would like to know it.
Juan vivirá conmigo.	Juan will live with me.

Probability Statements or Conjecture

The future tense is used to express **present** probability statements, while the conditional expresses **past** probability. These statements in English may be expressed a number of ways.

Present Probability	**Past Probability**
He **is** probably ill.	He **was** probably ill.
Estará enfermo.	*Estaría enfermo.*
[Debe de estar enfermo.] *	*[Debía de estar enfermo.]*
It **must** be 1:00.	It **must have been** 1:00.
Será la una.	*Sería la una.*
[Debe de ser la una.]	*[Debía de ser la una.]*
Where **can** he be?	Where **could** he be?
¿Dónde estará?	*¿Dónde estaría?*
I wonder who he **is**?	I wonder who he **was**?
¿Quién será?	*¿Quién sería?*

* ***Deber de*** + ***infinitive*** is another way to express probability statements.

Expressing "Would," "Wouldn't" with the Past Tense

When **would** means **used to**, the imperfect tense is used.
When **wouldn't** means **refused**, the negative preterite of *querer* is used.

Cuando era joven, iba al cine a menudo.
When he was young, he would go to the movies often.

No quiso verme.
He wouldn't (refused to) see me.

⬤ DRILL 2

1. Ninguna de las ventanas está sucia porque la criada las
    _____ ayer.

    (A) limpio   (C) limpió

    (B) limpiaba   (D) limpian

2. Ayer, al levantarme por la mañana, vi que_____un día estupendo.

    (A) hacía   (C) hizo

    (B) hará   (D) había hecho

3. Durante mi niñez siempre _____ a la casa de mis tíos.

(A) iría   (C) fui

(B) iba   (D) iré

4. Cuando tropezaron conmigo, _____ de salir del cine.

(A) acabaron   (C) acabé

(B) acababa   (D) acaban

5. Los jugadores no _____ jugar más.

(A) tuvieron   (C) quisieron

(B) trataron   (D) iban

6. Esta tarde mientras _____ el periódico, sonó el teléfono.

(A) miraré   (C) leía

(B) busqué   (D) estudio

7. Aunque ella vino temprano, no la _____.

(A) vi   (C) vea

(B) viera   (D) veré

8. Al despertarse Ramón se dio cuenta de que _____.

(A) llovió   (C) llovido

(B) llovía   (D) había llover

9. El ladrón entró por la ventana que _____ abierta.

(A) estuvo   (C) estará

(B) estaba   (D) estaría

10. La guerra de Vietnam _____ varios años.

(A) duraba   (C) duró

(B) durará   (D) hubo durado

11. _____ tres horas que regresó de su viaje.

   (A) Hacen   (C) Hace

   (B) Ha   (D) Desde

12. Yo_____ el colegio a los 10 años.

   (A) dejé   (C) dejara

   (B) dejaba   (D) dejase

13. Yo_____ dormido cuando me llamaste.

   (A) estaba   (C) estoy

   (B) estuve   (D) estaré

14. Lo_____ la semana que viene.

   (A) hicimos   (C) haremos

   (B) hacíamos   (D) habíamos hecho

15. Si yo fuera al centro, te_____ algo.

   (A) compraría   (C) compre

   (B) compré   (D) compraré

16. Cuando era niño, me _____ viendo pasar a la gente por las calles.

   (A) divertí   (C) divertiría

   (B) divertía   (D) divirtiera

17. ¿Cuánto tiempo_____ que hablabas cuando entraron?

   (A) hacía   (C) hacían

   (B) hizo   (D) había sido

18. Hacía dos horas que ellos_____ cuando sonó el teléfono.

   (A) charlaron   (C) habían charlado

   (B) charlan   (D) estaban charlando

19. Ayer al oír al testigo, el juez lo _____.

    (A) crea   (C) creyó

    (B) creía   (D) creerá

20. _____ las tres cuando el tren partió.

    (A) Eran   (C) Fue

    (B) Era   (D) Fueron

21. _____ dos años que terminó la guerra.

    (A) Hizo   (C) Hace

    (B) Hacía   (D) Hacen

22. Ayer yo _____ a Juan por primera vez.

    (A) conocía   (C) supe

    (B) conocí   (D) sabía

23. Hace dos semanas que no he visto a Ana. ¿_____ enferma?

    (A) Estará   (C) Va a estar

    (B) Esté   (D) Estás

24. Cuando Juan era joven, _____ al cine a menudo.

    (A) va   (C) iba

    (B) iría   (D) irá

25. Si tengo el tiempo, _____ el museo.

    (A) visitaría   (C) visitaré

    (B) visite   (D) visitaba

26. ¿Cuánto tiempo _____ que andas sin coche?

    (A) hacía   (C) hizo

    (B) haces   (D) hace

Drill 2—Detailed Explanations of Answers

1.   **(C)**   We know that a past tense is needed in this sentence because of the word "ayer" (yesterday). We must then choose between the two past tenses given among the choices: preterite and imperfect. The imperfect tense is often used to imply that a past action was incomplete, i.e., that it had not come to an end, that it was not concluded. In this sentence however, we know that the maid finished her task of cleaning the windows because we are told that for that very reason the windows are now clean. The preterite tense is used to show that a past action, as viewed by the speaker, is considered completed, over and done with.

2.   **(A)**   The use of the preterite of the verb "ver" tells us that we are talking about the past. In our sentence, we are describing what the weather was like yesterday morning. The imperfect tense, rather than the preterite, is most frequently used in sentences which describe the past, particularly if we do not wish to place undue emphasis on the idea that the situation described came to an end. This use of the imperfect tense is especially evident in contexts in which one is setting up the scene or describing the background against which other major events will take place, for example: "Era una tarde triste y lluviosa. No había nadie en la calle." (It was a sad and rainy afternoon. There was no one in the street.)

3.   **(B)**   In the sentence where you are to fill in the blank, the adverb "siempre" (always) is important. When we are talking about the past and we are referring to a customary or habitual action, as is the case in our sentence, we use the imperfect tense to place emphasis on the idea that the action was performed repeatedly (for an unspecified number of times). In (A), however, the verb "ir" is used in the conditional tense, not the imperfect. English speakers sometimes erroneously use the conditional tense in Spanish to express the idea of "would" in the sense of "used to," simply because English uses the word "would" both as a conditional and also to convey the concept of repeated and habitual past action. This cannot be done in Spanish. Compare the following two English sentences: (1) If he were here, I would know it. (2) Every Saturday when we were at the beach I would swim. Notice that only the second example has to do with a customary and habitual past action. It is in such a case that Spanish would use the imperfect tense instead of the conditional. Choice (C) is wrong because although the sentence refers to the past, it is in the preterite tense. Choice (D) is incorrect also because it is in the wrong tense, the future.

4.   **(B)**   The verb "tropezar" means "to stumble." The expression "tropezar **con**" means "to meet or encounter." Notice how the preposition "con," when followed by the prepositional pronoun "mí," results in the special form "conmigo."

The same thing happens in the second person singular (the familiar form) to produce the word "contigo." The expression "acabar de" + infinitive signifies "to have just" done something. This expression is normally only used in two tenses, the simple present and the imperfect. In the present it means "have or has just." In the imperfect it means "had just." Since our sentence contains a verb in the preterite tense, "tropezaron," we know that we are talking about the past. Therefore, we must logically use the only form of the imperfect that appears among the choices, "acababa."

5. **(C)** (A) is incorrect because "to have to" do something is "tener que" + infinitive, but we have omitted the "que." (B), "trataron," is wrong because we have not included the "de" from the expression "tratar de" + infinitive (to try to do something). In (D), "iban," the preposition "a" is lacking. Remember, "ir a" + infinitive means "to be going to" do something. (C), "quisieron," is the only answer which fits grammatically in our sentence. Try to recall the special meanings which the verb "querer" may have in the preterite tense. If the sentence is affirmative, it may be a synonym for "tratar de" (to try to). "Quisieron venir" would mean "They tried to come." If we simply mean "They wanted to come," we would use the imperfect tense: "Querían venir." If the sentence is negative, then "querer" in the preterite can mean "refused to," as is the case in our sentence. If we simply mean "They didn't want to come," then we would use the imperfect tense again: "No querían venir."

6. **(C)** In our sentence, "mientras" means "while," and "sonó" is the third person singular of the verb "sonar" (to ring—what a telephone does). Do not confuse "sonar" with "soñar" (to dream). Because "sonó" is a past tense, we know that neither (A), "miraré," the first person singular of the future of "mirar" (to look at), nor (D), "estudio" (I study), the first person singular of the present, can be used. Then we are faced with a choice between the first person singular of the preterite of "buscar" (to look for), in (B) "busqué," and "leía," the first person singular of the imperfect of "leer" (to read), in (C), which are both past tenses. When we are talking about the past and we wish to show that an action which was in progress was interrupted by another action, the action in progress is given the imperfect tense and the interrupting action appears in the preterite. In our sentence, the action which was in progress when something else cut across it or interrupted is "I was reading" ("leía"). The action which caused the interruption is "rang" ("sonó").

7. **(A)** After **aunque,** if the present tense is used, the independent clause is generally in the future. In this case, since it is in the past, the preterite indicative is correct. This sentence does not express any uncertainty, but fact. She did arrive, and early. Another statement of fact is that "I did not see her." Therefore, the subjunctive is not needed.

8.   **(B)**   The correct choice is "llovía" since the imperfect translates a sense of an ongoing event in the past (sometimes, as in this phrase, "intersected" by another discrete event, namely, "se dio cuenta"). The preterite, on the other hand, marks the start, end, or completed duration of an event. In this context such an event is the realizing and not the raining, which had already started outside the enunciation, so to speak. This is why choice (A) is incorrect. (As a rule of thumb, if a Spanish verb in the past can be translated into English by means of was + ing, then the Spanish verb can be rendered in the imperfect.) Choices (C) and (D) are wrong for other reasons: "llovido" is a past participle that requires an auxiliary verb ("haber") to function in the present context; and "había llover" is ungrammatical since compound tenses cannot be formed with the infinitive of the main verb.

9.   **(B)**   The window was already open. The real action of the phrase is the entering. By comparison, the reference to the window is in the mode of a **state** of things or in the mode of a **description**. This is why the correct answer involves an imperfect tense and not a preterite. Choices (C) and (D) do not correlate temporally with "entró."

10.   **(C)**   Again, the right answer is the preterite because the temporal function of the verb is to designate a duration. Choice (D) is a rarely used formation mostly reserved for literary style. It means the same as the preterite.

11.   **(C)**   The formula for this kind of expression is **hace** (never in the plural) + **time** + **que** + **preterite** (or **preterite** + **hace** + **time**). In English, this formula translates the particle "ago."

12.   **(A)**   Choices (C) and (D), both in the subjunctive, are ungrammatical, and (B) is not a good choice in view of the fact that the sentence is about temporal circumscription: the action of quitting school is "bound" by the point in time designated by "ten years." Remember that "imperfect" means incomplete and that an imperfect action is one that the sentence does not mark as ending (or beginning) in the past. The action described in this question, however, is complete; it is a point in time and not an open-ended line.

13.   **(A)**   Both (C) and (D) make no sense in terms of the temporal frame of the question. Now, the action of calling is in the preterite, which means it did not go on in time and that it is limited and complete in itself. But this is not true of sleeping, which becomes the temporal background for the instance of calling. And here we run into another criterion for learning the difference between preterite and imperfect: when there is a description in the past (as opposed to a main action), the verb used is in the imperfect.

14. **(C)**   This item simply tests your understanding that the future tense must be used in the sentence and your recognition of the future tense form of the verb "hacer" (to make or do), "haremos." We know that we must use the future because of the expression "la semana que viene" (next week) in our sentence. (A) "hicimos," is the first person plural of the preterite of "hacer." (B) and (D) give us, respectively, the first person plural of the imperfect, "hacíamos," and of the pluperfect, "habíamos hecho," of the same verb.

15. **(A)**   In an "if" clause in the past, using the subjunctive, the conditional is the appropriate form to follow.

16. **(B)**   You should first recognize the different forms of "divertirse" given as options and realize, for example, that "divirtiera" is a subjunctive form with no place in the sentence (because there is no "que" followed by a dependent verb). You can also eliminate (C) in order to avoid the contradiction in tense that would result if you put together an imperfect ("era") and a conditional. So the final choice boils down to a choice between the preterite form (A) and the imperfect one (B). The latter is correct because the action of having fun is not circumscribed temporally by any semantic element of the sentence. In other words, you may translate the second part of the sentence with "used to," and being able to do this automatically signals the use of the imperfect.

17. **(A)**   In time phrases that use the imperfect tense (hablabas), the third singular of the imperfect of "hacer" is needed. This would eliminate (C) because it is plural and (B) because it is preterite. Answer (D) is a form of the verb **ser**.

18. **(D)**   In time phrases beginning with "hacía," in either the imperfect tense or, in this case, the past progressive is correct. This would eliminate (A) the preterite and (B) the present tense of "charlar." Choice (C) could be used if it were negative.

19. **(C)**   Because the action occurred yesterday and "upon hearing" the witness, the preterite of the verb is necessary. If the sentence does not have any indications of past completion, the imperfect answer (B) would be preferred. This would eliminate (A) the subjunctive and (D) the future.

20. **(A)**   To express time in the past, the imperfect tense is used. Because it is "three" o'clock and, therefore, plural in Spanish, the plural form of the verb is required. Therefore, choice (B), which is singular, is incorrect. Because both (C) and (D) are in the preterite tense, they are incorrect.

21. **(C)** In order to express **"ago"** in Spanish, an "hace" statement of time will be followed by the preterite tense (in this case "terminó"). "Hace" will be written in the third person singular of the present tense in these statements. Therefore, choices (A), in the preterite, (B), in the imperfect, and (D), in the plural are all incorrect.

22. **(B)** Certain verbs change meaning in the preterite. "Conocer" means "met" in this tense. Because this happened yesterday (ayer) for the first time (por primera vez), we know that the preterite is necessary. This would make choice (A) in the imperfect incorrect. Also, to "meet or know" people requires the use of the verb **conocer**. Therefore, choices (C) "I found out" and (D) "I knew" for the verb **saber** are incorrect in this context.

23. **(A)** This question intimates probability in that it has been two weeks since Ana was seen last. To express present probability, the future tense is used. This may be translated a number of ways: I wonder if she is ill?; Can she be ill?; Is she probably ill? Choices (B), the present subjunctive, and (C), the immediate future, make no sense in this context. Choice (D) is the second singular to refer to Ana, but the third singular is required here.

24. **(C)** In English we often use "would" to refer to something we "used to" do in the past. In Spanish, however, this must be expressed with the imperfect tense, not the conditional. Choices (A), the present tense, (B), the conditional tense, and (D), the future tense, are incorrect in this context.

25. **(C)** In this question an understanding of **if** clauses is needed. Commonly when the **if** clause is in the present tense, the other clause will be written in the future tense. Choice (A) is conditional and would call for a past subjunctive to be used in the **if** clause. Choice (B), the present subjunctive, and (D), the imperfect, make no sense when translated in this context.

26. **(D)** Time expressions with **hace** have a certain formula. When asking "how long something **has been** going on," **hace** is paired up with the present tense (or present progressive tense). The other possible time expression would have **hacía** coupled with the imperfect (or past progressive tense). Since "andas" follows **que** and is in the present tense, "hace" must be used in the time expression. Choices (A), the imperfect, and (C), the preterite, are incorrect here. Choice (B) is in the wrong person to be used in an **hace** sentence.

FORMATION OF COMPOUND TENSES

Compound tenses are formed by adding an invariable past participle to the different forms of the auxiliary verb *haber*.

The Past Participle

The past participle in Spanish is formed by appending *–ado* to the stem of an *–ar* verb or *–ido* to the stem of an *–er* or *–ir* verb,

jugar – jugado (played)   *comer – comido* (eaten)
recibir – recibido (received)

The Irregular Past Participle

There are 12 irregular past participles.

abrir — abierto (opened)   *morir — muerto* (died)
cubrir — cubierto (covered)   *poner — puesto* (put)
decir — dicho (said)   *resolver— resuelto* (solved)
escribir — escrito (written)   *romper — roto* (broken)
hacer — hecho (done)   *ver — visto* (seen)
imprimir — impreso (printed)   *volver — vuelto* (returned)

Past Participles Ending in *–ido*

Most double-voweled infinitives will require an accent mark over the participle ending to separate the diphthong created when the weak vowel **i** follows the strong vowel of the stem.

oír – oído (heard)   *caer – caído* (fallen)   *leer – leído* (read)

Note: Verbs ending in *–uir* do not require accents in this form.

huir – huido (fled)   *construir – construido* (built)

Conjugation of *Haber*: Indicative Mood*

	Present	Preterite*	Imperfect	Future	Conditional
yo	*he*	*hube*	*había*	*habré*	*habría*
tú	*has*	*hubiste*	*habías*	*habrás*	*habrías*
él/ella/Ud.	*ha*	*hubo*	*había*	*habrá*	*habría*
nosotros, –as	*hemos*	*hubimos*	*habíamos*	*habremos*	*habríamos*
vosotros, –as	*habéis*	*hubisteis*	*habíais*	*habréis*	*habríais*
ellos/ellas/Uds.	*han*	*hubieron*	*habían*	*habrán*	*habrían*

* The preterite perfect is a literary tense not commonly used in everyday speech. It is always preceded by a conjunction of time:

luego que	as soon as	*apenas*	hardly, scarcely
en cuanto	as soon as	*cuando*	when
así que	as soon as	*después que*	after
tan pronto como	as soon as	*no bien*	no sooner

Conjugation of *Haber*: Subjunctive and Imperative Moods

	Present	Imperfect
yo	*haya*	*hubiera/hubiese*
tú	*hayas*	*hubieras/hubieses*
él/ella/Ud.	*haya*	*hubiera/hubiese*
nosotros, –as	*hayamos*	*hubiéramos/hubiésemos*
vosotros, –as	*hayáis*	*hubierais/hubieseis*
ellos/ellas/Uds.	*hayan*	*hubieran/hubiesen*

Names of Compound Tenses

Compound tenses are formed by combining different tenses of verbs to create a new one.

Perfect

The present indicative of *haber* with a past participle forms the **present perfect** tense:

He amado.
I **have** loved.

Han partido.
They **have** left.

Note: Only *haber* is conjugated. *Amado* and *partido* do not have to agree in gender and number with their respective subjects.

Pluperfect

The imperfect indicative of *haber* with a past participle forms the **pluperfect** or **past perfect** tense. This tense is used for a past action that precedes another past action:

Había amado.
I **had** loved.

Habíais comido.
You **had** eaten.

Habían partido.
They **had** left.

Future Perfect

The future of *haber* with a past participle forms the **future perfect**:

Habré amado.
I **will have** loved.

Habrán partido.
They **will have** left.

Note: This tense expresses an action that will take place **before** another. But very commonly the future perfect denotes probability in the past. Compare the following examples:

a) *¿Habrán partido antes de que comience a llover?*
   Will they **have left** before it starts to rain?

b) *Ya habrán partido.*
   They **probably left** already.

Conditional Perfect

The conditional of *haber* with a past participle forms the **conditional perfect**:

Habría amado.
I **would have** loved.

Habrían partido.
They **would have** left.

Perfect Subjunctive

The present subjunctive of *haber* with a past participle forms the **present perfect subjunctive**:

*Es increíble que no **haya amado** a nadie en su vida.*
It's incredible that he **has** not **loved** anyone in his life.

*Los extrañaremos cuando **hayan partido**.*
We'll miss them when they **have left**.

Pluperfect Subjunctive

The imperfect subjunctive of *haber* with a past participle forms the **pluperfect** or **past perfect subjunctive**:

*Yo no habría conocido la felicidad si no **hubiera amado**.*
I would not have known happiness if I **had** not **loved**.

*Él siempre había dudado de que sus amigos **hubieran partido** sin despedirse.*
He had always doubted that his friends **had left** without saying good-bye.

Past Participle as Adjective

When the past participle is used with **haber** to form the perfect tenses it is invariable. When not accompanied by some form of **haber**, it functions as an adjective and has four possible forms.

He roto la taza.	I have broken the cup.	[perfect]
La taza está rota.	The cup is broken.	[adjective]
Una ventana abierta	An open window	[adjective]

THE PRESENT PARTICIPLE

The present participle is formed by appending *-ando* to the stem of –*ar* verbs and *-iendo* to the stem of –*er* and –*ir* verbs.

andar–andando (walking)   *escribir–escribiendo* (writing)
vivir–viviendo (living)

Present Participles with a *y*

Double-voweled infinitives ending in –*er* and –*ir* (*creer, leer, oír, caer*, etc.) have a *y* in the present participle. It replaces the *i* of the participle ending.

caer–cayendo   *leer–leyendo*   *oír–oyendo*   *traer–trayendo*

Exception: *reír–riendo* (laughing)

Present Participles with Stem Changes

Verbs ending in –*ir* that have preterite tense stem changes use the same stem change in the present participle.

dormir–durmiendo   *pedir–pidiendo*   *servir–sirviendo*
(ue, **u**)   (i, **i**)   (i, **i**)

Irregular Present Participles

There are four irregular present participles.

ir–yendo   *poder–pudiendo*   *venir–viniendo*   *decir–diciendo*

The Present Formation of Compound Tenses
Participle with *Estar*

The present participle denotes an action in progress and commonly follows the verb *estar.* It corresponds to the "-ing" form of the verb in English. In Spanish it is always invariable. These are called progressive tenses.

Estoy comiendo.   I am eating.
Estaban leyendo.   They were reading.
Estaremos jugando al tenis.   We will be playing tennis.

The Present Participle with Motion Verbs

The present participle may also follow verbs of motion: *ir* (to go), *venir* (to come), *andar* (to walk), *entrar* (to enter), *salir* (to go out), etc.

Ella va corriendo por la calle.
She goes running down the street.

Juan entró riendo pero salió llorando.
Juan entered laughing but left crying.

The Present Participle with *Seguir/Continuar*

Present participles also follow forms of **seguir** (i, i) (to keep on) and **continuar** (ú) (to continue). In English, "to continue" is often followed by an infinitive. This will **not** occur in Spanish.

Siga leyendo.	Keep on reading.
Ellos continúan hablando.	They continue talking.
	They continue to talk.

The Present Participle Used Alone

The present participle does not need a helping verb to exist. It is often used alone.

Andando por la calle, se cayó.
Walking down the street, he fell down.

No conociendo bien la ciudad, se perdieron.
Not knowing the city well, they got lost.

When Not to Use the Present Participle

Never use the present participle as an **adjective**. Use a clause instead.

a crying child	*un niño que llora*
a frightening event	*un asunto que aterroriza*

Never use the present participle as a **noun** (gerund). Use the infinitive instead.

Seeing is believing.	*Ver es creer.*

Never use the present participle after a **preposition**. Use the infinitive instead.

después de comer	after eating

Never use the present participle of *ir* with the verb **estar**. Use *voy a, vas a, iba a,* etc.

Voy a salir.	I am going to leave.
Iban a comer.	They were going to eat.

REFLEXIVE PRONOUNS

Verbs whose action reflects back upon the subject are called reflexive. Infinitives of reflexive verbs in Spanish end in *–se*. Verbs of this type require the use of the reflexive pronoun group (*me, te, se, nos, os, se*). English uses pronouns such as myself, herself, themselves, etc. to designate reflexive actions. There are a number of reasons why a verb is reflexive.

1. The verb actually has a "reflexive" translation. I bathe "myself" = *Me baño.*

2. The pronoun is an inherent part of the verb and has no English translation: *atreverse a* (to dare to), *quejarse de* (to complain about), etc.

3. The pronoun alters the meaning of the verb in some way, other than reflexively: *irse* = to go **away**, *caerse* = to fall **down**, etc.

4. To render the meaning "get or become": *enfermarse* (to get ill), *casarse* (to get married), *enojarse* (to get angry), etc.

5. The pronoun is used with the verb when the subject is performing an action **on** his/her own body. *Me rompí la pierna.* = I broke my leg.

Placement of the Pronouns with Verbs

After selecting the pronoun that matches the subject of the verb, it will be placed either **before** the verb or **after** and **attached** to the verb. The following samples demonstrate the placement.

Quiero bañarme.	I want to bathe.	[infinitive]
¡Levántese!	Get up!	[+ command/formal]
¡No te sientes!	Don't sit down!	[– command/familiar]
Estás lavándote.	You are washing up.	[present participle]
Me llamo Juana.	I am called Juana.	[conjugated]

Uses of *Se*

The reflexive pronoun *se* is used in a number of ways.

1. To express the impersonal **one/people/they** statement with the third person singular of the verb.

   se dice = one says/people say/they say

2. To render "non-blame" statements when used with certain verbs: *perder* (to lose), *olvidar* (to forget), *romper* (to break), *quemar* (to burn). With statements such as these the speaker is indicating that something happened that was unintentional on his/her part. The *se* will precede the indirect object pronoun (which replaces the subject in English), and the verb will match the noun that follows it.

*se **me** rompió el vaso.*	**I** broke the glass.
*se **nos** perdió el dinero.*	**We** lost the money.
*se **le** olvidaron los libros.*	**He** forgot the books.

Reciprocal Actions

The plural reflexive pronouns (*nos, os, se*) are used to express "each other" in Spanish.

Se escriben.	They write to each other (to themselves).
Nos amamos.	We love each other (ourselves).

Note: Because the above statements could have a reflexive meaning (in parenthesis) as well, one may add the following phrase to clarify:

Se escriben	*uno a otro*	or	*el uno al otro*
	una a otra	or	*la una a la otra*
	unos a otros	or	*los unos a los otros*
	unas a otras	or	*las unas a las otras*

This additional clarifying statement is especially useful with verbs that are already reflexive. In those cases the reflexive pronoun cannot have dual meanings—it must act as a reflexive. As is often the case with these types, there is an accompanying preposition to be dealt with. This preposition is placed in the clarifying statement.

casarse con	to get married to
*Se casan uno **con** otro.*	They get married to each other.
burlarse de	to make fun of
*Se burlan uno **de** otro.*	They make fun of each other.

Reflexive Substitute for the Passive Voice

It is more idiomatic to replace the passive construction with a reflexive construction using the pronoun *se* and the verb in the third person singular or plural. This is especially true of passive sentences that have no expressed agent.

Aquí se habla español.   Spanish is spoken here.

➲ DRILL 3

1. Después de dos horas el orador siguió _____.

    (A) hablar   (C) habla

    (B) hablaba   (D) hablando

2. _____ olvidó lavar la ropa por la manaña.

    (A) Me   (C) Se me

    (B) Se   (D) Me lo

3. Los alumnos están _____ la composición.

    (A) escrito   (C) analizando

    (B) leen   (D) escriben

4. Los vampiros no _____ en el espejo.

    (A) lo ven   (C) le ven

    (B) se ven   (D) les ven

5. Los trabajadores han _____ su labor.

    (A) terminaron   (C) terminados

    (B) terminando   (D) terminado

6. Hace mucho tiempo que yo no _____ con mi mamá.

   (A) he hablado   (C) estaba hablando

   (B) había hablado   (D) hablado

7. _____ el trabajo, pudo salir a tiempo.

   (A) Haber terminado   (C) Al terminando

   (B) Estar terminando   (D) Habiendo terminado

8. Los problemas _____, cerró el libro y salió.

   (A) resueltos   (C) resolvidos

   (B) resueltas   (D) resuelven

9. Para este viernes ellos _____ la película.

   (A) habían visto   (C) habrán visto

   (B) habrían visto   (D) han visto

10. Ellos vinieron _____ por la calle.

    (A) andando   (C) andado

    (B) andar   (D) andados

11. _____, salió del cuarto.

    (A) Decírmelo   (C) Diciéndomelo

    (B) Me lo decir   (D) Deciéndomelo

12. Juan entró _____ después de oír el chiste.

    (A) reír   (C) reyendo

    (B) riendo   (D) riyendo

13. No continúes _____ en la iglesia por favor.

    (A) hablar   (C) hablado

    (B) a hablar   (D) hablando

14. Un niño_____ me causa pena.

    (A) que llora   (C) llorar

    (B) llorando   (D) a llorar

15. Esto es_____.

    (A) vivido   (C) viviendo

    (B) vivir   (D) viva

16. Los chicos_____por la calle cuando vieron al policía.

    (A) eran yendo   (C) yendo

    (B) estaban yendo   (D) iban

17. Al_____el ruido, todos corrieron.

    (A) oír   (C) oído

    (B) oyeron   (D) oyendo

18. ¡Ay de mí! ¡_____el vaso!

    (A) se me rompió   (C) se me rompieron

    (B) me rompí   (D) me rompieron

19. ¿Quieres_____antes de ir?

    (A) bañarse   (C) bañarte

    (B) báñate   (D) bañándote

20. Es importante_____la mano antes de hablar.

    (A) levantarse   (C) que te levantes

    (B) que levanta   (D) levantar

21. El sacerdote_____la pareja.

    (A) se casó   (C) casó a

    (B) se casó a   (D) casó con

22. Aunque vivimos en distintos lugares, _____ uno a otro cada semana.

(A) nos escribimos   (C) escribimos

(B) se escriben   (D) nos escriben

Drill 3—Detailed Explanations of Answers

1. **(D)** The gerund in Spanish may be used after a conjugated verb, as in this case. The only answer which is correct is **hablando. The siguió** is translated as "kept on" or "continued," i.e., verbs of motion.

2. **(C)** There are three different forms in which the verb "olvidar" (to forget) may be used. The simplest of these is "olvidar" used non-reflexively and followed by a noun or an infinitive, for example, "Olvidé lavar la ropa" (I forgot to wash the clothes). Another form is "olvidar**se de**" + noun or infinitive: "**Me** olvidé **de** lavar la ropa." The third form is also reflexive but does not use the preposition "de." It is always accompanied by an indirect object pronoun in addition to the reflexive pronoun: "**Se me** olvidó lavar la ropa." Notice that in this sentence the verb and the reflexive pronoun both are used in the third person singular. This is because the subject of the Spanish sentence is **not** "yo" (I), but rather the infinitive "lavar." In other words, the Spanish literally says "Washing forgot itself." In this sentence, "me" is an indirect object pronoun and means "to me." Therefore, "Se me olvidó lavar la ropa" literally means "Washing the clothes forgot itself to me." One would never say that in English. Instead, we would simply say "I forgot to wash the clothes." The indirect object pronoun, when used this way with the reflexive form of "olvidar," simply shows who is affected by the action of the verb. (A) "Me" will not work here. For it to be correct, we would have to change the verb to "olvidé" and then add the preposition "de."

3. **(C)** In order to form the present progressive tense, we use "estar" + –*ndo* verb form, meaning "to be doing (something)." Hence, we must say "están analizando" (are analyzing). The progressive tenses place very special emphasis on the fact that the action is (was, etc.) in progress or is (was, etc.) happening at a particular moment. If we do not wish to give that decided emphasis, we just use the simple tenses (present, imperfect, etc.) We can use the progressive form in all of the tenses simply by changing the tense of "estar," for example, "estaban analizando" (they were analyzing), etc. Choice (A) "escrito" is wrong because it is the past participle, not the present participle, of "escribir" (to write). (B) "leen" will not

function in our sentence because we cannot have two conjugated verbs, one immediately after the other ("están" and "leen"). The same is true for (D) "escriben."

4. **(B)** "Espejo" indicates that the pronoun needed is reflexive, and the only such pronoun among the choices is (B). The rest are direct object pronouns (A) or indirect, (C) and (D).

5. **(D)** What is needed to fill in the blank is a past participle, which eliminates the first two choices. You also must know that a past participle in a compound tense (following "haber") is invariable in person, gender, and number.

6. **(A)** "Time" statements beginning with **hace** are normally written using the present indicative or the present progressive tenses. Only in the case where the main verb is negative can a perfect tense be used. Choice (B) would be correct if the verb were negative and followed "hacía." Choice (C) also would be found in an "hacía" statement. Choice (D) makes no sense since it is the past participle by itself.

7. **(D)** The translation of this sentence indicates that a participle is required ("Having finished the work,") to make sense. In order for (A) to be correct in the infinitive form, it would have to act as a gerund (i.e., be the subject or object of the verb). Choice (C) is incorrect because **al** must be followed by an infinitive. Choice (B) makes no sense when translated and used in this context.

8. **(A)** The past participle may act as an adjective and in that capacity must match the noun it modifies. Because this noun is masculine and this participle is irregular, (A) is the correct answer. Choice (B) is feminine and (C) is an incorrect form of the past participle. Choice (D) is a conjugated verb and makes no sense in this context.

9. **(C)** By translating this sentence (By this Friday they will have seen the movie.) the proper perfect tense surfaces. Choice (A) "they had seen, (B) "they would have seen," and (D) "they have seen" make no sense in this context.

10. **(A)** Verbs of motion ("vinieron") can be followed by present participles, in this case "andando." They cannot, however, be followed by an infinitive (B) or the past participle (C) and (D).

11. **(C)** This sentence begins with the participial phrase meaning "Saying it to me." Because "Saying" is not the subject of the sentence, it will not be written as a gerund (the infinitive form in Spanish). Therefore, choice (A) is incorrect. Choice

(B) is incorrect not only because it is in the infinitive form but also because pronouns must be after and attached to infinitives. Choice (D) is misspelled.

12. **(B)** Again, verbs of motion may be followed by present participles. Choices (C) and (D) appear to be written in the present participle but are misspelled. Choice (A) is an infinitive and is, therefore, incorrect.

13. **(D)** Unlike English, the verb **continue** (continuar) in Spanish cannot be followed by either the infinitive or the present participle. In Spanish, only the present participle is correct with this verb. This would eliminate (A), the infinitive, (B), the infinitive preceded by an "a," and (C) the past participle.

14. **(A)** The present participle in Spanish may not act as an adjective. Phrases such as these must be converted to clauses such as the one found in this sample. Therefore, "a crying child" becomes "a child that cries" in the Spanish sentence. Therefore, (B), the present participle, (C), the infinitive, and (D), the infinitive with "a," are all incorrect.

15. **(B)** In Spanish, a verb used as a gerund, either as a subject or the object of the verb, must be in the infinitive form. Therefore, (A), the past participle, (C), the present participle, and (D), the present subjunctive, are all incorrect.

16. **(D)** "Ir" may not be used in the progressive tense in Spanish. In order to say that one "is or was doing something," a form of **ir a** (either in the present or in the imperfect tense) is used with the infinitive. Choice (B) is in the progressive tense and choice (A) is a form of **ser** with a present participle, which is never correct. Choice (C) is the present participle alone and makes no sense in the context of this sentence.

17. **(A)** The idiom **al** + **infinitive** means **upon** + **–ing**. Because choices (B), the preterite, (C), the past participle, and (D), the present participle, are not in the infinitive form, they are all incorrect.

18. **(A)** This sentence is considered a "non-blame" statement. Certain verbs (such as *perder, dejar, caer, romper*, etc.) are used in this manner so as to indicate that the subject did not commit the action on purpose. These sentences require using the reflexive pronoun **se**, the **indirect object** pronoun for the subject, and the verb in either the third person singular or plural depending on what follows it. In

this case "vaso" is singular and requires a singular verb. Choice (C) is, therefore, incorrect because the verb is plural. Choice (D) is plural and the reflexive pronoun is missing. Choice (B) would be correct if written as "rompí" alone but would then mean that this action occurred on purpose.

19. **(C)** After a conjugated verb the infinitive is necessary. In this case the subject (tú) requires adjusting the reflexive pronoun to match it. For this reason choice (A) is incorrect because the pronoun (se) does not match the subject (tú). Choice (B) is the familiar singular command and (D) is the present participle, neither of which would follow the conjugated verb in this sample.

20. **(D)** In order to answer this question, one must know the difference between "levantar" and "levantarse." The former means "to raise" while the latter means "to get up." This would then eliminate both (A) and (C). While choice (B) appears to be correct in that it is **not** reflexive, the verb form would need to be subjunctive to fit this particular sentence since it begins with an impersonal expression and there is a change in subject. "Levanta" in this sample is the present indicative.

21. **(C)** This sentence requires knowing the difference between "casarse con" (to get married) and "casar" (to marry). Because the priest is performing the ceremony, choice (C) is correct. The personal **a** precedes the direct object "pareja." Choice (A) is incorrect because it is reflexive and the meaning would not fit this sentence and (B), which is also reflexive, is followed by the wrong preposition. Choice (D) is not correct with "con."

22. **(A)** This is a statement calling for an "each other" translation. The phrase "uno a otro" also indicates this. In Spanish the plural reflexive pronouns are used in these statements. The phrase "uno a otro" is an additional piece so that the translation of the verb will not be confused for "we write to ourselves." Choice (B) is incorrect because the subject in this sentence is **we** (intimated in the first part of the sentence with "vivimos"). Choice (C) requires the matching reflexive pronoun "nos." Choice (D) means "they write to us" and doesn't fit the meaning implied by this sentence.

THE INFINITIVE

The Infinitive as the Subject of the Sentence

When the infinitive is used as the subject of the sentence (gerund) in English, it may be written in the infinitive form or end in "–ing." In Spanish this is written only in the infinitive form.

Seeing is believing.	*Ver es creer.*
Eating is important.	*Comer es importante.*

The Infinitive After Prepositions

In Spanish the only correct verb form that can follow a preposition is the infinitive.

antes de salir	before leaving
después de comer	after eating
al entrar	upon entering

The Infinitive with Verbs of Perception

The infinitive is used with verbs of perception **ver** (to see) and **oír** (to hear) when the sentence has a noun object.

Oí llorar al niño.	I heard the child cry.
Ella vio salir a Juan.	She saw Juan leave.

Verbs Requiring a Preposition Before the Infinitive

Certain verbs require an *a, en, de, por,* or *con* before the infinitive.

Verbs Requiring NO Preposition Before the Infinitive

aconsejar	advise to	*pensar (ie)*	think, intend to
deber	ought to	*permitir*	allow to
dejar	let, allow to	*poder (ue)*	be able to
desear	desire to	*prometer*	promise to
esperar	hope to	*querer (ie)*	wish to
impedir (i, i)	prevent from	*recordar (ue)*	remember to
lograr	succeed in	*rehusar*	refuse to

necesitar	need to	*saber*	know how to
oír	hear	*soler (ue)**	be accustomed to
pedir (i, i)	ask to	*temer*	be afraid to

* This verb is defective and commonly used in two tenses only—the present and the imperfect.

⇒ DRILL 4

1. Lavé la ropa después de _____.

   (A) cenar   (C) comida

   (B) comiendo   (D) había almorzado

2. Al _____ la alarma, todos abandonaron el hotel.

   (A) oyen   (C) oír

   (B) oyendo   (D) oído

3. Orlando oyó _____ a la puerta.

   (A) tocó   (C) tocando

   (B) tocar   (D) tocándola

4. El respirar no es _____.

   (A) vivir   (C) la vida

   (B) viviendo   (D) vive

5. Al _____ , le dije adiós.

   (A) salir   (C) salí

   (B) saliendo   (D) salido

6. _____ es bueno para el cuerpo.

   (A) Corriendo   (C) Correr

   (B) Corrido   (D) Fumar

7. _____ es bueno para la salud.

   (A) Dormir   (C) Dormido

   (B) Durmiendo   (D) Dormí

8. Sin_____, no puedo recomendar la película.

   (A) ver   (C) verla

   (B) veo   (D) verlo

9. Antes de _____ del autobús, Juan pagó el pasaje.

   (A) bajando   (C) bajar

   (B) el bajar   (D) baje

10. El policía vio _____ al ladrón del banco.

   (A) salida   (C) saliendo

   (B) salir   (D) salió

Drill 4—Detailed Explanations of Answers

1.   **(A)**   "Después de" (after) is a preposition. The only form of the verb we use directly following a preposition is the infinitive. Therefore, we cannot use the present participle, as in (B), "comiendo." The present participle in English is the verbal form ending in "–ing": for example, "eating." In English, this form may be used as a noun, in which case we call it a gerund. In a phrase such as "after eating," "eating" is a gerund and means "the act of eating." In Spanish, the form which corresponds to the "–ing," i.e., words ending in *–ando* and *–iendo*, do not follow a preposition. This is a mistake often made in Spanish by English speakers. Choice (C) is incorrect. If we want to say "after the meal" or "after the afternoon meal," we would have to use the definite article: "después de **la** comida." Choice (D) is also wrong. In Spanish, a conjugated form of the verb does not immediately follow a preposition. We could say, however, "después de haber almorzado" (after **having eaten** lunch). Then the verb is not in a conjugated form.

2.   **(C)**   Syntactically, the verb forms "oyen" (they hear), the third person plural of the present of "oír"; "oyendo" (hearing), the present participle; and "oído"

(heard), the past participle, will not fit correctly into this sentence. There is, however, an idiomatic construction based on **al** + **infinitive** which means "upon doing something." We find this form in (C).

3. **(B)** After verbs of perception (*oír, ver*), the infinitive is used. Therefore, (A), the preterite, and (C) and (D), the present participles, are incorrect.

4. **(A)** Verbs used as gerunds in Spanish (either as the subject or object of the verb) must be in the infinitive form. (B), the present participle, and (D), the present tense, are incorrect. (C) is incorrect because the infinitive is necessary to maintain parallel structure (infinitive/infinitive).

5. **(A)** The only verbal form that can follow "al" is the infinitive. It means "upon" + "–ing" in English.

6. **(C)** The key to this question is to remember that the infinitive can function as the subject of a sentence, but not the gerund (A) or the past participle (B). (D) "to smoke" is not good for "the body."

7. **(A)** This is another example of the use of the infinitive as the subject of the sentence. Therefore, (B), the present participle, (C), the past participle, and (D), the preterite are incorrect.

8. **(C)** After prepositions in Spanish the infinitive must be used. In the context of this sentence, the translation "without seeing it" makes most sense. "It" refers to *película,* which is feminine. (A) needs the direct object pronoun *la,* (D) has the incorrect direct object pronoun, and (B) is the present indicative, a conjugated verb form.

9. **(C)** The correct verb form after a preposition in Spanish is the infinitive. This would eliminate the present participle (A) and the subjunctive in (D). Choice (B) is a gerund and is not used after a preposition.

10. **(B)** After verbs of perception (ver/oír) the infinitive is used in Spanish. Therefore, the present participle (C), the preterite tense (D), and the noun meaning "departure" in (A) are incorrect.

FORMATION OF THE SUBJUNCTIVE

Present Subjunctive–Regular

	amar to love	*comer* to eat	*vivir* to live
yo	ame	coma	viva
tú	ames	comas	vivas
él/ella/Ud.	ame	coma	viva
nosotros, –as	amemos	comamos	vivamos
vosotros, –as	améis	comáis	viváis
ellos/ellas/Uds.	amen	coman	vivan

Present Subjunctive–Irregular

caber	quepa, quepas, quepa, quepamos, quepáis, quepan
caer	caiga, caigas, caiga, caigamos, caigáis, caigan
dar	dé, des, dé, demos, deis, den
decir	diga, digas, diga, digamos, digáis, digan
estar	esté, estés, esté, estemos, estéis, estén
haber	haya, hayas, haya, hayamos, hayáis, hayan
hacer	haga, hagas, haga, hagamos, hagáis, hagan
ir	vaya, vayas, vaya, vayamos, vayáis, vayan
oír	oiga, oigas, oiga, oigamos, oigáis, oigan
poner	ponga, pongas, ponga, pongamos, pongáis, pongan
saber	sepa, sepas, sepa, sepamos, sepáis, sepan
salir	salga, salgas, salga, salgamos, salgáis, salgan
ser	sea, seas, sea, seamos, seáis, sean
tener	tenga, tengas, tenga, tengamos, tengáis, tengan
traer	traiga, traigas, traiga, traigamos, traigáis, traigan
valer	valga, valgas, valga, valgamos, valgáis, valgan
venir	venga, vengas, venga, vengamos, vengáis, vengan
ver	vea, veas, vea, veamos, veáis, vean

Present Subjunctive–Spelling Changes

–*car*	*atacar*	ataque, ataques, ataque, etc.
–*gar*	*entregar*	entregue, entregues, entregue, etc.
–*zar*	*rezar*	rece, reces, rece, etc.
–*ger*	*coger*	coja, cojas, coja, etc.
–*gir*	*dirigir*	dirija, dirijas, dirija, etc.
–*guir*	*distinguir*	distinga, distingas, distinga, etc.
–*guar*	*averiguar*	averigüe, averigües, averigüe, etc.
–*uir*	*huir*	huya, huyas, huya, etc.
–*quir*	*delinquir*	delinca, delincas, delinca, etc.
–*cer*	*conocer*	conozca, conozcas, conozca, etc.
	vencer	venza, venzas, venza, etc.
–*cir*	*conducir*	conduzca, conduzcas, conduza, etc.

Present Subjunctive–Stem Changes

If a verb has only one stem change, it will appear in all persons except *nosotros* and *vosotros*. If there are two stem changes given, the second one will appear in the *nosotros/vosotros* forms of the present subjunctive while the first one will appear in all other persons.

(ú) **actuar** to act	(í) **enviar** to send	(ue, u) **morir** to die	(i, i) **pedir** to request	(ie, i) **sentir** to feel or regret
actúe	envíe	muera	pida	sienta
actúes	envíes	mueras	pidas	sientas
actúe	envíe	muera	pida	sienta
actuemos	enviemos	muramos	pidamos	sintamos
actuéis	enviéis	muráis	pidáis	sintáis
actúen	envíen	mueran	pidan	sientan

Past (Imperfect) Subjunctive–Regular

To form this tense, remove –*ron* from the end of the third person plural of the preterite and add the following endings:

–ra,	–ras,	–ra,	'–ramos,	–rais,	–ran
–se,	–ses,	–se,	'–semos,	–seis,	–sen

Either set of endings is correct, with the first set being the more widely used.

Past Subjunctive–Irregular

andar	*anduviera* or *anduviese*, etc.
caber	*cupiera* or *cupiese*, etc.
dar	*diera* or *diese*, etc.
decir	*dijera* or *dijese*, etc.
estar	*estuviera* or *estuviese*, etc.
haber	*hubiera* or *hubiese*, etc.
hacer	*hiciera* or *hiciese*, etc.
ir	*fuera* or *fuese*, etc.
poder	*pudiera* or *pudiese*, etc.
poner	*pusiera* or *pusiese*, etc.
querer	*quisiera* or *quisiese*, etc.
saber	*supiera* or *supiese*, etc.
ser	*fuera* or *fuese*, etc.
tener	*tuviera* or *tuviese*, etc.
traer	*trajera* or *trajese*, etc.
venir	*viniera* or *viniese*, etc.
–ducir	*condujera* or *condujese*, etc.
–uir	*huyera* or *huyese*, etc.

Past Subjunctive–Verbs with Stem Changes

Because the stem for the past subjunctive comes from the third person plural of the preterite, it will be affected by verbs that have stem changes in the preterite.

dormir (ue, u) to sleep	*sentir* (ie, i) to feel/regret	*pedir* (i, i) to ask for
durmiera	sintiera	pidiera
durmieras	sintieras	pidieras
durmiera	sintiera	pidiera
durmiéramos	sintiéramos	pidiéramos
durmierais	sintierais	pidierais
durmieran	sintieran	pidieran

Past Subjunctive–Verbs Like *Leer*

Because *–er* and *–ir* verbs with double vowels (*leer, oír, creer, caer*, etc.) have a *y* in the third person of the preterite, this *y* will be found in all forms of the past subjunctive.

oír   *oyera, oyeras, oyera, oyéramos, oyerais, oyeran*

COMMANDS: FORMAL AND FAMILIAR

The Formal Command

Formal commands (*Ud.* and *Uds.*) are always expressed by the present subjunctive. Some samples follow.

comer (eat)	(no) coma Ud.	(no) coman Uds.
volver (return)	(no) vuelva Ud.	(no) vuelvan Uds.
tener (have)	(no) tenga Ud.	(no) tengan Uds.
atacar (attack)	(no) ataque Ud.	(no) ataquen Uds.

The Familiar Command

Unlike the formal commands, which are derived from the same form (the present subjunctive), the familiar commands come from several different verb forms to cover the positive, negative, singular, and plural forms.

1. The singular (*tú*) form of the affirmative command is the same as the third person singular of the present indicative.

$$leer = lee \ (t\acute{u}) \quad lavar = lava \ (t\acute{u}) \qquad vivir = vive \ (t\acute{u})$$
read!   wash!   live!

2. The plural (*vosotros*) form of the affirmative command is formed by changing the *–r* ending of the infinitive to a *–d*.

$$leer = leed \quad lavar = lavad \qquad vivir = vivid$$
read!   wash!   live!

3. The negative forms come from the **tú** and **vosotros** forms of the present subjunctive.

$$leer = no \ leas \ (t\acute{u}) \quad lavar = no \ laves \ (t\acute{u})$$
      no leáis (vosotros)   *no lavéis (vosotros)*
      don't read!   don't wash!

Familiar Commands–Irregulars

The only irregular familiar commands occur in the affirmative singular. All other forms follow the rules stated above.

	tú	*vosotros*	*tú*	*vosotros*
decir	**di**	*decid*	*no digas*	*no digáis*
hacer	**haz**	*haced*	*no hagas*	*no hagáis*
ir	**ve**	*id*	*no vayas*	*no vayáis*
poner	**pon**	*poned*	*no pongas*	*no pongáis*
salir	**sal**	*salid*	*no salgas*	*no salgáis*
ser	**sé**	*sed*	*no seas*	*no seáis*
tener	**ten**	*tened*	*no tengas*	*no tengáis*
valer	**val**	*valed*	*no valgas*	*no valgáis*
venir	**ven**	*venid*	*no vengas*	*no vengáis*

Commands of Reflexive Verbs

Reflexive verbs require the use of reflexive pronouns. The formal command, singular and plural, uses *–se*. The familiar command uses *te* (singular) and *os* (plural). These pronouns **precede** the **negative command** and are **after** and **attached** to the **positive command**. Any time a pronoun is appended to a command form, an accent mark is required. Without it, the stress automatically moves to the next syllable, thus affecting the pronunciation.

Bañarse:	*báñese Ud.*	*no se bañe Ud.*
	báñense Uds.	*no se bañen Uds.*
	báñate tú	*no te bañes tú*
	bañaos vosotros*	*no os bañéis vosotros*

* When **os** is appended to the affirmative plural command, the final *–d* is dropped (**exception**: **idos**). If using an *–ir* verb, an accent is required over the *i* (*divertid + os = divertíos*) to split the diphthong and allow for the *i* to be pronounced separately.

"Let's" Statements

There are two ways to express this statement:

1. *Vamos a* + infinitive:

    | *Vamos a comer.* | Let's eat. |
    | *Vamos a sentarnos.* | Let's sit down. |
    | *Vamos a leérselo.* | Let's read it to him. |

2. First person plural present subjunctive:

    | *comamos* | Let's eat. | (*no comamos*) |
    | *leámoselo** | Let's read it to him. | (*no se lo leamos*) |
    | *sentémonos*** | Let's sit down. | (*no nos sentemos*) |

Exception: *Vámonos* = Let's go. *No nos vayamos.* = Let's not go. The affirmative is not derived from the subjunctive, but from the indicative.

* Because double *s* does not exist in Spanish, this verb form will eliminate one (*leámoselo*).

** Before adding **nos** to the reflexive verb form, the final *–s* is dropped. An accent mark is needed.

"Have"/ "Let"/ "May" Statements

Que + third person singular/plural present subjunctive

Examples:	Have her go.	*Que vaya ella.*
	Let him read it.	*Que lo lea.*
	May they do it well.	*Que lo hagan bien.*
	Have them give it to me.	*Que me lo den.*

Note: Pronouns precede these verb forms because they are the conjugated verb of the noun clause.

Dejar is also used to express **let**, with direct object pronouns.

Déjame ver.	Let me see.
Déjanos salir.	Let us leave.

➡ DRILL 5

1. No te _____ en el cuarto de Felipe.

   (A) acueste   (C) acuesten

   (B) acostéis   (D) acuestes

2. ¡No _____ Ud., por favor!

   (A) me hable   (C) me habla

   (B) hábleme   (D) me hables

3. ¡Que lo _____ Ud. bien!

   (A) pasar   (C) pases

   (B) pase   (D) pasa

4. Hola, mis amigos. ¡ _____ para hablar conmigo!

   (A) Siéntense   (C) Sentados

   (B) Siéntese   (D) Sentaos

5. La madre le dijo a su hijo, –¡ _____ al supermercado!

   (A) vete   (C) no vaya

   (B) váyase   (D) no va

6. Antes de salir mi madre me dijo, –¡ _____ el abrigo, hijo!

   (A) póngase   (C) pónete

   (B) póngate   (D) ponte

7. Hijos, no _____ mientras estoy hablando.

   (A) os reís   (C) os reíais

   (B) os riáis   (D) reíos

8.   Juanito, cuando salgas, _____ la luz.

    (A) apaga   (C) apagues

    (B) apague   (D) apagaste

9.   _____ aquí para poder ver mejor.

    (A) Nos sentamos   (C) Sentémosnos

    (B) Sentémonos   (D) Sentámonos

10.   No _____ con vuestros amigos esta noche.

    (A) os vayáis   (C) os vais

    (B) se vayan   (D) idos

Drill 5—Detailed Explanations of Answers

1.   **(D)**   This item tests your knowledge of the various forms of the imperative. The choices given are all command forms. We know that we are searching for the "tú" command, i.e., the second person singular imperative, because of the second person singular reflexive pronoun, "te," which is given in the sentence. Furthermore, we know that we must choose a negative imperative from the list because of the "No" in the sentence. Negative familiar singular commands in Spanish correspond to the second person singular of the present subjunctive, which, for "acostarse" (ue) (to go to bed), is "No te acuestes." Choice (A), "acueste," will not work because it is the command form for the third person singular (the "Usted" command), but we are given the second person singular of the reflexive pronoun in the sentence, "te." Choice (B), "acostéis," is the negative command for the "vosotros" form of the verb. Being a negative command, it is also like the corresponding form of the subjunctive of "acostarse," i.e., the second person plural. "Vosotros" is used only in Spain. In all of Central and South America, the third person plural (the "Ustedes" form) is used in its place. "Acostéis" is an incorrect answer here because the reflexive pronoun "te" is not the second person plural form. For (B) to be correct, we would have to say "No os acostéis... ." (C), "acuesten," is wrong also because the reflexive pronoun for it would have to be "se," the third person plural form.

2.   **(A)**   The negative formal singular command (Ud.) is required in this sentence. Object pronouns precede negative commands. Choice (B) is incorrect because the pronoun is after and attached to the positive command. Choice (C) is not in a command form, and (D) is the negative familiar command form.

3. **(B)** The exclamatory statement ("May it go well for you!") requires the use of the present subjunctive, which in this sample is the same as the formal command for "Ud." Choice (A), an infinitive, (C), the "tú" form of the verb, and (D), the present indicative form, are all incorrect.

4. **(D)** The familiar plural positive command is required in this statement ("amigos"). This is formed by removing the –d from the infinitive before attaching the reflexive pronoun **os** to the end. Choice (C) is incorrect because the –d has been retained. Choices (A) and (B) are both formal commands.

5. **(A)** Because the mother is speaking to her son, the familiar positive command is required in this sample. The familiar singular positive command of **irse** is irregular. Choice (B) is the formal command, (C) is the present subjunctive, and (D) is the present indicative.

6. **(D)** The mother is again addressing her son in this sentence, which requires the use of the familiar positive singular command of **ponerse** (to put on). This is irregular. Both (A) and (B) are formal command forms but (B) also has the incorrect reflexive pronoun attached. Choice (C) is an incorrect verb form.

7. **(B)** Because the children are being asked **not** to laugh in this sentence, the negative familiar plural command form is required. This form comes from the second person plural of the present subjunctive. Choice (A) is the second person plural of the present indicative. Choice (C) is the second person plural of the conditional tense, and (D) is the familiar plural positive command form.

8. **(A)** Because Juanito is being addressed in the familiar ("salgas"), the familiar positive singular command is required. For regular verbs this comes from the third person singular of the present tense. Choice (B) is the formal command, (C) is the second person singular of the present subjunctive, and (D) is the preterite tense.

9. **(B)** One way to express **let's** in Spanish is by using the "nosotros" form of the present subjunctive. If the verb is reflexive, the pronoun **nos** is attached to the end of this form, after removing the –s. Choice (A) is the present indicative. Choice (C) has retained the –s of the verb, and (D) is not in the present subjunctive.

10. **(A)** Because "vuestros" indicates that the command should be familiar plural and because the sentence is negative, the command form here will come from the "vosotros" form of the present subjunctive. Pronouns precede negative commands. Choice (B) is the third plural of the present subjunctive, (C) is the second plural of the present indicative, and (D) is the familiar plural positive command form.

THE SUBJUNCTIVE–USES

Subjunctive vs. Indicative

The indicative mood tenses express certainty or factual knowledge. The subjunctive mode is used to convey ideas in the realm of all areas other than those of objective fact: concepts that are hypothetical, contrary to fact, those which embody the expression of feelings of the speaker toward a state or action. Because the subjunctive is a **subjoined, subordinate, dependent** verb form, it is logical that it will occur in the **dependent clause** of the sentence. There are four types of clauses that could contain the subjunctive: noun, adjective, adverb, and "if."

The Noun Clause

The noun clause is a group of words that acts as the subject or object of the main clause. The subjunctive will occur in this clause if two conditions are met:

1. a change of subject between two clauses,

2. a specific category of verb is used in the main clause: wishing/wanting, emotion, impersonal expression, doubt/denial, or indirect command

To join the independent clause to the dependent clause, the relative pronoun *que* (that) is required in Spanish. In English we often leave this word out. Note the two possible ways to express the following statement in English.

I hope he's here.   I hope **that** he's here.

Category I–Wishing/Wanting

querer (to want)   *Quiero **que Juan vaya.***
                                      I want Juan to go.

Others: *desear* (to want), *preferir* (to prefer), *gustar* (to like), etc.

Category II–Emotion

temer (to fear)   *Temo **que Juan vaya.***
                                      I fear Juan (may, will) go.

Others: *tener miedo de* (to be afraid of), *lamentar* (to regret), *ojalá que* (if only), *sentir* (to regret/feel)

Category III–Impersonal Expression

An impersonal expression is a combination of **to be** with an adjective. The subject is always **it**. In Spanish, **to be** will come from *ser*.

es importante	*Es importante **que Juan vaya**.*
	It's important for Juan to go.

Others: *Ser* + adjective (*necesario, natural, probable, posible, mejor, lástima, triste,* etc.)

Note: Some impersonal expressions will **not** prompt a subjunctive if they imply **no doubt**. See exceptions on the next page. These expressions will require subjunctive only if negative.

Category IV–Doubt/Denial

dudar (to doubt)	*Dudo **que Juan vaya**.*
	I doubt Juan will go/is going.

Others: *negar* (to deny), *suponer* (to suppose), *puede ser* (it may be), *creer* (to believe),* *pensar* (to think),* *tal vez/quizás* (perhaps)

* *Creer/pensar* commonly take subjunctive if they are negative or in a question. This is dependent upon the speaker's point of view. If he/she actually believes or thinks what he/she is saying, the indicative will be used.

Category V–Indirect Command

pedir (to ask for)	*Le pido a **Juan que vaya**.*
	I ask Juan to go.

Others: *decir* (to tell), *sugerir* (to suggest), *exigir* (to demand), *insistir en* (to insist on), *aconsejar* (to advise), *rogar* (to beg)

Note: Several verbs from this category may be used with the infinitive or the subjunctive.

permitir (to permit)	*dejar* (to allow)
hacer (to make)	*aconsejar* (to advise)
impedir (to prevent)	*mandar* (to command)
prohibir (to prohibit)	*recomendar* (to recommend)

*(Te) aconsejo que **vayas**.* or *Te aconsejo ir.*
I advise you to go.

*No (me) permiten que **fume**.* or *No me permiten fumar.*
They do not permit me to smoke.

Many verbs in this category require the use of the indirect object pronoun in the independent clause used with the second subject: *rogar, pedir, decir, aconsejar,* etc.

Example: *Te ruego que (tú) hables con ella.*
                             I beg you to speak with her.

Exceptions

The following expressions are used with the **indicative unless** they are **negative**.

occurre que	it happens that
sucede que	
es evidente que	it's evident that
es cierto que	it's certain that
es verdad que	it's true that
es seguro que	it's sure that
es obvio que	it's obvious that
es que	it's that
se sabe que	it's known that
parece que	it seems that
no es dudoso que	it's not doubtful that

Sequence of Tenses

Whether the present or past subjunctive is used in the dependent clause is based on the tense used in the independent or main clause. Sequence primarily means the present subjunctive will follow present tense forms, while past subjunctive will follow past tense forms. Following is a list of tenses with sequence indicated.

Independent Clause (Indicative)		Dependent Clause (Subjunctive)
Present	*espero*	
Present Progressive	*estoy esperando*	***que vaya***
Future	*esperaré*	
Present Perfect	*he esperado*	
Future Perfect	*habré esperado*	***que haya ido***
Command	*espere/espera*	
Preterite	*esperé*	***que fuera***
Imperfect	*esperaba*	
Past Progressive	*estaba esperando*	
Conditional	*esperaría*	***que hubiera ido***
Past Perfect	*había esperado*	***que hubiese ido***
Conditional Perfect	*habría esperado*	

The Adjective Clause

An adjective clause is one that modifies or describes a preceding noun. This noun is called the antecedent and it will determine if the subjunctive will exist in the adjective clause itself. This antecedent must be (1) negative or (2) indefinite for the subjunctive to exist in the adjective clause.

To determine this, one must focus not solely on the antecedent itself but the surrounding words (the verb and/or any articles used with that noun).

Compare these two adjective clauses:

Indicative:	Subjunctive:
Tengo un coche que es nuevo. (antecedent=coche) [exists because he **has** it]	***Busco*** *un coche que sea nuevo.* [does not yet exist]
Busco **el** *libro que tiene la información.* (antecedent=libro) [a specific book exists with the information]	*Busco* **un** *libro que tenga la información.* [no specific book]

*Hay **varios** hombres que van*
con nosotros
(antecedent=hombres)
[these men exist]

*No hay **ningún** hombre que vaya*
con nosotros.
[a negative antecedent]

The Adverbial Clause

An adverbial clause answers the questions when? where? how? why? etc. These clauses are introduced by conjunctions. These conjunctions can be broken down into three separate types:

1. conjunctions **always** followed by the subjunctive

2. the *–quiera* group conjunctions (which are **always** followed by the subjunctive)

3. conjunctions **sometimes** followed by the subjunctive

Always Subjunctive

a fin de que/para que	so that
a menos que/salvo que	unless
con tal que	provided that
antes (de) que	before
en caso de que	in case (that)
sin que	without
a condición de que	on condition that

Examples: *Salió sin que yo lo supiera.*
He left without my knowing it.

Lo haré antes de que lleguen.
I'll do it before they arrive.

The *–quiera* Group

dondequiera que	wherever
cualquier (a) que	whatever
quienquiera que	whoever
quienesquiera que	whoever
cuandoquiera que	whenever
por + adj/adv + *que*	however, no matter how

Examples: *Dondequiera que vayas, serás feliz.*
Wherever you go, you'll be happy.

Por enferma que esté, ella asistirá.
No matter how sick she is, she'll attend.

Sometimes Subjunctive

Adverbial clauses begun with these conjunctions will have subjunctive only if there is speculation or doubt as to whether the action will take place in the future.

aunque	although
cuando	when
después (de) que	after
en cuanto	as soon as
luego que	as soon as
tan pronto como	as soon as
así que	so that
hasta que	until
mientras	while

Subjunctive	**Indicative**
*Aunque **cueste** mucho, lo quiero.* Although it may cost a lot, I want it.	*Aunque **costó** mucho, lo compré.* Although it cost a lot, I bought it.
*Léalo hasta que **llegue.*** Read it until he arrives.	*Lo leí hasta que **llegó**.* I read it until he arrived.
*Dijo que lo haría cuando **llegara**.* He said he would do it when he arrived. [hasn't gotten here yet]	*Lo hizo cuando **llegó.*** He did it when he arrived.

Normally, if the verb in the independent clause is in the future or command form, the subjunctive will be needed in the dependent clause. However, as is noted in the last example, this is not always the case. One must always think in terms of "has this happened yet or not?" and use the subjunctive accordingly.

The "If" Clause

The imperfect and pluperfect subjunctives are used in contrary-to-fact statements, as follows:

If Clause	Result Clause
Si yo estudiara/estudiase más,...	*recibiría (recibiera) buenas notas.*
If I studied more,...	I would get good grades.
Si yo hubiera/hubiese estudiado más,...	*habría (hubiera) recibido buenas notas.*
If I had studied more,...	I would have gotten good grades.

Note: The present subjunctive is **never** used in the **if** clause. Instead, the proper sequence (present indicative with future) follows:

Si yo estudio más,...	*recibiré buenas notas.*
If I study more,...	I will get good grades.

Como Si (as if) Statements

"As if" statements are always followed by the imperfect or the pluperfect subjunctive.

Habla como si la conociera bien.
He speaks as if he knew her well.

Me castigó como si lo hubiera hecho.
He punished me as if I had done it.

The *–ra* Form as Polite Request

The *–ra* forms of the imperfect subjunctive of *querer, poder*, and *deber* are often used instead of the conditional of these verbs to express a polite request or statement.

Quisiera hacerlo.	I would like to do it.
¿Pudieras pasarme la sal?	Could you pass me the salt?
Debieran comprarlos.	They should buy them.

➔ DRILL 6

1. Mis padres no deseaban que yo _____ eso.

   (A) hiciera   (C) haría

   (B) hacía   (D) haga

2. Si estuviera aquí, _____ hablar con ella.

   (A) me gustará   (C) trataría de

   (B) podemos   (D) me negué a

3. Te lo dirán cuando te _____.

   (A) ves   (C) visitemos

   (B) lo venden   (D) ven

4. Dijeron que nos enviarían el paquete tan pronto como _____.

   (A) lo recibieron   (C) tengan tiempo

   (B) llegara   (D) sabrán nuestra dirección

5. Me aconsejó que _____.

   (A) no siguiera la ruta de   (C) voy al médico
        la costa

   (B) duerma más   (D) venga inmediatamente

6. ¡Ojalá que me _____ un recuerdo de París!

   (A) traen   (C) enviarán

   (B) han comprado   (D) den

7. María le dio el periódico a Enrique para que él lo _____

   (A) lee   (C) lea

   (B) leyeran   (D) leyera

8. Si yo fuera al centro, te _____ algo.

    (A) compraría   (C) compre

    (B) compré   (D) compraré

9. Yo conozco a un señor que _____ español muy bien.

    (A) hable   (C) hablando

    (B) habla   (D) hablara

10. Su madre le dijo que _____ todo o no podría tener postre.

    (A) come   (C) comía

    (B) coma   (D) comiera

11. Lo harán cuando _____.

    (A) llegas   (C) puedan

    (B) entran   (D) tienen tiempo

12. Si _____ dinero, iría a Bolivia.

    (A) tenía   (C) tengo

    (B) tuviera   (D) tuve

13. _____ que tienes razón.

    (A) Creo   (C) Niego

    (B) Dudo   (D) Me alegro de

14. Siento que ellos _____ con Uds. ayer.

    (A) no estuvieron   (C) no estaban

    (B) no estuvieran   (D) no estarán

15. Si yo tuviera tiempo en Roma te _____

    (A) visito   (C) visitaré

    (B) voy a visitar   (D) visitaría

16. No estoy seguro, pero tal vez él _____

    (A) viniera   (C) viene

    (B) vendrá   (D) venga

17. Mi consejero me dijo que no dijera nada hasta que alguien me lo _____.

    (A) pide   (C) ha pedido

    (B) pidiera   (D) va a pedir

18. Se lo expliqué en detalle para que lo _____.

    (A) comprendiera   (C) comprende

    (B) comprenda   (D) comprendió

19. Mi madre dice que está bien que vaya mi hermano, con tal de que se lo _____.

    (A) cuida   (C) cuidaba

    (B) cuidara   (D) cuide

20. Le pedí que _____ temprano para acabar temprano.

    (A) venga   (C) venir

    (B) viniera   (D) venía

21. No quiere que su hijo _____ malas costumbres.

    (A) tenga   (C) tengan

    (B) tiene   (D) tienen

22. No creo que mis amigos me _____ abandonado.

    (A) han   (C) hayan

    (B) habían   (D) hubieran

23. Si él te _____ un beso, ¿cómo reaccionarías?

    (A) daba   (C) diera

    (B) da   (D) dar

24. No vendrías si_____ lo que te espera.

    (A) sabías   (C) sabes

    (B) supieras   (D) supiste

25. Mis padres me compraron un automóvil para que_____ a pasear.

    (A) salgo   (C) salga

    (B) salir   (D) saliera

26. Por bien que_____ Ana, no quiero jugar con ella.

    (A) juega   (C) está jugando

    (B) juegue   (D) jugara

27. Habla con ella como si la_____ bien.

    (A) conoce   (C) conociera

    (B) conozca   (D) conoció

28. Es evidente que los chicos no_____ en sus cuartos.

    (A) están   (C) son

    (B) estén   (D) sean

29. Mi mamá quería que_____ nuestra tarea a tiempo.

    (A) hagamos   (C) hiciéramos

    (B) hacemos   (D) hicimos

30. Si yo hubiera sabido la respuesta, se la_____.

    (A) diría   (C) había dicho

    (B) habría dicho   (D) diga

Drill 6—Detailed Explanations of Answers

1. **(A)** The verb "desear" can express volition, or desire that something happen. With verbs of this type, if there are two different subjects in the two clauses of the sentence, i.e., if someone is bringing his will to bear on someone or something

else, then the subjunctive is required. In our sentence the two different subjects are "Mis padres" and "yo." My parents were exerting their will on me. The sentence, however, requires the imperfect subjunctive, "hiciera," rather than the present subjunctive "haga," because the first verb, "deseaban," is in a past tense, the imperfect. Spanish normally observes a logical tense sequence in sentences requiring the subjunctive. If the first verb, the one that **causes** the subjunctive (in this case, "deseaban"), is in a past tense or the conditional tense, a past subjunctive is required (in this case, the imperfect subjunctive). On the other hand, if the verb that causes the subjunctive is in a present tense or the future, a present subjunctive is used. Note that we would not use the subjunctive, but rather the infinitive, if there were not two separate subjects involved: "Yo no deseaba decir eso" (I didn't want to say that).

2. **(C)** Sentences with subordinate clauses beginning with "si" (if), which establish an unreal or hypothetical situation, contain a past tense of the subjunctive (imperfect or pluperfect subjunctive). Our statement begins with such a clause. In these cases, the other clause (the one which shows what would happen if the "si" clause were true) is in the conditional or conditional perfect tense. Since the "si" clause (the hypothesis) is given here in a simple imperfect subjunctive, rather than the pluperfect subjunctive, we also should use the simple conditional tense in the result clause, rather than the conditional perfect. Note that there are times when one might use the future tense in a result clause, but in those cases the verb of the "si" clause is in the simple present or the present perfect. In such instances, the situation is viewed as much less hypothetical and possible of happening. Compare the following examples: "Si estudia, entonces sacará buenas notas" (If he studies...and it is possible he will..., then he will get good grades); "Si estudiara, entonces sacaría buenas notas" (If he were to study...but he doesn't..., then he would get good grades.) Only choice (C) could be used in this sentence because it is the only one which appears in the conditional tense. Choice (A) is in the future, (B) is in the present, and (D) is in the preterite. Remember that "tratar de" + infinitive is an idiom meaning "to try to." The expression "negarse a" + infinitive signifies "to refuse to."

3. **(C)** The word "cuando" in our sentence is an adverb which pertains to time. When adverbs of time such as "cuando," "hasta que," "tan pronto como," "así que," "luego que," and "mientras" refer to the future, we are obliged to use the subjunctive following them. Of the four possible choices, the only verb form which is subjunctive is found in (C), "visitemos," the first person plural of the present subjunctive of "visitar" (to visit). In (A), "ves," we find the second person singular of the present indicative of "ver" (to see); (B) gives us the third person plural of

the present indicative of "vender" (to sell); in choice (D), we find the third person plural of the present indicative of "ver." Remember that we do not always use the subjunctive after these adverbs of time. If the sentence does not refer to some future time, or if it expresses a customary or habitual situation, the indicative is used: "Siempre los veo cuando **vienen** a nuestro pueblo." (I always see them when they come to our town.) There are even situations in the **past** in which we may refer to some action that was **yet to happen** at some future time. In such instances, a subjunctive is also used following the adverb of time: "Iban a hablarles cuando **llegaran**" (They were going to speak to them whenever they arrived). Note that here we have had to use the imperfect subjunctive of "llegar," rather than the present subjunctive, because we are talking about something that was yet to happen in the past. This sentence implies that they had not yet arrived but were to arrive at some future time. Now, compare the following sentences: "Tratarán de hacerlo cuando tengan tiempo" (They will try to do it whenever they have time); "Dijeron que tratarían de hacerlo cuando tuvieran tiempo" (They said that they would try to do it whenever they had time). In the first example, the verb of the main clause, "tratarán," is future. If the verb of the main clause is future or some present form, then we use a form of present subjunctive. In the second example, the principal verb, "tratarían," is conditional. If the main verb is conditional or a past tense, we use a past form of the subjunctive, in this case, the imperfect subjunctive: "tuvieran."

4.   **(B)**   For a complete explanation of the use of the subjunctive following adverbs of time such as "tan pronto como" (as soon as), see the explanation for question 3. Also, pay particular attention to the example there which illustrates the use of the past subjunctive after these expressions if the main verb is in a past tense, as is the case in our sentence here. Choice (A) does not qualify because it is in the preterite tense of the indicative. Choice (C) is given in the present subjunctive, rather than the imperfect subjunctive. (D) appears in the future tense of the indicative.

5.   **(A)**   The verb "aconsejar" (to advise) embodies an expression of will or desire that someone else do something. It carries an implicit command. After such verbs it is necessary to use a subjunctive form in the dependent clause. Because the main clause of our sentence uses a past tense (preterite) of the verb "aconsejar," we must use a past tense of the subjunctive, the imperfect subjunctive. Choice (B) employs the present subjunctive of the verb; (C) offers us the present indicative; in (D), we once again find a present subjunctive.

6.   **(D)**   The noun "recuerdo" in our sentence means "souvenir." "Ojalá" and "Ojalá que" both mean "Oh, if only…" or "I wish or hope that…" They are expressions of desire. Unlike many such expressions, they do not require a change

of subject to produce a subjunctive in the following verb. In fact, if there is a verb after them, the subjunctive is obligatory. For that reason, choices (A), (B), and (C), are not useful to us. (A) is the third person plural of the present indicative of "traer" (to bring). (B) gives us the third person plural of the present perfect tense of "comprar" (to buy). (C) is the third person plural of the future of "enviar" (to send). Following "Ojalá" and "Ojalá que," if the present or present perfect subjunctive is used, the implication is that the situation is feasible and possible of happening. When we say "¡Ojalá que me den un recuerdo de París!," we mean "I hope that they will give me a souvenir from Paris!" (and it is **possible** that they will). On the other hand, we use a past subjunctive (imperfect or pluperfect) after these two expressions to show that the situation is highly hypothetical, unreal, or impossible: "¡Ojalá que **fuera** millonario!" (I wish I were a millionaire!...but I'm not, and probably never will be...).

7.   **(D)**   After the expression **para que,** the subjunctive must be used, and this sentence is in the past. The imperfect subjunctive is used after a principle clause containing the preterite, imperfect, or conditional tenses. Choice (D) is the only one in the imperfect subjunctive which is also singular.

8.   **(A)**   In an "if" clause in the past, using the subjunctive, the conditional is the appropriate form to follow.

9.   **(B)**   A known individual or thing does not require the subjunctive, but an unknown, i.e., an indefinite person or thing, does. In this case, it is known, present tense, and indicative. Therefore, choice (B) is correct.

10.   **(D)**   The imperfect subjunctive is necessary since the verb of the main clause is in the past and it requires the subjunctive following the rule of a verb of request (or similar meaning) directing an action of an object or person different from the subject.

11.   **(C)**   In our sentence, the word "cuando" is what we term an adverb of time. We can tell from the verb "harán" that we are talking about the future. Whenever an adverb of time refers to the future, we are required to use a subjunctive form of the verb in the following clause. Generally, if the main verb appears in the future or present tenses, we use the present tense of the subjunctive. Among the verbs which are your possible choices, only "puedan" is a present subjunctive form. All of the other choices appear in the present indicative. Even sentences whose main verb is in a past tense may occasionally refer to some future time, e.g., "Dijeron que lo harían cuando **pudieran**" (They said that they would do it whenever they could). Observe that here we cannot use the present subjunctive.

We must, on the other hand, use the imperfect subjunctive because we are referring to the past. When the verb does not refer to a future time or when it indicates a customary action, we use an indicative tense following adverbs of time: "Siempre me llaman cuando pueden" (They always call me when they can). Other common adverbs of time which have the same effect are: "hasta que," "tan pronto como," "mientras que," "así que," "luego que," and "en cuanto."

12. **(B)** Dependent clauses beginning with "si" (if) require the use of the **imperfect subjunctive** if they set up an impossible, hypothetical, or unreal situation. Then, in the other clause, we use the **conditional** tense to show what would happen (what the result would be) if that hypothesis were true. The only imperfect subjunctive form appearing among the choices is (B) "tuviera." (A) "tenía" is the imperfect indicative; (C) "tengo" is the present indicative; (D) "tuve" is the preterite. When we say "Si tuviera dinero, iría a Bolivia," we mean "If I had money (but I don't), I would go to Bolivia." In other words, we are emphasizing the unreality or impossibility of my having enough money. If, on the other hand, we wanted to imply that it is not totally unfeasible that I will have the money, we would say in English, "If I have the money, I will go to Bolivia." Notice that here, in the "if" clause, we have used the **present indicative**, and in the result clause, the **future** tense. This pattern would be observed also in Spanish: "Si tengo dinero, iré a Bolivia." Suppose we were talking about a situation in the past and we wanted to set up an unfeasible hypothesis or assumption: "If I had had money, I would have gone to Bolivia" ("Si hubiera tenido dinero, habría ido a Bolivia"). Here we have used compound or perfect tenses: in the "si" clause, the **pluperfect subjunctive**; in the result clause, the **conditional perfect**. Remember this caution: we never use a present or a present perfect subjunctive immediately after the word "si."

13. **(A)** How much do you remember about the uses of the subjunctive as opposed to the indicative? A careful scrutiny of the possible choices reveals that (B) "Dudo" (I doubt), (C) "Niego," (I deny), and (D) "Me alegro de" (I am happy) would require a subjunctive following them if we were to use them in the sentence. This sentence does not give the subjunctive form of "tener," "tengas," but rather the indicative, "tienes." Consequently, we must use (A) Creo (I believe), which does not require a subjunctive following it if it is used affirmatively. There are only two possible times when we **may** use the subjunctive after "creer": (1) if "creer" is used negatively, e.g., "No creo que tengas razón" (I don't believe you are right) and (2) if "creer" is used in a question, e.g., "Crees que llueva mañana?" (Do you think it will rain tomorrow?). Even when "creer" is used negatively or interrogatively, the speaker has the **option** of using the indicative, rather than the subjunctive, following "creer" if he wishes to show that he himself feels no doubt about the situation. Earlier, we indicated that the verb "dudar" requires the subjunctive. That is because expressions which cast doubt

on the second clause of the sentence bring about a subjunctive in the subordinate verb. The verb "negar" (ie) (to deny) produces a subjunctive in the following clause whenever it denies the validity or truth of the subordinate clause. Expressions of emotion, such as "alegrarse de" (to be happy), bring about a following subjunctive only if there is a change of subject between the two verbs. Otherwise, simply the infinitive is used.

14. **(B)**   "Siento" is the first person singular of the present tense of "sentir" (ie, i) (to be sorry). "Sentir" is a verb of emotion. It requires a subjunctive in the second part of the sentence when we have two different subjects. For this reason, (A) "no estuvieron," the preterite of "estar" (to be), (C) "no estaban," the imperfect of "estar," and (D) "no estarán," the future of "estar," are all wrong. (B), however, "no estuvieran," the imperfect subjunctive of "estar," is correct. Notice that although "Siento" is given in the present tense, we must use a past tense of the subjunctive because the action of the subordinate clause took place in the past. The word "ayer" (yesterday) is our clue.

15. **(D)**   In an "if" clause in the present tense, the independent clause is usually in the future and the dependent clause in the present subjunctive. If, however, the "if" clause is in the past, the independent clause is in the conditional. None of the other answers is correct.

16. **(D)**   After the expression **tal vez** indicating a future idea, the present subjunctive is used. Choice (A) is past subjunctive. Only choice (D) is correct.

17. **(B)**   The use of the subjunctive is required after **hasta que**. In this case, the sentence is in the past, so the imperfect subjunctive is required, even though the idea of the sentence indicates some action in the future.

18. **(A)**   After the expression **para que** the subjunctive can be expected. The introductory sentence begins in the preterite, so the imperfect subjunctive should be chosen.

19. **(D)**   After the expression **con tal de que** one expects the subjunctive. It should be noticed that this sentence is in the present tense. The only answer in the present subjunctive is (D). The reflexive in this answer is sometimes referred to as the dative of interest, or it could be considered as the indirect object meaning "for her."

20. **(B)**   First you have to decide between the subjunctive and the indicative mood (choice (C), an infinitive, is ungrammatical in the context), and once you decide that the correct mood is the subjunctive (because it is governed by a verb—

"pedir"—that always requires a subjunctive), then you have to opt between (A) and (B), that is, the present and the past. Since the main verb is in the past, the subjunctive form to follow must be in the same tense.

21. **(A)**   You should first eliminate the last two choices as ungrammatical since they are plural and "hijo" is not. Then you must decide between subjunctive (the correct choice because "querer" always requires the subjunctive) and indicative.

22. **(C)**   The four choices break down into two indicatives and two subjunctives. You must choose a subjunctive form at this point because when "creer" is preceded by a negative, it requires the subjunctive mood. Finally, this subjunctive verb must be (like "creo") in the present.

23. **(C)**   Three of these choices are ungrammatical, (A), (B), and (D) the first two because there is no tense correlation between "daba" (an imperfect form) or "da" (a present) and "reaccionarías" (a conditional form), and the third one because the infinitive must be conjugated. You should also realize that the structure of the sentence is of the "if/then" type, which always requires a subjunctive in the "if" clause.

24. **(B)**   This is also an "if/then" clause (inverted: "then/if"). Consequently, the "if" clause must contain a subjunctive form, the only one available being (B).

25. **(D)**   Your task in this question is easy if you know that "para que" always takes a subjunctive, though you still have to decide between (C) and (D). The key to this part of the answer is the main verb ("compraron"), which is in the past; therefore, the subjunctive verb that depends on it must also be in the past.

26. **(B)**   This adverbial phrase requires the use of the present subjunctive to follow sequence. Therefore, (A) the present tense, (C) the present progressive, and (D) the past subjunctive are incorrect.

27. **(C)**   "Como si" is always followed by the past subjunctive. Therefore, choice (A) the present indicative, (B) the present subjunctive, and (D) the preterite are incorrect.

28. **(A)**   Although this sentence begins with an impersonal expression and there is a change in subject (i.e., a second clause follows), the subjunctive is not required in the noun clause because there is no doubt implied. Other expressions of this type are "es verdad," "es cierto," "no es dudoso," and "es obvio que." This will

eliminate choices (B) and (D), which are both in the present subjunctive. Choice (C) is incorrect because this sentence points out location for which the verb **estar** is used.

29. **(C)** This sentence requires the use of the subjunctive because it begins with a verb of volition and there is a change in subject (from "mamá" to "we"). Because the verb in the independent clause (quería) is in the imperfect tense, to maintain proper sequencing, the past subjunctive is required in the dependent clause. Choice (A) is present subjunctive. Choice (B) the present indicative and (D) the preterite are incorrect since this sentence requires the use of the subjunctive.

30. **(B)** An "if" clause containing a compound verb form (the perfect tense) in the past subjunctive requires the use of a compound tense in the other clause, commonly written in the conditional tense. Choice (A), although it is in the conditional tense, is not compound. Choice (D) is in the present subjunctive and is, therefore, incorrect in this context. Choice (C) is a compound tense but in the pluperfect, not in the conditional perfect tense.

CONJUGATION OF *SER*

Indicative

	Present	Imperfect	Preterite	Future	Condit.
yo	soy	era	fui	seré	sería
tú	eres	eras	fuiste	serás	serías
él/ella/Ud.	es	era	fue	será	sería
nosotros, –as	somos	éramos	fuimos	seremos	seríamos
vosotros, –as	sois	erais	fuisteis	seréis	seríais
ellos/ellas/ Uds.	son	eran	fueron	serán	serían

Subjunctive

	Present	Imperfect
yo	sea	fuera/fuese
tú	seas	fueras/fueses
él/ella/Ud.	sea	fuera/fuese
nosotros	seamos	fuéramos/fuésemos
vosotros	seáis	fuerais/fueseis
ellos/ellas/Uds.	sean	fueran/fuesen

Imperative

Singular	Plural
sé (tú)	sed (vosotros)
no seas (tú)	no seáis (vosotros)
(no) sea (Ud.)	(no) sean (Uds.)

Participles

Past Participle: *sido*
Present Participle: *siendo*

CONJUGATION OF *ESTAR*

Indicative

	Present	Imperfect	Preterite	Future	Condit.
yo	estoy	estaba	estuve	estaré	estaría
tú	estás	estabas	estuviste	estarás	estarías
él/ella/Ud.	está	estaba	estuvo	estará	estaría
nosotros, –as	estamos	estábamos	estuvimos	estaremos	estaríamos
vosotros, –as	estáis	estabais	estuvisteis	estaréis	estaríais
ellos/ellas/ Uds.	están	estaban	estuvieron	estarán	estarían

Subjunctive

	Present	Imperfect
yo	esté	estuviera/estuviese
tú	estés	estuvieras/estuvieses
él/ella/Ud.	esté	estuviera/estuviese
nosotros, –as	estemos	estuviéramos/ estuviésemos
vosotros, –as	estéis	estuvierais/estuvieseis
ellos/ellas/Uds.	estén	estuvieran/estuviesen

Imperative

Present	Imperfect
está (tú)	estad (vosotros)
no estés (tú)	no estéis (vosotros)
(no) esté (Ud.)	(no) estén (Uds.)

Participles

Past Participle: *estado*
Present Participle: *estando*

Uses of *Ser*

"To be" followed by a predicate noun (a noun that is the same person as the subject) is always *ser*.

Él es médico.
He **is** a doctor.

Somos hombres con una misión.
We **are** men on a mission.

To express origin, ownership, or material consistency.

¿Es Ud. de Atlanta?
Are you from Atlanta?

Ese libro es de la biblioteca.
That book **is** the library's.

Esta mesa es de madera.
This table **is** (made) of wood.

Ser is used to mean "to take place."

La fiesta fue ayer.
The party **was** yesterday.

La reunión es mañana.
The meeting **is** tomorrow.

The use of *ser* with an adjective denotes that the speaker considers the quality signified by the adjective an essential or permanent component of the noun.

El agua es clara.
Water **is** clear.

La madera es dura.
Wood **is** hard.

Mi hermano es alto.
My brother **is** tall.

To tell time/dates/seasons:

Son las dos y media.	It is 2:30.
Es verano.	It is summer.
Es el primero de enero.	It is January 1.
Será tarde.	It will be late.

With "impersonal expressions"—these are expressions with adjectives whose subject is "it."

Es posible.	It's possible.
Será imposible.	It will be impossible.
Ha sido necesario.	It has been necessary.

To express religion or occupation:

Soy católica.	I am Catholic.
Son doctores.	They are doctors.

With the adjective *feliz:*

Ella es feliz.	She is "happy go lucky."

To express "passive voice"—when the agent (doer) is expressed:

La información fue leída por el profesor.
The information was read by the teacher.

With personal pronouns:

Soy yo.	It is I.
Es ella.	It is she.

Uses of *Estar*

Estar is used to express location.

*El estadio **está** a dos cuadras.*
The stadium **is** two blocks away.

*Los pañuelos **están** en el cajón.*
The handkerchiefs **are** in the drawer.

Estar is used with the present participle of other verbs to form the progressive tense.

__Está__ lloviendo.
It **is** raining.

__Están__ comprando los boletos.
They **are** buying the tickets.

Estar is used with adjectives to indicate a change from the norm, a temporary state of the subject, or a subjective reaction.

Estaba gordo cuando lo vi.
He **was** fat when I saw him.

El postre está rico.
The dessert **is** good.

To express the result of a previous action:

La tarea está hecha.
The homework **is** done.

La casa está bien construida.
The house **is** well built.

With certain idiomatic expressions:

Mi primo está de médico allí.
My cousin "***acts*** as" a doctor there.

Estamos por salir ahora.
We **are** in favor of leaving now.

Estoy por llorar.
I **am** about to cry.

Adjectives that Change Meaning with *Ser* or *Estar*

Mi tío es bueno.	My uncle is **good.**
Mi tío está bueno.	My uncle is **in good health.**
Tú perro es malo.	Your dog is **bad.**
Tu perro está malo.	Your dog is **sick.**
La función es aburrida.	The show is **boring.**
Mi esposa está aburrida.	My wife is **bored.**
Mi hijo es listo.	My son is **smart.**
Mi hijo está listo.	My son is **ready.**
Este edificio es seguro.	This building is **safe.**
El portero está seguro.	The porter is **sure.**
Ese hombre es cerrado.	That man is **narrow-minded.**
La puerta está cerrada.	The door is **closed.**
Su hija es callada.	His daughter is **taciturn.**
La noche está callada.	The night is **silent.**

Use of *Lo* with *Estar/Ser*

In Spanish, when a question with a form of *ser* or *estar* is followed by an adjective, the neuter object pronoun *lo* replaces that adjective in the reply.

¿Estás enfermo?	Are you ill?
Sí, lo estoy.	Yes, I am.
¿Son ricos los García?	Are the Garcías rich?
Sí, lo son.	Yes, they are.

➲ DRILL 7

1. ¿De dónde_____ Uds?

   (A) van   (C) son

   (B) se dirigen   (D) están

2. Esos cocos_____ de Cuba, ¿verdad?

   (A)   están   (C)   son

   (B)   estarán   (D)   sean

3. La boda_____ en la iglesia.

   (A) estuvo   (C) fue

   (B) fueron   (D) estando

4. Yo_____ dos noches en la selva.

   (A) esté   (C) estuve

   (B) era   (D) fui

5. El padre de Alicia_____ médico.

   (A) está   (C) estaba

   (B) es   (D) estará

6. Tú_____ equivocado cuando dijiste que yo no iría a la fiesta.

   (A) eres   (C) eras

   (B) estás   (D) estabas

7. Los niños han_____ tristes desde que sus padres les pro-hibieron ver televisión.

(A) sido   (C) estado

(B) sidos   (D) estados

8. El accidente_____ en la esquina, cerca de la tienda.

(A) estuvo   (C) está

(B) fue   (D) estaría

9. Los deportistas_____ débiles porque no han comido en tres días.

(A) son   (C) eran

(B) están   (D) habían sido

10. _____ posible hacer la tarea.

(A) Serán   (C) Está

(B) Ha sido   (D) Estaría

Drill 7—Detailed Explanations of Answers

1.   **(C)**   The question we most likely want to ask is, "Where are you from?" The verb "ser" is used when we are talking about origin; for example, "Soy de los Estados Unidos" (I am from the United States). In our question we are not talking about where these people are, i.e., what their location is. Consequently, "están" (D) would be wrong here. "Estar" does not refer to origin but to location. "Van" (A), and "se dirigen," (B) are normally followed by the preposition "a" (to), because people "go" or "direct themselves" **to** a place, not **from** a place, as "de" would mean.

2.   **(C)**   The origin of people and things is expressed in the verb **ser**. The subjunctive form is not needed here.

3.   **(C)**   **Ser** is used for an event or time, and in this case it is singular and in the past.

4.   **(C)**   To answer correctly, you must understand the differences between the two verbs in Spanish which mean "to be": "ser" and "estar." Only the latter is

used to refer to position or location. This immediately eliminates choice (B) "era" (the imperfect of "ser") and (D) "fui" (the preterite of "ser"). (A) "esté" is a form of "estar" but not the right one. It is the first person present of the subjunctive, and there is no reason to use a subjunctive form in this sentence. On the other hand, (C) "estuve" (I was), the first person preterite of "estar," works fine. We have used the preterite of "estar" rather than the imperfect because we know that the action came to an end. The expression "dos noches" puts a limit on the duration of my stay in the jungle ("selva"). Therefore, "estaba" (the imperfect) should not be used here. This particular use of the preterite of "estar" means the same as "pasé" (I spent).

5. **(B)** The only correct way to translate the verb "to be" when the complement is a noun is by means of "ser" and not "estar."

6. **(D)** The primary choice is between "ser" and "estar." In the expression "to be wrong," only "estar" can be used. In addition, you have to realize that the blank has to be filled with a verb in the past to correlate with "dijiste." This eliminates (B).

7. **(C)** The first thing you should notice here is that a form of "haber" is to be followed by some form of "to be." If you analyze the problem in this way, you'll immediately eliminate (B) and (D), provided you remember that a past participle is invariable in gender and number. Now you are left with the choice between "ser" and "estar," which should go in favor of "estar" because the action (or description "to be sad") began at a certain point and is thus a deviation from the norm (not to be sad).

8. **(B)** If you chose any of the forms of "estar" you might be confusing the sense of location with the notion of occurrence or happening that is translated into Spanish with "ser." To take place ("ser") is not the same as "to be located."

9. **(B)** Now an anomalous element (not eating in three days) has been introduced in the picture of normality described in the previous question, which explains why the right choice is "están" and not any of the other forms of "ser."

10. **(B)** Impersonal expressions (the subject of the verb **to be** is **it** followed by an adjective) require the third person singular of the verb **ser** in Spanish. This would eliminate (C) and (D) since they are both from **estar** and (A) because it is plural.

PRONOUNS

Personal Pronoun Chart

Subject	Prepositional	Direct	Indirect
yo	mí	me	me
tú	ti	te	te
él	él	le*	le–a él
ella	ella	la	le–a ella
ello	ello	lo	le–a ello
Ud.	Ud.		le–a Ud.
	sí		(se)
nosotros, –as	nosotros, –as	nos	nos
vosotros, –as	vosotros, –as	os	os
ellos	ellos	los	les–a ellos
ellas	ellas	las	les–a ellas
Uds.	Uds.		les–a Uds.
	sí		(se)

* *Le* is used to translate **him** or **you**. In Spain the direct object pronouns *lo* and *los* are often replaced by *le* and *les* when the pronoun relates to a person or to a thing personified. For the CLEP Spanish exam, one should follow the Latin American usage and avoid this substitution.

SUBJECT PRONOUNS

These pronouns are usually omitted in Spanish, as the verbal form by itself indicates person and number. (For the sake of clarity, *Ud.* and *Uds.* are usually not omitted.) Naturally, subject pronouns are used when confusion would result otherwise and in order to emphasize a statement. Often the particle *mismo (misma, mismos, mismas)* is used to add emphasis.

Fue *a comprar vino.*
He went to buy wine.

Ud. **fue** *a comprar vino.*
You went to buy wine.

Ud. **mismo fue** *a comprar vino.*
You yourself went to buy wine.

Second Person Subject Pronouns

Tú (you, singular) differs from *usted* in terms of familiarity. *Tú* is more intimate; *usted* is more formal. As a rule of thumb, *tú* is used with those people with whom the speaker is on a first-name basis.

In certain parts of Latin America (Argentina, Uruguay, Paraguay, Central America), the form *vos* is often used instead of *tú*.

Vos comes with its own verbal forms: *Vos venís a la hora que querés (Tú vienes a la hora que quieres).* You come at whatever time it pleases you.

Vosotros (you, plural) differs from *ustedes* regionally. In Latin America and in southern Spain, *vosotros* has been replaced by *ustedes*.

Ser Followed by a Subject Pronoun

In Spanish, the subject pronoun follows "to be."

*Soy **yo.***
It is **I**.

*Fue **ella** quien me envió el regalo.*
It was **she** that sent me the present.

OBJECT PRONOUNS

The direct object pronouns answer the question "whom" or "what"; the indirect object pronouns answer the question "to (for) whom" or "to (for) what."

*Ella **me** dió un regalo.*
She gave **me** a present. (**To whom** did she give a present?)

*Nosotros **lo** vimos.*
We saw **him**. (**Whom** did we see?)

Prepositional Complement with Indirect Object Pronoun

The indirect object pronoun can be clarified or emphasized by the addition of a prepositional complement (*a* + prepositional pronoun).

*Yo **le** hablé ayer.*
Yesterday I spoke to **him/her/you**.

*Yo **le** hablé **a ella** ayer.*
Yesterday I spoke to **her**.

Special Uses of the Indirect Object Pronoun

a) **Redundant Indirect Object Pronoun**. An indirect object pronoun is used in Spanish even when the indirect object noun is present in the sentence. The latter, however, must designate a person.

Les dije a **los empleados** que trabajaran más.
I told the employees to work harder.

Common verbs of this type are: *pedir* (to ask for), *preguntar* (to ask), *dar* (to give), *decir* (to tell), *gustar* (to like), and *regalar* (to give).

¡Pídaselo a Jorge!   Ask George for it!

b) **Dative of Interest**. Indirect object pronouns are also used to represent the interested party involved in the action designated by the verb. (In these cases English uses a possessive adjective or pronoun.)

Also, when the action results in some disadvantage or loss to the person directly concerned with the action, the indirect object is used. These are usually expressed with **from + person** in English.

***Me** robaron la billetera.*
They stole my wallet.

***Le** mataron al perro.*
They killed his dog.

*Ella siempre **le** esconde la medicina **al paciente**.*
She always hides the medicine from the patient.

c) **for + person** is often expressed in Spanish by an indirect object rather than by *para* + **person**, particularly when a service is rendered.

***Le** lavé la ropa a ella.*
I washed the clothes for her.

*Ella **me** cocinó la comida.*
She cooked the meal for me.

*Juan **nos** arregló la puerta.*
Juan fixed the door for us.

Exceptions: With *ser*– *Este té es para ti.*
This tea is for you.

Where the indirect object is receiving a concrete object, either way is acceptable.

Te traje flores. **or**
Traje flores para ti.

d) **Use the definite article** and indirect object pronoun if the subject of the sentence performs an action on a part of someone else's body.

*Ella **le** lavará la cara a María.*
She will wash Mary's face (for her).

*Julio **le** cortó el pelo a su hijo.*
Julio cut his son's hair (for him).

e) **After *ser* used impersonally**, the indirect object pronoun may be employed to denote the person **to** whom the impersonal expression is applicable.

***Le** será fácil hacerlo.*
It will be easy **for him** to do it.

When Not to Use the Indirect Object Pronoun

In the following two instances, the indirect object pronoun should be avoided and the prepositional phrase used in its place.

a) **After verbs of motion** (*ir, venir, correr,* etc.)

*¡Ven **a mí**, Paco!* Come to me, Paco!
*El niño corrió **a ellos**.* The boy ran to them.
*¡No se acerque **a él**!* Don't approach him!

b) **When the direct object is in the first or second person** (that is when it is **me, te, nos, os***)*, Spanish uses the prepositional phrase instead of the indirect object pronoun.

*Me presentaron **a él**.*
They presented **me** (D.O.) to him (prepositional phrase).

*Nos mandó **a ellos**.*
He sent **us** (D.O.) to them (prepositional phrase).

Special Uses of the Direct Object Pronoun

a) **Neuter Direct Object Pronoun**. In English the verb "to be" does not require a direct object pronoun, but in some cases both *estar* and *ser* need a **neuter** direct object pronoun to make the sentence grammatical. In these cases *lo* refers back to the whole idea expressed in the previous sentence.

¿Es Ud. médico? Sí, lo soy.
Are you a doctor? Yes, I am.

¿Estáis enfermos? No, no lo estamos.
Are you sick? No, we are not.

The neuter direct object pronoun may also be used with the verb "to know."

¿Sabes que Catalina se casó ayer? Sí, lo sé.
Do you know that Catalina got married yesterday? Yes, I know.

¿Tienes dinero que prestarme? ¡Ya lo creo!
Do you have money to lend me? You bet!

b) *Haber* **with Direct Object Pronoun**. The verb *haber* sometimes requires the use of a direct object pronoun unknown in English. Note that the direct object pronoun in the following example is no longer neuter.

¿Hay chicas en la fiesta? Sí, las hay.
Are there girls at the party? Yes, there are.

c) *Todo* **with Direct Object Pronoun**. A direct object pronoun is required before the verb when the object of the verb is *todo*. Note that the object pronoun agrees in number and gender with *todo*.

Lo he visto todo.
I have seen everything.

Las aprendí todas.
I learned them all.

d) **Verbs that contain prepositions in their meaning** (*esperar*–to wait **for**, *mirar*–to look **at**, *buscar*–to look **for**, *escuchar*–to listen **to**, etc.) will use the direct object pronouns.

La miré.
I looked at her.

Los buscaré para siempre.
I'll look for them always.

e) **Verbs used with D.O. + infinitive** = *dejar* (to let), *hacer* (to make), *ver* (to see), and *oír* (to hear).

*No **lo** dejen jugar.*
Don't let him play.

***Lo** hizo recitar.*
He made him recite.

***La** vi entrar.*
I saw her enter.

f) **Redundant direct object pronouns** are needed as follows:

1. With the noun when the object is a person or proper name.

   *Conociénd**ola** a Eloisa…*
   Knowing Eloisa…

   *Ojalá que **lo** cojan al ladrón.*
   I hope they catch the thief.

2. When the object precedes rather than follows the verb.

   La salida (D.O.) ***la** encontrará a su derecha.*
   The exit, you'll find it to your right.

Position of Object Pronouns in the Sentence

Unlike English, object pronouns in Spanish precede the conjugated verb (see examples above). However, they are attached at the end of the verb when the verbal form is an affirmative command, an infinitive, or a present participle.

*Ud. **le** escribe.* You write **to him.**	conjugated—present tense
*¡Escríba**le**! (or) ¡Escríb**ele**!* Write **to him!** (or her)	positive command
*Uds. **la** perdonaron.* You forgave **her.**	conjugated—preterite tense
*Hubo que perdonar**la**.* It was necessary to forgive **her.**	infinitive
***Los** dejó sobre la mesa.* He left **them** on the table.	conjugated—preterite tense

Salió dejándolos sobre la mesa.   present participle
He went out leaving **them** on the table.

Note: When the infinitive or the present participle is subordinated to an auxiliary verb such as *querer, ir, poder,* or *estar,* the direct object pronoun can go before these verbs or after, and attached to the infinitive or present participle:

I'm going to see **him.**	*Voy a ver**lo.***
I'm going to see **him.**	***Lo** voy a ver.*
I'm looking at **her.**	***La** estoy mirando.*
I'm looking at **her.**	*Estoy mirándo**la.***

Syntactic Order of Object Pronouns

When a verb has two object pronouns, the indirect object pronoun precedes the direct object pronoun.

Envían una carta.	They send a letter.
***Nos** envían una carta.*	They send a letter **to us.**
***Nos la** envían.*	They send **it to us.**
*¡Enví**ennosla**!*	Send **it to us!**
*¡No **nos la** envíen!*	Don't send **it to us!**

But when the two object pronouns in the sentence are third person pronouns, the **indirect** object pronoun (*le* or *les*) is replaced by *se.*

Escribes una carta.	You write a letter.
***Les** escribes una carta.*	You write a letter **to them.**
***Se la** escribes.*	You write **it to them.**
*¡Escríbe**sela**!*	Write **it to them!**

Prepositional Pronouns

Prepositions are words or phrases that relate words to one another. They may be followed by nouns, pronouns, or verbs (in the infinitive form in Spanish).

Here is a basic list of prepositions:

a	to, at	*excepto**	except
bajo	under	*hacia*	toward
como*	like	*hasta*	until, as far as, to

(continued)

Prepositions *(continued)*

*con***	with	*menos**	except
contra	against	*para*	for
de	from, of	*por*	for
desde	from, since	*salvo**	except
durante	during	*según**	according to
en	in, at, on	*sin*	without
*entre**	between, among	*sobre*	on, upon, over, above

*These prepositions are used with **subject** pronouns, not the prepositional group.

    según él y yo   according to him and me

**With this preposition the prepositional pronouns *mí, ti*, and *sí* combine to form *conmigo, contigo, consigo*. These combinations are invariable; there are no plural or feminine forms.

Here is a basic list of compound prepositions:

además de	besides	*encima de*	on top of
alrededor de	around	*en cuanto a*	in regard to
antes de	before	*enfrente de*	in front of
a pesar de	in spite of	*en lugar de*	instead of
cerca de	near	*en vez de*	instead of
debajo de	under	*frente a*	in front of
delante de	in front of	*fuera de*	outside of
dentro de	within	*lejos de*	far from
después de	after (time)	*para con**	toward
detrás de	behind	*por + inf*	because of

*To show an attitude toward, as in *"Es muy cariñoso (para) con su mujer."*

Use of *Sí, Consigo*

Sí is a special prepositional form of the pronoun *se*. It is often combined with a form of *mismo (–a, –os, –as)* to express "self." Note the difference between these two examples.

Ella no se refiere a sí misma.
She is not referring to herself.

vs.

Ella no se refiere a ella.
She is not referring to her (someone else).

Están disgustados consigo mismos.
They are disgusted with themselves.

vs.

Están disgustados con ellos.
They are disgusted with them (others).

Use of *Ello*

Ello means **it** when referring to situations or statements, but not to nouns.

Todo fue horrible; no prefiero hablar de ello.
It was all horrible; I prefer not to talk about it.

Para vs. *Por*

In general, *por* expresses the ideas contained in "for the sake of," "through," and "exchange," whereas *para* expresses destination, purpose, end, intention.

a) *Por* means "through"; *para* refers to destination.

Iba **por** *el parque.*	I was walking **through** the park.
Iba **para** *el parque.*	I was **on** my **way to** the park.

b) *Por* refers to motive; *para* to purpose or end.

Lo hizo **por** *mí.*
He did it **for** me (for my sake, on my behalf).

El artesano hizo una vasija **para** *mí.*
The artisan made a vase **for** me.

c) *Por* expresses the idea of exchange.

Lo cambié **por** *una camisa.*   I exchanged it **for** a shirt.

d) *Por* denotes a span of time; *para* designates an endpoint in time.

*Los exiliados caminaron **por** tres días y tres noches.*
The exiles walked **for** (during, for the space of) three days and three nights.

*El traje estará listo **para** el lunes.*
The suit will be ready by Monday.

e) *Para* translates "in order to."

*Fui a su casa **para** hablar con él.*
I went to his house **in order to** speak to him.

f) *Por* and *para* have set meanings in certain idiomatic constructions.

por *ejemplo*	**for** example
por *lo menos*	at least
para *siempre*	**for**ever
*No es **para** tanto.*	It's not that serious.

g) Other expressions using *por*.

por ahora	for now
por avión	by plane
por consiguiente	consequently
por desgracia	unfortunately
por ejemplo	for example
por encima	on top of
por escrito	in writing
por eso	therefore
por fin	finally
por lo común	generally
por lo contrario	on the contrary
por lo general	generally
por regla general	as a general rule
por lo tanto	consequently
por lo visto	apparently
por otra parte	on the other hand
por poco	almost
por si acaso	in case
por supuesto	of course
por teléfono	by phone
por todas partes	everywhere

IDIOMS WITH *A, DE, EN, SIN*

a) Idioms with *a*

a caballo	on horseback
a casa/en casa	at home
a causa de	because of
a eso de	at about (with time)
a fines de	at the end of
a fondo	thoroughly
a fuerza de	by dint of
a la derecha	to the right
a la izquierda	to the left
a la orden	at your service
a la vez	at the same time
a lo largo (de)	in the long run
a lo lejos	in the distance
a lo menos (al menos)	at least
a mano	by hand
a mas tardar	at the latest
a mediados (de)	in the middle
a menudo	often
a mi parecer	in my opinion
a pie	on foot
a pierna suelta	without a care
a principios de	at the beginning of
a saltos	by leaps and bounds
a solas	alone
a tiempo	on time
a través de	across
a veces	at times
a la española (francesa, etc.)	in the Spanish/French way
a la larga	in the long run
a la semana	per week
al aire libre	outside

al amanecer	at dawn
al anochecer	at nightfall
al cabo	finally
al contrario	on the contrary
al día	up to date
al fin	finally
al lado de	next to
al parecer	apparently
al por mayor	wholesale
al por menor	retail
al principio	at first

b) Idioms with *de*

de antemano	ahead of time
de arriba	upstairs
de balde	freely
de broma	jokingly
de buena gana	willingly
de cuando (vez) en cuando	from time to time
de día (noche)	by day, at night
de día en día	from day to day
de esta (esa) manera	in this (that) way
de este (ese) modo	in this (that) way
de hoy (ahora) en adelante	from today (now) on
de mala gana	unwillingly
de mal humor	in a bad mood
de manera que/de modo que	so that
de memoria	by heart
de moda	in style
de nada	you're welcome
de ninguna manera/de ningún modo	by no means
de nuevo	again
de otro modo	otherwise

(abrir) de par en par	(to open) wide
de pie	standing
de prisa	in a hurry
de pronto/de repente	suddenly
de rodillas	kneeling
de todos modos	anyway
de uno en uno	one by one
de veras	really

c) Idioms with *en*

en bicicleta	by bike
en broma	jokingly
en cambio	on the other hand
en caso de	in case of
en contra de	against
en cuanto	as soon as
en cuanto a	as for, in regard to
en efecto	in effect
en este momento	at this time
en lugar (vez) de	instead of
en marcha	under way, on the way
en medio de	in the middle of
en ninguna parte	nowhere
en punto	sharp (telling time)
en seguida	at once
en suma	in short, in a word
en todas partes	everywhere
en vano	in vain
en voz alta (baja)	in a loud (low) voice

d) Idioms with *sin*

sin aliento	out of breath
sin cuento	endless
sin cuidado	carelessly

sin duda	without a doubt
sin ejemplo	unparalleled
sin embargo	nevertheless
sin falta	without fail
sin fondo	bottomless
sin novedad	same as usual

VERBS WITH PREPOSITIONS

a) Verbs with *con*

amenazar	to threaten to
casarse	to get married to
contar (ue)	to rely on
cumplir	to keep (one's word)
encontrarse (ue)	to run into by chance
enojarse	to get angry with
estar de acuerdo	to agree with
meterse	to pick a quarrel with
quedarse	to keep
soñar (ue)	to dream about
tropezar (ie)	to meet by chance with

b) Verbs with *en*

apoyarse	to lean on
confiar (i)	to trust in
consentir (ie, i)	to consent to
consistir	to consist of
convenir	to agree to/on
convertirse (ie, i)	to become, change into
empeñarse	to insist on
especializarse	to major in
fijarse en	to notice, stare at
influir	to influence
insistir	to insist on
meterse	to get involved in

pensar (ie)		to think about
reparar		to notice
quedar		to agree to
tardar		to delay in

c) Verbs with *de*

acabar de + inf	*Acabo de comer.*	I just ate.
	Acababa de comer.	I'd just eaten.
	Acabé de comer.	I finished eating.

acordarse (ue)	to remember
alegrarse	to be glad
alejarse	to go away from
apoderarse	to take possession of
aprovecharse	to take advantage of
arrepentirse (ie, i)	to repent
*avergonzarse (ue)**	to be ashamed
burlarse	to make fun of
carecer	to lack
constar	to consist of
cuidar	to take care of
darse cuenta	to realize
dejar	to stop (doing something)
depender	to depend on
despedirse (i, i)	to say good-bye to
disfrutar	to enjoy
enamorarse	to fall in love with
encargarse	to take charge of
enterarse	to find out about
fiarse (i)	to trust
gozar	to enjoy
olvidarse	to forget about
oír hablar	to hear about
pensar (ie)	to think about
preocuparse	to be worried about

quejarse	to complain about
*reírse (i, i)***	to laugh at
servir (i, i)	to serve as
servirse (i, i)	to make use of
tratar	to try to + inf.
tratarse	to be a question of

*This verb will have a dieresis mark over the *ü* in the present indicative and subjunctive, in all forms except *nosotros* and *vosotros*: *me avergüenzo,* but *nos avergonzamos*

**This verb is conjugated as follows:

Present Indicative	Present Subjunctive	Preterite	Imperfect Subjunctive
me río	*me ría*	*me reí*	*me riera/se*
te ríes	*te rías*	*te reíste*	*te rieras/ses*
se ríe	*se ría*	*se rió*	*se riera/se*
nos reímos	*nos riamos*	*nos reímos*	*nos riéramos/semos*
os reís	*os riáis*	*os reísteis*	*os rierais/seis*
se ríen	*se rían*	*se rieron*	*se rieran/sen*

Present Participle: *riendo*

Past Participle: *reído*

Formal Commands: *ríase, no se ría*   *ríanse, no se rían*

Familiar Commands: *ríete, no te rías*   *reíos, no os riáis*

d) Verbs with *por*

acabar	to end up by
dar	to consider, to regard as
esforzarse (ue)	to make an effort
interesarse	to be interested in
preguntar + person	to ask for (a person)
tomar	to take (someone) for

e) Verbs with *a*

Verbs of beginning, learning, and motion are followed by an a in Spanish.

Beginning	Learning	
comenzar (ie) a	*aprender a*	to learn
echarse a	*enseñar a*	to teach
empezar (ie) a		
ponerse a		
principiar a		

Motion	
acercarse a	to approach
apresurarser a	to hurry to
dirigirse a	to go toward
ir a	to go to
regresar a	to return to
salir a	to leave to
subir a	to go up
venir a	to come to
volver a (ue)	to return to

Other verbs followed by *a*:

acertar (ie) a	to happen to
acostumbrarse a	to become used to
alcanzar a	to succeed in (doing something)
asistir a	to attend
asomarse a	to appear at
aspirar a	to aspire to
atreverse a	to dare to
ayudar a	to help
condenar a	to condemn to
convidar a	to invite to
cuidar a	to take care of (person)
decidirse a	to decide to
dedicarse a	to devote oneself to

detenerse a	to pause to
disponerse a	to get ready to
exponerse a	to run the risk of
invitar a	to invite to
jugar (ue) a	to play (game)
negarse (ie) a	to refuse to
obligar a	to obligate to
oler (ue) a*	to smell like
parecerse a	to resemble
querer (ie) a	to love
resignarse a	to resign oneself to
saber a	to taste like
ser aficionado, –a a	to be fond (a fan) of
someter a	to submit to
sonar a	to sound like
volver (ue) a + verb	to (do something) again

*This verb in the present indicative and subjunctive (except for *nosotros* and *vosotros*) will begin with "h." *El huele a ajo.* He smells like garlic.

CONJUNCTIONS

Conjunctions are words or phrases that connect clauses to one another. The following is a basic list of conjunctions:

o (u)	or
y (e)	and
pero, mas, sino que	but
ni	nor, neither
que	that
si	if, whether

Uses of the Basic Conjunctions

a) *O* changes to *u* in front of words beginning with *o* or *ho:*

No sé si lo dijo Roberto **u** Horacio.
I don't know whether Roberto **or** Horacio said it.

b) *Y changes to e in front of words beginning with i or hi:*

Padre e hijo viajaban juntos.
Father **and** son were traveling together.

Note: *Y does not change in front of y or hie:*

| *fuego y hielo* | fire **and** ice. |
| *Tú y yo.* | You **and** I. |

Pero vs. *Sino*

Pero, mas, and *sino* mean "but." (*Mas* with an accent mark, however, is an adverb meaning "more.") *Pero* and *mas* are interchangeable, but *pero* and *sino* have different uses. *Sino* (or *sino que*) has the sense of "rather" or "on the contrary." For *sino* or *sino que* to be used, the first part of the sentence must be negative.

*No dije roca **sino** foca.*
I didn't say "rock" **but** "seal."

*No vino para quedarse **sino que** vino y se fue.**
She didn't come to stay **but** came and left.

*Mi abuelo ya murió **pero** me dejó un buen recuerdo.*
My grandfather already died **but** he left me good memories.

*When the contrast is between clauses with different verb forms, *que* is introduced.

Correlative Conjunctions

Conjunctions such as *ni...ni* (see above) are not uncommon in Spanish. Other pairs are:

o...o	either...or
ya...ya	whether...or, sometimes...sometimes
no sólo...sino también	not only...but also

*Decídete. **O** te vas **o** haces lo que te digo.*
Make up your mind. **Either** you leave **or** you do as I say.

*Ella **no sólo** gana el dinero sino que también lo gasta.*
She not only earns the money but also spends it.

Conjunctive Phrases

Some conjunctions may require the use of the subjunctive. (See subjunctive–the adverbial clause.) The others follow:

apenas...cuando	hardly...when
a pesar de que	in spite of
conque	so then, and so, then
desde que	since
empero	however
entretanto que	meanwhile
más bien que	rather than
mientras tanto	meanwhile
no bien...cuando	no sooner...than
no obstante	notwithstanding

➲ DRILL 8

1. Mi viejo amigo Fernando trabaja_____ la Compañía Equis.

   (A) por   (C) cerca

   (B) a   (D) para

2. Miguelín_____ trajo café de Colombia.

   (A) ti   (C) mí

   (B) nos   (D) ella

3. _____ a él, no a ella.

   (A) Le parecen   (C) Se negaron

   (B) Se lo enseñaron   (D) Los vieron

4. Ayer compré unas sillas nuevas; son muy elegantes y juegan bien con los otros muebles. Son nuevecitas y no quiero que la gente se siente en_____.

   (A) las   (C) les

   (B) ellas   (D) ella

5. María me dijo un secreto. _____ dijo el otro día.

   (A) Me lo   (C) Me los

   (B) Lo me   (D) No me lo

6. Cuando entramos en el dormitorio, nos dimos cuenta de que los ladrones sólo habían robado nuestras corbatas nuevas. _____ llevaron toditas.

   (A) Las nos   (C) Se las

   (B) Nos la   (D) Me la

7. Invité a Carmela a que fuera _____.

   (A) conmigo   (C) con yo

   (B) con mi   (D) de aquí

8. Siempre al comer me gusta el pan con mucha mantequilla. A la mesa tengo que decirles a los otros que _____.

   (A) me pasen   (C) me la pasen

   (B) pásenmela   (D) se la pasen

9. —Mamá, prepáreme la comida. Ella me dice, _____.

   (A) "Te lo estoy preparando."

   (B) "Estoy preparándotela."

   (C) "La te preparo."

   (D) "Prepárotela."

10. Como era natural, el perro salió _____ la puerta.

    (A) para   (C) a

    (B) por   (D) de

11. Raúl no entendía el subjuntivo; el profesor _____.

    (A) se lo explicó   (C) lo explica

    (B) se los explica   (D) los explicó

12. Nuestros enemigos están trabajando_____.

   (A) con nos   (C) contra nosotros

   (B) contra nos   (D) connos

13. La silla estaba_____ la mesa.

   (A) antes de   (C) en cuanto a

   (B) detrás de   (D) después de

14. Mi novia quería casarse conmigo pero nunca_____dijo.

   (A) se le   (C) me lo

   (B) se lo   (D) lo me

15. Al presidente_____trataron de asesinar hace varios años.

   (A) se   (C) ello

   (B) lo   (D) les

16. Carmen es muy bella. Ayer_____vi.

   (A) la   (C) les

   (B) lo   (D) se

17. Me pidieron que_____entregara el informe directamente al jefe.

   (A) lo   (C) se

   (B) le   (D) la

18. El fugitivo ha regresado; yo mismo_____vi.

   (A) lo   (C) les

   (B) te   (D) se

19. Él_____dio un beso al despedirse.

   (A) lo   (C) le

   (B) la   (D) se

20. Este político sabe mucho_____la poca educación que tiene.

    (A) a causa de   (C) por

    (B) para   (D) porque

21. Todos mis amigos van al mercado menos_____.

    (A) mí   (C) conmigo

    (B) mi   (D) yo

22. Ella no es alta_____baja.

    (A) pero   (C) también

    (B) sino   (D) sino que

23. Yo no conozco al niño_____me gusta su coche nuevo.

    (A) pero   (C) pero que

    (B) sino   (D) sino que

24. Ella siempre_____esconde su dinero a mi madre y a mí.

    (A) nos   (C) les

    (B) le   (D) los

25. No puedo ver a mis amigas; tengo que_____.

    (A) buscarles   (C) buscarlas

    (B) las buscar   (D) las busco

26. Fue horrible; prefiero no pensar en_____.

    (A) lo   (C) ella

    (B) él   (D) ello

27. Esta taza es_____el café. ¡Démela, por favor!

    (A) por   (C) en

    (B) para   (D) con

28. La semana pasada me quedé en casa _____ tres días.

(A) por   (C) en

(B) para   (D) de

29. ¿Cuánto dinero me dará Ud. _____ mi trabajo?

(A) por   (C) de

(B) en   (D) para

30. _____ el viernes tenemos esta lección.

(A) En   (C) Para

(B) Por   (D) De

Drill 8—Detailed Explanations of Answers

1. **(D)** To work **for**, in the sense of "to be employed by," requires the use of "para" rather than "por." For this reason, (A) is wrong, but (D) is right. Thinking that you wanted to say "at," you might have mistakenly chosen answer (B), but the word "a" normally means "at" only when it follows verbs of motion: "Tiró la pelota a la pared" (He threw the ball at the wall). When motion is not involved, we use the preposition "en" to mean "at": "Mi madre está en el mercado" (My mother is at the market). Choice (C) is wrong because "near to" is "cerca **de**" and not simply "cerca."

2. **(B)** In the sentence, the verb "trajo" is the third person preterite of "traer" (to bring). We know that Miguelín brought someone coffee, i.e., Miguelín brought coffee **to** someone. The indirect object pronouns, which mean "to" or "for," are "me" (to or for me), "te" (to or for you, familiar singular), "le" (to or for him, her, you, polite singular), "nos" (to or for us), "os" (to or for you, familiar plural), and "les" (to or for them, you, polite plural). In the list of possible answers, we encounter only one pronoun from this list, "nos." In (A), we see the second person singular familiar form of the prepositional pronoun, i.e., a pronoun which is used following a preposition. Since there is no preposition this choice is incorrect.

3. **(B)** Choice (A) is incorrect because "parecerse a" (to resemble) requires a reflexive pronoun, but we are given the third person singular indirect object pronoun. In (C), we find the reflexive form of "negar," which is used in the idiomatic expression "negarse a" + infinitive (to refuse to). The "a" in our sentence, however, is not followed by an infinitive, but rather by a prepositional pronoun, "él." In (D),

we have used the third person plural masculine form of the direct object pronoun. Since we are referring to "él" (him), for this to be correct, we would have to use the masculine singular form of that pronoun, "lo." (B) is correct. It says, "Se lo enseñaron" (They showed or taught it to him). Observe the two object pronouns at the beginning of this answer. Remember that if we have two third person object pronouns (the first indirect, the second direct), the first of these automatically changes to "se." In our sentence, then, the "Se" would actually stand for the word "le." English speakers might question why the indirect object pronoun appears here since later in the sentence we find the prepositional phrase "a él," which means "to him." Nevertheless, the redundant use of the indirect object pronoun is typical of Spanish style, even though there may be a prepositional phrase later in the sentence which explicitly states the same idea.

4. **(B)** After a preposition, the object pronoun is expressed by the subject pronoun with the exception of the first and second persons singular. In this case, **ellas** is plural and would be the only correct answer because it refers to "chairs."

5. **(A)** The indirect object pronoun always precedes the direct. Both precede the verb unless this is in the infinitive. **Me lo** is the only correct answer because **lo** refers to **secreto**. Choice (D), although grammatically correct, does not follow the train of information given in the first sentence.

6. **(C)** The passive voice in Spanish can be translated by the reflexive **se**, and choice (C) is the only possible one because **las** refers to **corbatas**. (A) has the plural **las**, but the indirect object does not precede the direct.

7. **(A)** The first and second persons singular with the preposition **con** are always **conmigo** and **contigo**. Occasionally **consigo** is used, meaning **con él, con ella**, or **con usted**. The verb **invitar** is one of the verbs which, when followed by a change in subject, requires the subjunctive, and in this case, it is in the past. **Fuera** is the imperfect subjunctive form of **ir**.

8. **(C)** The indirect object pronoun always precedes the direct. In this case, the subjunctive is required because of the verb **decir**, as a request with a change of subject. The **la** refers to **mantequilla**. (A), (B), and (C) have **me**, but only (C) includes both the indirect and the direct objects in their proper position.

9. **(B)** The use of the auxiliary **estar** is correct with the present participle. The indirect and direct objects are joined in that order following the present participle. **Te** is used because the familiar form is appropriate, and the **la** refers to **comida**.

10. **(B)** **Por** is correct. It is the correct word for "through" in this context.

11. **(A)** The indirect object pronoun **le** is changed to **se** when used in conjunction with a direct object pronoun. **Lo**, in this sentence, refers to the subjunctive in the sentence. Choice (C) is a remote possibility, but is not totally correct grammatically.

12. **(C)** After a preposition, the subject pronoun should be used except for the first and second persons singular. Our enemies are supposedly working "against us," so choice (C) is the only correct answer.

13. **(B)** The preposition "antes de," in (A), means "before." It refers to time, not location. The sentence is talking about the position of the "chair" ("silla"). If we meant "before" in the sense of "in front of," we would have to use the preposition "delante de." The contrary of "delante de" is "detrás de" (behind, in back of), which fits well in our sentence. In (D), "después de" (after), we have another preposition which refers to time, not location. In (C) "en cuanto a" means "about" in the sense of "concerning."

14. **(C)** Neither of the first two choices can be the correct answer because in both "se" refers to a third person not to be found in the question. Choice (D) has the right object pronouns but in the wrong order. Choice (C) is the right answer because it contains the appropriate indirect object pronoun ("she said **to me**) and direct object pronoun ("she said **it** to me) in the correct sequence.

15. **(B)** The correct answer is the only direct object pronoun available. This is a peculiar but common use of the pronoun, which wouldn't be necessary if the sentence were in the normal syntactic order, namely, with the subject in front (an implicit "ellos") and the direct object ("presidente") in back. When the usual order is inverted, then a redundant object pronoun must be introduced.

16. **(A)** The question calls for a direct object pronoun. Of the two available, you need to choose the feminine form to go with "Carmen."

17. **(B)** This question calls for the indirect object pronoun, which you have to identify (there is only one) from the choices offered. The reason for this type of pronoun is that Spanish tends to reinforce the indirect object ("jefe") when it refers to a person.

18. **(A)** Here you need a direct object pronoun that refers to "el fugitivo" and the only possibility among the four choices is "lo."

19. **(C)** The direct object in this sentence is "un beso" and since it is present in the phrase there is no need for a direct object pronoun (such as "lo" or "la"). What the sentence does need is an indirect object pronoun referring to the implicit person (or pet or whatever) in the statement.

20. **(B)** "Para" is used whenever the idea of "considering" is implied.

21. **(D)** After certain prepositions (menos, excepto, salvo, entre, como, and según), subject pronouns are used in Spanish. Therefore, choice (A), which is prepositional, is incorrect. Choice (B) means "my" and choice (C) means "with me."

22. **(B)** "Sino" has the sense of "rather" or "on the contrary" and is used as the conjunction in a negative sentence where the second part directly contradicts the first. It is important to note that direct contradictions must be between equal parts of speech, in this case, between the adjectives "alta" and "baja." Choice (A) is incorrect because it cannot be used where a direct contradiction is implied. Choice (C) "also" makes no sense in this context. Choice (D) is used when the direct contradiction is between two conjugated verbs (i.e., Ella no quiere sentarse sino que quiere levantarse).

23. **(A)** Even though the first part of this sentence is negative, the second part is not a direct contradiction of the first. Therefore, choice (B) and (D) are incorrect. Choice (C) "pero que" (but that) makes no sense.

24. **(A)** When the action results in some disadvantage or loss ("hides") to the person directly concerned with the action, the indirect object pronoun is used. In English these statements are commonly expressed with **from + person**. Choice (A) is correct because the indirect object must correlate with the phrase "a mi madre y a mí," which is equivalent to **us**. Choices (B) "to him," (C) "to them," and (D) "to you" are also indirect object pronouns but do not correlate with the previously mentioned phrase.

25. **(C)** Verbs which include a preposition in their meaning (buscar–to look for, esperar–to wait for, mirar–to look at) are used with direct object pronouns. Choice (A) is incorrect because it has an indirect object pronoun. Choice (C) has the correct direct object pronoun but it is incorrectly placed. Choice (D) is incorrect because the conjugated verb "busco" cannot follow "tengo que," which requires the use of the infinitive.

26. **(D)**   The neuter pronoun "ello" (it) is used to refer to entire happenings, events, or occurrences previously alluded to. Choice (A) is a direct object pronoun and cannot be used after a preposition. Choices (B) "he/it (m)" and (C) "she/it (f)" are incorrect since there is no reference to anything specific that is either masculine or feminine in gender.

27. **(B)**   To indicate what something is intended for, use **para**. The intended use of the cup is for coffee.

28. **(A)**   **Por** is used to express a length of time. In this example, the length of time is three days.

29. **(A)**   **Por** is used when "in exchange for" is intended. In this sample it is money in exchange for work.

30. **(C)**   **Para** is used to express some point in future time. In this sample the future time indicated is Friday.

GUSTAR

Gustar and verbs like it follow a certain pattern that is unlike English. These verbs are commonly used in the third person singular and plural in conjunction with the indirect object pronoun group.

Gustar's Pattern

Because ***gustar*** means "to be pleasing to," its translation into Spanish from the English "to like" will require setting the verb up according to the following pattern:

I like cars.   = Cars **are pleasing** to me.
              = *Me **gustan** los coches.*

In the example given, after rearranging the sentence to fit the Spanish pattern, the indirect object surfaces (to me). In addition, one can see that the new subject (cars) will require using the verb in the third person plural. The following chart shows the indirect object pronoun group with **all** six persons "explained" with the prepositional phrase.

me	*– a mí*	*nos*	*– a nosotros*
te	*– a ti*	*vos*	*– a vosotros*
le	*– a él*	*les*	*– a ellos*
le	*– a ella*	*les*	*– a ellas*
le	*– a Ud.*	*les*	*– a Uds.*

This additional prepositional phrase that can accompany each of the indirect object pronouns can be used to:

1. further emphasize the indirect pronoun itself.

    *A **mí** me gusta la música clásica.*
    I really like classical music.

2. further clarify the meaning of le/les.

    *A **ella** le gustaban las películas de horror.*
    She liked horror movies.

3. provide a place to put names/nouns/proper nouns.

    *A **Juan** le gustará ir al cine conmigo.*
    Juan will like to go to the movies with me.

    *A **los chicos** les gustan los coches.*
    Boys like cars.

"*Gustar*" Types

Verbs that follow the "*gustar* pattern":

agradar	to be pleasing	*Nos agrada ir.* It pleases us to go.
bastar	to be enough	*Me basta un traje.* One suit is enough for me.
doler (ue)	to be painful	*Me duele la cabeza.* My head aches.
parecer	to seem	*A él le parece imposible.* It seems impossible to him.
placer	to be pleasing	*Nos place verte.* It pleases us to see you.
quedar	to have left	*Me quedó un buen libro.* I had one good book left.
sobrar	to be left over	*Les sobran tres dólares.* They have $3.00 left over.
tocar	to be one's turn	*A María le toca.* It's Mary's turn.

"To Need"

"To need" can be expressed three ways: *faltar, hacer falta,* and *necesitar.*

I need a car.	*Me falta un coche.* *Me hace falta un coche.* *Necesito un coche.*
I needed a car.	*Me faltó/faltaba un coche.* *Me hizo/hacía falta un coche.* *Necesité/Necesitaba un coche.*

Note: The verb "*faltar/hacer falta*" is commonly used in the present, preterite, and imperfect tenses. If one needs to express "need" in other tenses, use *necesitar.*

DRILL 9

1. A Roberto_____gusta ir a la playa todos los días durante el verano.

   (A) se   (C) le

   (B) os   (D) te

2. _____ chico le gusta jugar al tenis.

   (A) El   (C) A

   (B) Al   (D) nothing needed

3. A Rob y a mí_____ el helado.

   (A) les gusta   (C) nos gusta

   (B) les gustan   (D) nos gustan

4. Me encanta_____ dinero.

   (A) gastar   (C) gastaré

   (B) gastando   (D) pasar

5. _____ falta dos dólares.

   (A) Me hace   (C) Me haces

   (B) Me hacen   (D) Me hago

6. ¿A quiénes_____ toca?

   (A) lo   (C) les

   (B) le   (D) los

7. A mis amigos_____ el chocolate.

   (A) les gustó   (C) le gustó

   (B) les gustaron   (D) nos gustó

8. _____ nos encantó la cuidad.

   (A) A María   (C) A vosotros

   (B) A las mujeres   (D) A los niños y a mí

9. A José _____ dos cursos difíciles.

   (A) le bastará   (C) se bastarán

   (B) le bastarán   (D) bastarán

10. A Juan no le importaba _____.

   (A) los coches   (C) estudiando

   (B) ir al cine   (D) a trabajar

Drill 9—Detailed Explanations of Answers

1. **(C)** Normally, with the verb "gustar" and similar verbs, we use indirect object pronouns (me, te, le, nos, os, les). Although we usually translate "gustar" to mean "to like," we should remember that it literally means "to be pleasing **to**." This explains the use of "A" before "Roberto" in the sentence. It is pleasing "**to** Roberto." The indirect object pronoun can mean "to" or "for." It is for this reason that the indirect object pronoun is required here. Because "Roberto" is a singular noun, we must then use the third person singular indirect object pronoun "le."

2. **(B)** "Gustar" type verbs use indirect object pronouns, which can be further clarified by using prepositional phrases. These phrases begin with "a" and normally precede the indirect object pronoun that they go with. Choice (A) is incorrect because the preposition "a" is required. Choice (C) is missing the article "el" which is needed before the noun "chico."

3. **(C)** The "a" phrase contains the hint as to which indirect object pronoun to select. By including "me" with "Rob" the corresponding pronoun is "we" (nos). The verb is singular because the noun "helado" is singular. Choices (A) and (B) have the incorrect object pronoun. Choice (D) has the incorrect form of "gustar."

4. **(A)**   If a verb follows any verb used like "gustar," it must be in the gerund form (infinitive) since it is acting as the actual subject of the statement. Choices (B) the present participle and (C) the future tense are both in the incorrect form. Choice (D), although it is an infinitive, is incorrect because this verb means to spend "time" not "money."

5. **(B)**   The main verb in this expression (hacer), which means "to need" must match the item(s) needed. In this case two dollars are needed, which is plural. Answer (A) is singular and will not match the subject. Answer (C) the "tú" form of the verb and answer (D) the "yo" form of the verb **hacer** are not acceptable forms of this verb when used in this manner. It must either be third singular or third plural.

6. **(C)**   This "gustar" type means "to be one's turn." The prepositional phrase ("a quiénes) contains the hint as to which indirect object pronoun to select. Choices (A) and (D) are direct object pronouns and are not used with "gustar" types. Choice (B) is singular and will not match "a quiénes."

7. **(A)**   Because the noun "chocolate" is singular, a singular form of **gustar** is required. The prepositional phrase "A mis amigos" corresponds to the indirect object pronoun "les," Choice (B) is incorrect because the verb is plural. Choices (C) and (D) have the incorrect I.O. pronouns.

8. **(D)**   Because the indirect object pronoun "nos" has been used in this sentence, the corresponding prepositional phrase must match it. "A María" (A) would require "le," "A las mujeres" (B) would require "les," and "A vosotros" (C) would require using "os."

9. **(B)**   The verb must be plural to match "dos cursos difíciles," and the indirect object pronoun must correspond to the prepositional phrase "A José." Choice (A) has the incorrect verb form. Choice (C) has a reflexive pronoun, and (D) is missing the indirect object pronoun entirely.

10. **(B)**   After the verb "importaba" either an infinitive or a singular noun may be used. Choice (A) has a plural noun, and (C) is the present participle of "estudiar." Choice (D) has an additional "a" before the infinitive, which is unnecessary.

DEMONSTRATIVES: ADJECTIVES/PRONOUNS

These two groups share identical forms except that the accent mark is used over the pronouns.

Adjective		Pronoun	
this	*este, esta*	this one	*éste, ésta*
that	*ese, esa*	that one	*ése, ésa*
that*	*aquel, aquella*	that one*	*aquél, aquélla*
these	*estos, estas*	these	*éstos, éstas*
those	*esos, esas*	those	*ésos, ésas*
those*	*aquellos, aquellas*	those*	*aquéllos, aquéllas*

*These demonstratives are used to indicate greater distance from the speaker as well as distance in time. *Ése* (etc.) refers to something near the listener but removed from the speaker, whereas *aquél* (etc.) refers to something far from **both** the speaker and listener.

> *En aquella época...*   At that time...
> *Aquellas montañas...*   Those mountains...

Note: The definite article (*el, la, los, las*) followed by *de* or *que* is often translated as a pronoun.

> *mi corbata y **la de** mi hermano*
> my tie and **that of** my brother

> *Este libro y **el que** tiene Juan son interesantes.*
> This book and **the one that** Juan has are interesting.

NEUTER FORMS

The neuter forms (*eso, esto, aquello*) are used when the gender is not determined or when referring to vague or general ideas. These words do not vary in gender or number.

> *¿Qué es esto?*
> What is this?

> *Estoy enfermo y esto me enoja.*
> I'm ill and this makes me angry.

Former and Latter

The pronoun *éste* (*–a, –os, –as*) is used to translate **the latter** (the latest or most recently mentioned), while *aquél* (*–la, –los, –las*) expresses **the former** (the most remotely mentioned).

Juana and Pablo are siblings; the former is a doctor, the latter is a dentist.
Juana y Pablo son hermanos; éste es dentista, aquélla es doctora.

Note: In English we say "the former and the latter," but in Spanish this order is reversed.

➡ DRILL 10

1. Querida, ¿no crees que_____ anillo es tan lindo como los otros?

    (A) esto   (C) este

    (B) aquello   (D) esa

2. Mis nietos me regalaron_____ televisor.

    (A) eso   (C) aquel

    (B) esto   (D) esté

3. Muéstreme otro apartamento, no me gusta_____.

    (A) esto   (C) esté

    (B) este   (D) éste

4. _____ problemas son fáciles de resolver.

    (A) Estos   (C) Estas

    (B) Estes   (D) Esas

5. Llegó tarde y_____ me hace enojar.

    (A) eso   (C) esta

    (B) ésta   (D) aquel

6.   ¿Qué es_____?

(A) éste   (C) ésto

(B) esto   (D) ésta

7.   Estas camisas y_____a lo lejos son caras.

(A) ésos   (C) aquellas

(B) aquéllas   (D) ésas

8.   Rolando y Antonia son hermanos; ésta es alta y_____es inteligente.

(A) este   (C) aquél

(B) aquel   (D) ése

9.   Me gustan_____guantes porque son de cuero.

(A) estos   (C) estas

(B) éstos   (D) éstas

10. Mi corbata y_____Juan son de seda.

(A) ella de   (C) éste de

(B) ésa de   (D) la de

Drill 10—Detailed Explanations of Answers

1.   **(C)**   The masculine demonstrative adjective "este" means "this" and should be used to modify a masculine singular noun, just as is required by the sentence. "Esto" (this) in (A) and "aquello" (that) in (B) are pronouns, not adjectives, and they are neuter, i.e., they are neither masculine or feminine. The neuter pronouns "esto," "eso" (that), and "aquello" (that) are used to refer to ideas or concepts (not specific nouns), for example "Llueve mucho aquí. **Eso** no me gusta." Here the word "eso" does not refer to any particular word, nor does it modify anything. Rather, as a pronoun, it stands for or takes the place of the whole idea which was previously expressed, "Llueve mucho aquí." "Esa" in (D) is clearly wrong because we cannot use a feminine form of the adjective to modify a masculine noun.

2. **(C)** The verb "regalar" means "to give a gift." A "televisor" is a "television set." Choice (D) is inappropriate because it is a form of the present tense of the subjunctive "estar." The syntax of the sentence does not require a verb in the blank. All of the remaining choices are demonstratives, but only one, "aquel" (that), may function as an adjective, which is what we need in the blank in order to modify the word "televisor." (A) "eso" (that) and (B) "esto" (this) are not adjectives, but rather **neuter demonstrative** pronouns. Because they are neuter (neither masculine nor feminine), they cannot be used to refer to any specific noun. Instead, they are used to refer to whole concepts or ideas which have previously been mentioned: "Hace mucho calor en esta región y **esto** no me gusta" (It's very hot in this region, and I don't like this). The word "esto" in this sentence refers to no specific noun, but rather to the whole idea previously stated, "Hace mucho calor en esta región…"

3. **(D)** The demonstrative adjective form for "this" is converted into a pronoun by using the orthographic accent. (A) "Esto" is considered neuter, since it does not refer to a masculine or feminine noun. Choice (B) is the correct form for the masculine, but it needs the accent. Choice (C) is the correct form for the imperative. Only choice (D) is the proper form.

4. **(A)** "Problema" is masculine, which eliminates (C) and (D). The plural form of "este" (B) is "estos."

5. **(A)** When referring to an entire event, happening, or occurrence, the neuter form "eso" is used. Choice (B) is the feminine singular demonstrative pronoun meaning "this one." Choice (C) is the feminine singular demonstrative adjective meaning "this." Choice (D) is the masculine singular demonstrative adjective meaning "that" (in the distance).

6. **(B)** The neuter demonstrative is used when one doesn't know the gender of the item asked about. Choice (A) is the masculine singular demonstrative meaning "this one." Choice (C) is incorrect because the neuter forms do not require accent marks. Choice (D) is the feminine singular demonstrative pronoun meaning "this one."

7. **(B)** Because this demonstrative is replacing "camisas," it is being used as a pronoun and must, therefore, have the accent mark to differentiate it from the adjective. Also, "a lo lejos" (in the distance) requires some form of "aquél." Although (A) and (D) are pronouns, neither one is used for distance and (A) is the wrong gender. (C) is the demonstrative adjective meaning "that" and must precede a noun, *not* replace it.

8. **(C)** "Latter" (a form of "éste") and "former" (a form of "aquél") are expressed using the demonstrative pronouns. Whereas we say "the former...the latter," in Spanish this is reversed. In this sentence the former, Rolando, is being referred to by the statement "...es inteligente." Therefore, the masculine singular form "aquél" is needed to express "former." Choices (A) and (B) are incorrect because they are demonstrative adjectives. Choice (D) means "that one" and is not used to express "former or latter" in Spanish.

9. **(A)** "Guantes" (gloves) is the masculine noun requiring the demonstrative adjective. Choice (C) is incorrect because it is feminine. Choices (B) and (D) are demonstrative pronouns and cannot be used to modify nouns.

10. **(D)** Before the preposition **de**, the demonstrative is replaced by the definite article which will have the same gender as the noun referred to, in this case "corbata." Choices (B) and (C) are still in the demonstrative forms. Choice (C) also has the incorrect gender. Choice (A) makes no sense when translated ("she of").

RELATIVE PRONOUNS

Relative pronouns come in both a long and short form, as follows:

que	who, that, which, and whom	*el que/el cual*
quien		*la que/la cual*
quienes		*los que/los cuales*
		las que/las cuales

*El hombre **que** vi es médico.*
The man that I saw is a doctor.

*La mujer con **quien** hablé es mi hermana.*
The woman with whom I spoke is my sister.

*Las chicas con **quienes** ando son estudiantes.*
The girls with whom I walk are students.

Note: When referring to people, after a preposition only *quien* or *quienes* may be used.

*La madre de Juan, **la que/la cual** está allí, llegó tarde.*
John's mom, who is there, arrived late.

*La madre de Juan, **que/quien** es médico, llegó.*
Juan's mom, who is a doctor, arrived.

*Aquí está la mesa, sobre **la que/la cual** está la caja.*
Here's the table upon which is the box.

Note: The difference between **el que/el cual** is one of formality, **el cual** being more formal and less idiomatic than **el que**.

Use of the Long Forms

With reference to the samples above, the long form of the relative pronoun is preferred when:

1. *introducing a parenthetical clause whose antecedent is ambiguous; the long form always refers to the antecedent farthest away from that clause.*

   Note: When referring to the closest of the double antecedent, use the shorter form.

2. *using a long preposition followed by a relative pronoun.*

   Note: *por, sin,* and *para* must be included since putting *que* after these words will result in a change in meaning.

por qué = why	*por la que* = through which
sin que = without + subj.	*sin la que* = without which
para que = so that + subj.	*para la que* = for which

The Neuter Pronouns

1. *lo que*   that which, what
   Lo que dijo es verdad.   What you said is true.

2. *lo que/lo cual*
   "which" when referring to an entire idea, event, etc.

   *Todos los estudiantes salieron bien, **lo que/lo cual** le gustó a la maestra.*
   Everyone passed, which the teacher liked.

Note: *Lo que/lo cual* are only interchangeable when used as in (2) above. *Que* standing alone cannot be used.

Idiomatic Uses of the Pronouns

el que/quien	he who
la que/quien	she who
los que/quienes	those who
las que/quienes	those who (f)

Note: There are **no** accent marks. *Quien* is most commonly used in proverbs.

Whose = *Cuyo* vs. *De Quién*

Cuyo (*–a, –os, –as*) acts as an adjective and will agree with the noun following it.

El hombre cuya hija acaba de graduarse…
The man whose daughter has just graduated…

Note: When referring to parts of the body, use *a quien* instead of *cuyo*.

La niña, a quien la madre lavó las manos, es bonita.
The girl, whose hands her mother washed, is pretty.

De quién/de quienes is an interrogative and is followed by a verb.

¿De quién es este libro?   Whose is this book?
No sé de quien es.   I don't know whose it is.

DRILL 11

1. Los señores de_____ te hablo son extranjeros aquí.

    (A) que   (C) cuyos

    (B) cuales   (D) quienes

2. Marta,_____ hijo es ingeniero, vive en Buenos Aires.

    (A) quien   (C) de quien

    (B) cuya   (D) cuyo

3. _____ que no puedo entender es por qué se fue sin decir adiós.

    (A) Lo   (C) El

    (B) Ello   (D) Esto

4. ¿Conoces a los hombres con_____ el jefe acaba de hablar?

    (A) quien   (C) las cuales

    (B) quienes   (D) que

5. _____ estudia, aprende.

    (A) Quienes   (C) El que

    (B) Lo que   (D) Él que

6. La chica,_____ la madre cortó el pelo, es mi amiga.

   (A) a que   (C) de quién

   (B) a quien   (D) cuya

7. El padre de Anita,_____ es profesora, acaba de morir.

   (A) quien   (C) el cual

   (B) la cual   (D) a quien

8. La puerta, por_____ entró la reina, es del siglo IX.

   (A) quien   (C) qué

   (B) cual   (D) la cual

9. Mi hija Anita juega bien al tenis,_____ es bueno.

   (A) que   (C) cual

   (B) lo cual   (D) quien

10. En este edificio hay una gran ventana,_____ se ve las montañas.

    (A) por la cual   (C) por que

    (B) por cual   (D) por el que

Drill 11—Detailed Explanations of Answers

1. **(D)** We need a relative pronoun to complete the sentence correctly. A relative pronoun is one that relates back to a specific noun, pronoun, or idea stated earlier in the sentence (in this case, "señores"). The most common relative pronoun for both people and things is "que," but **following a preposition** (in this case, "de"), if we are referring to people, we may **not** use "que." On the contrary, we use "quien" (if we are referring back to a singular noun) or "quienes" (if we are referring back to a plural noun, as is the case in our sentence). The longer forms of the relative pronoun, "los que" and "los cuales," may also be used in this same situation, but are perhaps less frequent. Note that these must agree in number and gender with the noun to which they refer. Choices (A) and (B) could be correct only if we placed "los" in front of them.

2.   **(D)**   In our sentence, the word "ingeniero" means "engineer." "Cuyo" is a relative adjective which means "whose." By "relative" we mean a word which relates back to a noun which is previously mentioned in the sentence. In this instance, "cuyo" relates back to "Marta." It is she whose son is an engineer. Since "cuyo" is an adjective, it must agree in number and gender with the noun which follows it. In this case, then, "cuyo" agrees with "hijo," not with "Marta," and must be masculine singular. "Cuyo" and its other forms ("cuya," "cuyos," and "cuyas") are not used as interrogatives, i.e., to ask questions. If we want to ask "Whose is this book?", we would have to inquire "¿De quién es este libro?" Choice (A) "quien" is incorrect, for it is not the masculine form and cannot modify "hijo." (C) "de quién" will not fit because it cannot be followed immediately by a noun. It means "of whom."

3.   **(A)**   For this answer you need to remember that "que" is preceded by "lo" (a particle that never varies regardless of the context) when the construction can be translated as "that which."

4.   **(B)**   After a preposition when referring to a person or persons, a form of "quien" or "quienes" is needed. Because the antecedent (hombres) is plural, choice (B) is correct. Choice (C) could have qualified if it were masculine and choice (D) cannot refer to people.

5.   **(C)**   Although this sentence translates as "he who studies, learns," the relative pronoun without the accent is the correct answer. Choice (A) does not qualify because it is plural. Choice (B) means "that which" and choice (D) has an accent and is, therefore, incorrect.

6.   **(B)**   When referring to parts of the body, use **a quien** instead of a form of **cuyo**, which eliminates choice (D). Choice (C) is incorrect because it means "whose," as an interrogative and would be followed by a verb. Choice (A) means "to which" and makes no sense in this sentence. Also, after a preposition, when referring to people, use "quien" or "quienes."

7.   **(A)**   When referring to the last person mentioned in the double antecedent, a form of "quien" is used. Because it is stated that this person is a "profesora," we know the clause refers to Anita. Choice (C) would be correct if referring to the "padre." Choice (B) is the long form and would need to refer to "padre" which is the wrong gender, and choice (D) means "whom" or "to whom" which is not grammatically correct.

8. **(D)** The longer forms of the relative pronouns follow long prepositions or, as in this case, ones that would change meaning if used with the short form. In this case the translation "through which" cannot be stated using choice (C) "por qué" since that would mean "why." Choice (A) refers to people and choice (B) requires a definite article (in this case **la**) to be correct.

9. **(B)** The neuter form **lo cual** is correct since the second part of the sentence ("which is good") refers to the entire event or occurrence (the fact that Anita plays tennis well) stated in the first part of this sentence. Choices (A) and (C) would each need "lo" to be correct. Choice (D) would refer to people.

10. **(A)** Choices (A) and (D) each mean "through which," however, because the antecedent is feminine (ventana), choice (A) is correct. Choice (B) would need the definite article "la" to be correct. Choice (C) is confusing since it could be "why" if it had an accent.

AFFIRMATIVES AND NEGATIVES

The Affirmative and Negative Words

no	no	*sí*	yes
nadie	nobody, no one	*alguien*	someone
nada	nothing	*algo*	something
tampoco	neither	*también*	also
sin	without	*con*	with
ni…ni	neither…nor	*o…o*	either…or
jamás	never, not ever	*siempre*	always
nunca	never, not ever		
ninguno	none	*alguno*	some, any

Negative Expressions

ni (yo, Juan, ella) tampoco	nor (I, Juan, she) either
ni siquiera	not even
ya no	no longer
todavía no	not yet
sin novedad	nothing new
no…más que	only
no…más de	no more than
ahora no	not now
más que	more than
mejor que	better than
peor que	worse than
antes de	before
de ningún modo	by no means
de ninguna manera	by no means
apenas	hardly
no sólo…sino también	not only…but also

The Rules for Usage

Unlike English, statements with double (or more) negatives are correct. A negative sentence in Spanish, whether it has only one negative word or many, **must have** one negative **before** the verb. If there is more than **one** negative, the Spanish sentence may be written two ways.

*No tengo **nada**.*   ***Nada** tengo.*
*No veo a **nadie**.*   ***A nadie** veo.*
*No como **ni** pan **ni** queso.*   ***Ni** pan **ni** queso como.*

Sentences with multiple negatives are common.

*No dije **nunca nada a nadie.***
I **never** said **anything to anyone**.

If a personal *a* is required, it must accompany the negative.

Use of *Ninguno*

The plural forms of ***ninguno**, –a –os, –as* are no longer used. This word may be used with the noun or to replace the noun. *Ninguno, –a* and *Alguno, –a, –os, –as* have shortened forms before masculine, singular nouns: *ningún, algún.*

Ningún** libro…no tengo **ninguno
No book…I don't have any.

***Ninguna** pluma…no hay **ninguna** aquí*
No pen…there isn't any here.

***Ninguno** de ellos salió.*
None of them left.

***Ninguna** de ellas irá.*
None of them will go.

¿Tiene amigos Juan?
Does Juan have friends?

*No tiene **ninguno**.*
He hasn't any.

Use of *Alguno*

When *alguno*, *–a* follows a noun in Spanish, it makes the negative more emphatic (= at all). This happens with singular nouns only.

*Juan **no** tiene **ninguna** novia.*
Juan doesn't have **any** girlfriend.

*Juan **no** tiene novia **alguna**.*
Juan doesn't have a girlfriend **at all**.

Uses of *Jamás* and *Nunca*

The English **"never"** is normally expressed by *nunca* and **"never again"** by *nunca más*. In modern Spanish, *jamás* is a learned form mainly in literature. In spoken Spanish it is used to give great emphasis to **never**. In that case it means **absolutely never**.

*No volvió **jamás** a ver a su novia.*
He never again saw his girlfriend.

***Jamás** lo sabrás.*
You'll absolutely never know it.

*¡Nunca **jamás**!*
Never again!

Jamás also means **ever** in a question expecting a negative answer.

*¿Ha visto Ud. **jamás** nada que iguale a esto? ¡**Nunca**!*
Have you **ever** seen anything to equal this? **Never**!

Nada as Intensifier

Nada may be used adverbially with the meaning "not at all."

Manuel no trabaja nada.
Manuel does absolutely no work.

No hemos dormido nada.
We haven't slept a wink.

No ha sido nada cómodo el cuarto.
The room wasn't comfortable at all.

Algo to Mean "Somewhat"

Algo may be placed before an adjective to express the meaning "somewhat."

Este curso es algo fácil.
This course is somewhat easy.

Estamos algo inquietos.
We are somewhat worried.

Note: *¿Sabes una cosa?*
Do you know something?

¿Sabes algo?
Do you know anything?

Pero vs. *Sino/Sino Que*

Pero, sino, and *sino que* all mean **but**. However, *sino* and *sino que* are used:

(a) when the first clause is negative **and**

(b) the second clause contradicts the first—this contrast must be between two equivalent parts of speech (noun–noun, adjective–adjective, infinitive–infinitive). **Sino que** connects the same way, but must be followed by a **conjugated** verb.

*No habla español, **sino** inglés.*   noun–noun
He doesn't speak Spanish, but English.

*No le gusta el blanco, **sino** el azul.*   adjective–adjective
He doesn't like white, but blue.

*No quiere estudiar, **sino** jugar.*   infinitive–infinitive
He doesn't want to study, but to play.

*No cerró la puerta, **sino que** la dejó abierta.*   conjugated verb–
He didn't leave the door open, but left it closed.   conjugated verb

But: *No habla bien, **pero** me gusta su traje.*
He doesn't speak well, but I like his suit.

Note: *Pero* = "but nevertheless"
Sino = "but on the contrary"

1. Viene a vernos _____.

    (A) nunca   (C) nadie

    (B) alguien   (D) jamás

2. No me dijo _____ sobre el asunto.

    (A) nadie   (C) algo

    (B) nada   (D) ninguno

3. ¿Tienes algunos amigos íntimos? No, no tengo _____.

    (A) ningunos   (C) ningún

    (B) nadie   (D) ninguno

4. _____ día voy a hacerme médico.

    (A) Alguna   (C) Ninguno

    (B) Algún   (D) Alguno

5. Nunca hace nada por nadie. No tiene _____.

    (A) amigo alguno   (C) algún amigo

    (B) ningunos amigos   (D) amigos algunos

6. Él juega mejor que _____.

    (A) algo   (C) alguien

    (B) ninguno   (D) nadie

7. Nadie va con ellos, ni con Juan _____.

    (A) ni   (C) nadie

    (B) tampoco   (D) también

8. _____ de las camisas me queda bien.

    (A) Nada   (C) Ningún

    (B) Ninguna   (D) Ningunas

9. _____ veo en el estadio.

    (A) Nadie   (C) A nada

    (B) Ningún   (D) A nadie

10. Sin decirme_____, se fue para siempre.

    (A) algo   (C) nada

    (B) alguna cosa   (D) ninguno

Drill 12—Detailed Explanations of Answers

1. **(B)** Choices (A), (C), and (D) are all negatives. None of them can be used in the blank because, if a negative word such as "nunca" (never), "nadie" (no one), "ninguno" (none, not any, no one), or "jamás" (never) come after the verb, then there must be a "no" in front of the verb. In other words, we must use a double negative. This does not happen in this sentence. Of the four choices, only the indefinite "alguien" (someone) is acceptable.

2. **(B)** In Spanish the double negative is required when "no" is at the beginning of the sentence, which eliminates (C) because "algo" is a positive particle. Choice (A) is not appropriate because "nadie" refers to persons, and (D) is equally inappropriate because there is no specific antecedent in the question to which "ninguno" could refer.

3. **(D)** "Ninguno" is used exclusively in the singular forms either to modify or refer to previously mentioned nouns. Choice (A) is incorrect because it is plural. Choice (B) means "nobody" and cannot be used to replace the noun "amigos." Choice (C) is apocopated, which is not necessary since it does not precede a masculine noun.

4. **(B)** Both "alguno" and "ninguno" have apocopated forms (drop the –o) before masculine singular nouns. "Día" is a masculine singular noun, which makes (A) incorrect because it is feminine. Choices (C) and (D) would need to be apocopated to be used correctly before "día."

5. **(A)** When a form of "alguno" is used **after** the noun, it makes the statement more negative and is commonly translated with "at all." Because it is being used like "ninguno" in this type of statement, it will only be correct in the singular

forms. Because both (B) and (D) are plural, neither is correct. Although (C) is singular, because "algún" precedes the noun, it no longer is a negative and would only be correct in this statement written as "ningún."

6. **(D)** Comparative expressions like "mejor que" (better than), "peor que" (worse than), and "más que" (more than), for example, are negative. Therefore, (A) and (C), which are both affirmative, cannot follow this expression. Choice (B), although negative, is incorrect since there is no noun to which it refers.

7. **(B)** The expression "ni…tampoco" (nor…either) is used in statements such as this one. "Tampoco" is the negative form of "también" (also). Choice (A) is incorrect because "ni" must be followed by something, a noun, pronoun, verb, etc., in order to be used. It cannot stand alone. Choice (C), which means "no one" or "nobody," makes no sense in this statement. "También" (also) is affirmative and cannot be used after the negative "ni."

8. **(B)** Forms of "ninguno" are used only in the singular and modify or refer to nouns. In this statement, this word refers to "camisas," which is feminine. "Ninguna" in this sample is also the subject of "queda." Choice (D) is incorrect because it is plural. Answer (C) is incorrect because it is apocopated and this can only occur before a masculine singular noun. "Nada" (A) cannot be used to modify or refer to nouns.

9. **(D)** Because "nadie" is the direct object of the verb "veo" in this example and also refers to a person, the personal "a" is required before it whether it precedes or follows the verb. Choice (A) needs a personal "a." Choice (B) can only be used before masculine singular nouns. Choice (C) means "to nothing" and makes no sense in this context.

10. **(C)** "Sin" is a preposition that is considered negative. Choices (A) and (B) are both affirmative forms. Choice (D) must have a noun either to modify or to refer to.

INTERROGATIVES

Interrogative Words

qué	what, which, what a + noun
quién, quienes	who, which one(s)
cuál, cuáles	which, what, which one(s)
cuánto, –a, –os, –as	how much, how many
cuándo	when
dónde	where
adónde	(to) where
por qué	why (answer uses *porque*)
para qué	why (answer uses *para*)
cómo	how
a quién, a quiénes	whom
de quién, de quiénes	whose

Note: **All** interrogatives have accent marks.

Common Interrogatory Expressions

¿De qué trata?

¿Por qué debería uno...?

¿Dónde tiene lugar?

¿Cuál es el problema?

¿Qué le pasó a...?

¿Cuánto cuesta?

¿Cómo se caracteriza mejor?

¿Qué tiene que hacer...?

¿A qué se debe...?

¿Para qué... (verb)?

¿Qué opina?

¿Qué puede afectar...?

¿En qué consiste...?

¿De qué... (verb)

¿A qué se refiere esta conversación?

¿Qué tipos...?

¿Qué podrán hacer...?

¿Qué hará...?

Uses of *Qué*

a) To ask a definition:

¿Qué es el amor?
What is love?

b) To ask about things not yet mentioned (choice involved):

¿Qué prefieres, manzanas o peras?
Which ones do you prefer, apples or pears?

c) To express **what a**!:

¡Qué día (tan/más) hermoso!
What a beautiful day!

d) To precede a noun:

¿Qué clases te gustan?
What/which classes do you like?

Uses of *Cuál/Cuáles*

a) Followed by *de* = which one(s) of several:

¿Cuál de los libros es más necesario?
Which of the books is most necessary?

b) Refers to a definite object already mentioned (choice involved):

Hay dos vestidos, ¿cuál prefieres?
There are two dresses, **which** do you prefer?

c) Followed by *ser* when there are a number of possibilities:

¿Cuál es la fecha?
What is the date?

¿Cuál es la capital?
What is the capital?

Por Qué, Para Qué, and *Porque*

Por qué and *para qué* both mean *why*. The former is used if the expected answer will begin with *porque* (because). The latter starts a question where the expected answer will begin with *para* (in order to).

*¿**Por qué** vas al cine?*
Why do you go to the movies?

***Porque** me gusta la película.*
Because I like the film.

*¿**Para qué** vas al cine?*
Why do you go to the movies?

Para ver a mi actor favorito.
In order to see my favorite actor.

Dónde/Adónde vs. Donde

a) *Adónde* is used with verbs of motion.

   *¿**Adónde** vas?*

b) *Donde* (without the accent) requires a noun to refer to.

   *La casa **donde** vivo es vieja.*

c) *Dónde* (with accent) is the interrogative.

   *¿**Dónde** está la casa?*

Note: There are other combinations with *dónde... de dónde, por dónde*, etc.

Cuándo vs. Cuando

a) *Cuando* (without accent) can be replaced by **as** and not change the meaning drastically.

   *Te lo diré **cuando** venga Julio.*
   I'll tell you **when/as** Julio arrives.

b) *Cuándo* (with accent) is the interrogative.

   *¿**Cuándo** vas a salir?*

Quién/Quiénes

a) With prepositions to refer to people:

   *¿**Con quién** hablas?*
   With whom do you speak?

b) With **de** to express **whose**:

> *¿De quién es el carro?*
> **Whose** is the car?
> (Whose car is it?)

Note: The word order must be changed to express the Spanish sentence correctly: **Of whom** is the car?

A Quién/A Quiénes

Whom is often misused in English. It is used as the object of the verb. **Who**, on the other hand, can only be the subject of the verb. Note the differences below.

Who is the subject of "is."

Who is going with me?   *¿Quién va conmigo?*

Whom is the object of "see"; the subject is **you**.

Whom do you see?   *¿A quién ves?*

In Spanish, the **whom** statements are actually a combination of the **personal** *"a"* and the words *quién/quienes*. In some sentences, the *"a"* may act as an actual preposition and have a translation.

¿A quién escribiste?
To whom did you write?

¿A quiénes enviaron el paquete?
To whom did they send the package?

➡ DRILL 13

1.   ¿_____ es tu número de teléfono?

(A) Qué   (C) Que

(B) Cual   (D) Cuál

2.   ¿_____ día es hoy?

(A) Cuál   (C) Cómo

(B) Qué   (D) A cuál

3. ¿_____ de los libros es mejor?

    (A) Cuáles   (C) Qué

    (B) Cuál   (D) Quiénes

4. Mamá, ¿_____ sirven los anteojos?

    (A) porque   (C) para qué

    (B) por qué   (D) para

5. ¿_____ vestidos quieres comprar?

    (A) Cuál   (C) Cuáles

    (B) Qué   (D) Cómo

6. El pueblo_____ vivo es viejo.

    (A) donde   (C) a donde

    (B) dónde   (D) que

7. No sé_____ es ese carro.

    (A) quién   (C) que

    (B) de quien   (D) de quién

8. ¡_____ día más hermoso!

    (A) Qué un   (C) Qué

    (B) Cuál   (D) Qué una

9. ¿_____ es la astronomía?

    (A) Qué   (C) Quién

    (B) Cuál   (D) A quién

10. ¿_____ son los meses del año?

    (A) Cuál   (C) Qué

    (B) Cuáles   (D) De quién

Drill 13—Detailed Explanations of Answers

1. **(D)** From the question marks in our sentence we can tell that we need an interrogative pronoun, a pronoun which asks a question, in the blank. There are only two of these given in the list of possible answers: (A) "Qué" and (D) "Cuál." How do we know that these two are interrogative pronouns? Because this type of pronoun always bears an accent mark. The word "Que," in (C), is a relative pronoun, one that relates back to a previous noun in a sentence: "Los turistas **que** hablan francés..." Here the "que" refers back to "turistas." In (B), the word "Cual" is part of another relative pronoun, "el cual," "la cual," "lo cual," which is designed to show gender and is used for the sake of clarity when we have previously been talking about two nouns: "La madre de José, la cual tiene dos hermanos, viaja por España." If we did not use this longer, feminine form ("la cual"), i.e., if we were to say instead "que" or "quien," we would be referring to the noun immediately preceding the relative pronoun ("José"). But since we want to show that it is José's mother, and not José, who has two brothers, then we must use this longer pronoun or its alternate form, "la que." In English, we say "What is your telephone number?" In Spanish, the interrogative word "qué" asks for a definition. If we ask "¿Qué es la física?" we are asking for a definition of what physics is. In our sentence, we do not want to ask for a definition of what one's telephone number is, which is what (A) "Qué" would imply. Instead, we must ask, "Which one" ("Cuál"), out of all the possible numbers in the directory, is your phone number. In other words, "cuál" asks for a choice or selection from a number of possibilities.

2. **(B)** Before a noun, "qué" means "what/which." Choice (A) is not correct because it cannot modify a noun. Choice (C) means "how" and (D) means "to which."

3. **(B)** "Cuál" is used with a form of **ser** to mean "which." It is also the subject of the verb, which is singular. Choice (A) is incorrect because it is plural. Choice (D) means "who" and choice (C), which can also mean "what/which," cannot be used before a "de" phrase where there is an indication of choice.

4. **(C)** "Para qué" is used when the question intimates "for what purpose/ use." Choice (A) "because" and (D) "in order to" are not interrogatives and make no sense. Choice (B) means "why" and does not fit within the intended meaning of this question.

5.   **(B)**   "Qué" is used before a noun to mean "what/which". Therefore, choices (A) and (C) are incorrect since neither can precede a noun. Choice (D) means "how."

6.   **(A)**   "Donde" without an accent requires a noun to refer to, in this case "pueblo." Because an indirect question is not being asked, choice (B) is incorrect since all interrogatives have accent marks. Choice (C) is used in questions with verbs of motion (i.e., Where are you going?). Choice (D) is the relative pronoun meaning "that."

7.   **(D)**   Because an indirect question is being asked, the accented form of "whose" is required. This would make choice (B) incorrect. Choice (A) means "who" and choice (C) is a relative pronoun meaning "that."

8.   **(C)**   Because "¡qué!" in this context means "What a!" and the indefinite article (a) is included in its translation, choices (A) and (D) would be incorrect. Choice (B) is never used to mean "What a!" and again a form of "cuál" is not correct before a noun.

9.   **(A)**   "Qué" is used before a form of **ser** when asking for a definition, as in this example. Choices (C) "who" and (D) "whom" make no sense. "Cual" precedes a form of **ser** when there are a number of possibilities, which makes choice (B) incorrect.

10.   **(B)**   A form of "cuál" will precede a form of **ser** when a number of possibilities are given to choose from (i.e., months). Because it is the subject of the verb and because the verb is plural, choice (A) is incorrect. Answer (D) means "whose" and makes no sense in this context. Choice (C) can only be used before a form of **ser** when asking a definition.

THE PERSONAL *A*

Normally the preposition *a* means **to** or **at** in Spanish. There are instances when this preposition will appear in the sentence with **no** apparent translation into English. In this case, this preposition is called the personal *"a."* This *a* will appear in the Spanish sentence if the **direct object** of the verb:

a) *refers to a person in some way:*

No veo a Juan/a su amigo/al ejército/a nadie.
I don't see Juan/his friend/the army/anyone.

b) *refers to a domestic animal:*

Juan ama mucho a su perro, Spot.
Juan loves his dog, Spot.

c) *refers to a specific geographical location (if they do **not** have an article):*

Visito a España/a Barcelona/a México.
I visit Spain/Barcelona/Mexico.

But: Visito **el** Perú.

Omission of the Personal *A*

a) After the verb *tener*, unless it means "keep/hold":

Tengo dos hermanos.   I have two brothers.

But: *Tengo al culpable en la cárcel.*
                               I have the guilty one in jail.

b) Before an indefinite personal direct object (usually modified by a numeral or an indefinite article):

Vi tres hombres en el bosque.
I saw three men in the forest.

Oí un ladrón dentro del banco.
I heard a thief inside the bank.

c) *When the personal "a" would be in close proximity to another a (such as one meaning "to," "at," "toward" or the a preceding an indirect object):*

Presenté mi esposo a mis amigos.
I introduced my husband to my friends.

POSSESSIVES: ADJECTIVES/PRONOUNS

The possessive adjectives:

my	*mi, mis*	our	*nuestro, –a, –os, –as*
your	*tu, tus*	your	*vuestro, –a, –os, –as*
his/her/your	*su, sus*	their/your	*su, sus*

The possessive adjectives precede the noun they modify and match it as closely as possible in gender and number.

mi casa, mis casas   my house, my houses
nuestra pluma, nuestras plumas   our pen, our pens

Because the third person adjective has several possible translations, the following may be done for clarification:

su casa =   his house   *la casa de él*
           her house   *la casa de ella*
           your house (s)   *la casa de Ud.*
           their house (f)   *la casa de ellas*
           their house (m)   *la casa de ellos*
           your house (pl)   *la casa de Uds.*

The Possessive Pronouns

The pronoun group is used **to replace** the noun already stated and, therefore, takes on the properties of that noun. This includes retention of the definite article. Also note the difference in translation.

mine   *el mío, la mía*
                  los míos, las mías
yours   *el tuyo, la tuya*
                  los tuyos, las tuyas
his/hers/yours   *el suyo, la suya*
                  los suyos, las suyas
ours   *el nuestro, la nuestra*
                  los nuestros, las nuestras
yours   *el vuestro, la vuestra*
                  los vuestros, las vuestras
theirs/yours   *el suyo, la suya*
                  los suyos, las suyas

Again, because the third person pronouns have several possible meanings, clarification with the prepositional phrase is also possible. With the pronouns, however, the definite article must be retained.

mi coche y el suyo	my car and his	*y el de él*
	my car and hers	*y el de ella*
	my car and yours	*y el de Ud.*
	my car and theirs (f)	*y el de ellas*
	my car and theirs (m)	*y el de ellos*
	my car and yours	*y el de Uds.*

Uses of the Pronouns

The possessive pronouns are used primarily in three areas:

a) *As the replacement for the noun:*

   my house and **ours**   *mi casa y **la nuestra***

b) *As an "adjective" with nouns, as follows:*

   several friends of **mine**   *unos amigos **míos***

   Note: "of" is **not** expressed.

c) *As the possessive used after ser:*

   | *¿Este vestido?* | This dress? |
   | *Es **tuyo**.* | It is **yours**. |

   | *¿Estos carros?* | These cars? |
   | *Son **nuestros**.* | They are **ours**. |

   Note: The definite article is normally omitted after *ser*.

Possessives with Clothing/Body Parts

Normally, with parts of the body and clothing, the possessive adjective is replaced by the definite article. However, in the following instances, the possessive is correct.

a) With body parts:

   1. When ambiguity would result without it.

   2. When the body part is modified.
      Ella levantó sus grandes ojos azules.

3. When the body part is the subject.
   Tus manos tienen callos.

b) With clothing:

   1. When the article worn is the subject.
      Su camisa está allí.

   2. When the article is not being worn by the subject.
      *Encontré **mis** calcetines allí.*

➡ DRILL 14

1. Ayer vimos_____ señorita Corrales.

   (A) a la   (C) a

   (B) la   (D) la a

2. Mi hermana es más alta que_____.

   (A) la suya   (C) su

   (B) el suyo   (D) mía

3. ¿Conoce Ud._____ padres?

   (A) mi   (C) a mis

   (B) mis   (D) míos

4. Su amigo es más inteligente que_____.

   (A) la nuestra   (C) los míos

   (B) el nuestro   (D) el mío

5. Los hombres se pusieron_____ antes de salir.

   (A) el sombrero   (C) su sombrero

   (B) sus sombreros   (D) sombreros

6. Se quitaron_____ al entrar en la casa.

   (A) sus abrigos   (C) sus guantes

   (B) su abrigo   (D) el abrigo

7. ¿De quién es este lápiz? –Es _____.

 (A) mío   (C) de mi

 (B) el mío   (D) de mí

8. Mis hermanas y _____ Isabel son bellas.

 (A) las que   (C) las

 (B) las de   (D) aquellas

9. Tu casa es más grande que _____.

 (A) el mío   (C) mío

 (B) mi   (D) la mía

10. Sus pirámides y _____ vienen de épocas distintas.

 (A) los nuestros   (C) las nuestras

 (B) nuestros   (D) nuestras

11. Tengo _____ padre en el hospital.

 (A) mi   (C) a mi

 (B) a mí   (D) el

Drill 14—Detailed Explanations of Answers

1. **(A)** The personal "*a*" must be used when speaking about a person, and the article should accompany a title when not in direct address. The answer (A) is the only one fulfilling these requirements.

2. **(A)** The long form of the possessive is used when the noun is replaced. Because the possessive is now being used as a pronoun, it will take on the properties of the noun it has replaced, including the definite article. The noun in this example is "hermana." Choice (B) is incorrect because it is the wrong gender. Choice (C) is a possessive adjective and must be used with a noun. Choice (D) is the possessive pronoun but needs an article.

3.   **(C)**   The possessive adjective is required to match the noun "padres." Also, because "padres" is the direct object of the verb and refers to a person, the personal *a* is also required. Choice (A) needs to be plural and have a personal *a*. Choice (B) needs the personal *a* and choice (D) is the possessive pronoun, which cannot precede the noun.

4.   **(B)**   All choices are possessive pronouns but only (B) is the correct gender for "amigo."

5.   **(A)**   With parts of the body and clothing in Spanish, the possessive is replaced by the definite article. The ownership is established by the reflexive pronoun. In addition, in Spanish, each person wears only **one** hat at a time and even if the subject is plural, the article of clothing remains singular. Answer (C) has the possessive and is incorrect. Choice (B) is plural and has the possessive, and choice (D) needs to be singular with a definite article to be correct.

6.   **(D)**   For the same reason given in number 5 above, each person wears only one coat and the possessive must be replaced by the definite article. Choice (A), therefore, is incorrect because it is plural and has retained the possessive. Choice (B) needs to replace the possessive with the article "el." Choice (C) would be correct if "sus" were replaced with "los" since gloves are worn in pairs.

7.   **(A)**   The long form of the possessive is used to replace a noun previously referred to. In this example, the noun is "lápiz." Normally, the long form has a definite article. However, after **ser** the article is omitted. Choice (B) is incorrect because it has the article. Choice (C) means "of my," and choice (D) is incorrect because in spoken Spanish "of me" is not used in this manner. Forms of "mío" are used instead.

8.   **(B)**   To eliminate **'s** in Spanish, an **of** phrase is used. When replacing a possessive such as this one (Isabel's) wherein there is a name to deal with, the definite article is retained followed by **de**. Because the noun here is "hermanas," the feminine plural article is needed. Neither (C) nor (D) make sense when placed directly before Anita. Choice (A) can be translated "those that or those who" but neither make sense in front of Anita.

9.   **(D)**   The long form of the possessive with the definite article is needed to replace the noun previously mentioned ("casa"). Choice (A) is the wrong gender. Choice (B) is the possessive adjective which means "my" and must precede a noun, and choice (C) needs to be feminine with an article to be correct.

10.   **(C)**   Again, the long form of the possessive with the definite article is needed to replace the noun previously mentioned ("pirámides") which is feminine plural. Choice (A) is the wrong gender. Choice (B) is the wrong gender and needs an article, and choice (D) needs a definite article to be correct.

11.   **(C)**   The personal "a" is used after **tener** when it means "keep or hold" as it does in this sample. Also, the possessive adjective "mi" has no accent. Choice (A) needs a personal "a." In choice (B) the accented "mí" means me and is prepositional, not possessive. Choice (D) needs a personal "a."

THE PASSIVE VOICE

The passive voice is the "mirror image" of the active voice. In passive voice statements, the subject receives the action of the verb instead of actually doing it.

Active: I built the house.
Construí la casa.

Passive: The house was built by me.
La casa fue construida por mí.

The combination of *ser* with the **past participle** of the transitive verb constitutes the "true passive" in Spanish. The past participle is used as an adjective and must agree with the subject in number and gender. The formula follows:

ser + **past participle** + *por* + **agent** (doer)

Whenever the agent is expressed, this formula is used.

Agent Expressed by *De*

By is normally translated by *por*. If, however, the past participle expresses feelings or emotion, **by** is translated by *de*.

*Juana es amada (respetada, odiada, admirada) **de** todos.*
Juana is loved (respected, hated, admired) by all.

Reflexive Substitute for the Passive Voice

Commonly, when the agent is **not** expressed and the subject is a thing, the passive "Spanish" statement will be written using the third person singular or plural of the verb with the pronoun *se*.

*Aquí **se habla** español.* Spanish is spoken here.
***Se vendieron** guantes allí.* Gloves were sold there.

Note: The subject follows the verb.

Third Person Plural Active Equivalent for Passive Voice

The best way to avoid using a passive construction is to convert the passive statement to an active one by using the subject **they**.

The house was sold.	=	They sold the house.
Se vendió la casa.	=	*Vendieron la casa.*

No Agent Expressed, Person Acted Upon

In sentences where the agent is indefinite (not mentioned or implied) and a person is acted upon, the indefinite *se* is coupled with the **third singular** of the verb.

The man was killed.	He was killed.
Se mató al hombre.	*Se le mató.*
The girls will be punished.	They will be punished.
Se castigará a las chicas.	*Se las castigará.*

Note: The person acted upon is the direct object of the Spanish sentence. Therefore, direct object pronouns are used to replace it, with one expection— *les* is used instead of *los* for the masculine plural.

The men will be killed.	They will be killed.
Se matará a los hombres.	*Se les matará.*

Idiomatic Expressions with *Se*

Se plus the third person singular of the verb will render "impersonal" subject statements. In English we say **people**, **one**, **they**, **you**, and the like. This type of statement may also be translated as a passive construction.

se dice =	it is said	*se cree* =	it is believed
[dicen]	people say	*[creen]*	people believe
	they say		they believe
	one says		one believes
	you say		you believe

This may also be rendered with the third person plural of the verb.

The Apparent Passive: *Estar* Plus the Past Participle

The true passive in Spanish is formed with *ser* and a past participle. Constructions formed with *estar* and a past participle are different. Instead of expressing an action carried out by an explicit or implicit agent, the apparent passive denotes a state or a condition resulting from a previous action. The past participle becomes an adjective. Compare the following examples:

Apparent Passive

*La puerta **está** abierta.*
The door **is** open. (The action of opening it happened earlier.)

True Passive

*La puerta **es abierta** (por el niño).*
The door **is opened** (by the boy). (We see the action happening now.)

Apparent Passive

*La pieza **estaba** reservada.*
The room **was** reserved. (Someone reserved it earlier.)

True Passive

*La pieza había **sido reservada** (por el turista).*
The room had **been reserved** (by the tourist).

➲ DRILL 15

1. _____ la mujer.

   (A) Asesinaron a   (C) Asesinamos

   (B) Se asesinaron a   (D) Fue asesinado

2. La universidad_____ por el presidente Juárez.

   (A) fundó   (C) fue establecida

   (B) estaba fundado   (D) se estableció

3. El asesino fue_____ por el policía.

   (A) muerto   (C) morido

   (B) matado   (D) muriendo

4. La ventana_____ abierta por el viento.

   (A) sido   (C) estaba

   (B) estuvo   (D) fue

5. La señora García es respetada_____todos los alumnos.

   (A) de   (C) a

   (B) por   (D) con

6. _____ que va a mejorar la economía.

   (A) Se dicen   (C) Se dice

   (B) Es dicho   (D) Está dicho

7. Aquí_____español e inglés.

   (A) es hablado   (C) son hablados

   (B) se habla   (D) se hablan

8. ¿Los traidores?_____matará mañana.

   (A) Se les   (C) Se

   (B) Se los   (D) Los

9. Al entrar, vi que las ventanas_____abiertas.

   (A) fueron   (C) han sido

   (B) estaban   (D) han estado

10. Esas casas fueron_____por un arquitecto famoso.

    (A) construida   (C) construidos

    (B) construido   (D) construidas

Drill 15—Detailed Explanations of Answers

1. **(A)** When a person is acted upon in a passive voice sentence, the statement may be expressed three ways: by using true passive ("ser" + past participle) which matches the noun (thus eliminating answer choice (D)), by using an active voice statement requiring the personal *a* (thus eliminating choice (C)), or by using the third singular of the verb preceded by the reflexive **se** followed by the personal *a* (thus eliminating choice (B)). (A) is correct in the active voice with the personal *a*.

2.   **(C)**   Choice (A) "fundó" means "founded," but it will not function in the sentence because the "university" ("universidad") did not found anything. On the contrary, it was founded "**by** President Juárez." This gets us into what is called the passive voice. In a passive sentence, the subject is acted upon by someone or something. In our sentence, the subject, "universidad," is acted upon by "el presidente Juárez." To form the passive voice in Spanish, we follow this pattern: the proper tense and form of the verb "ser" + past participle. Look at the correct answer: "fue establecida." You will see that we have followed this pattern. One other thing you will notice is that in the passive voice, the past participle always agrees in number and gender with the subject. In our sentence, "establecida" is feminine singular to agree with "universidad." Observe also that the verb "fue" is third person singular since the subject, "universidad," is a singular noun. The passive voice must always be used when the subject is acted upon and the doer of the action is expressed by a "por" phrase ("por el presidente Juárez"). (B) "estaba fundado" is incorrect because (1) we have not used the verb "ser," but rather "estar" (therefore, we are not indicating an action; we are merely describing a state), and (2) the past participle does not agree with the subject "universidad." Now look at (D), "se estableció." Sometimes the reflexive form of the verb can be used as a substitute for the true passive voice, but never when we have a "por" phrase which indicates who did the action, as is the case in our sentence.

3.   **(A)**   The last two choices are ungrammatical. In order to identify the correct answer, you have to know that the past participle of the verb "matar" is "muerto" when the sentence refers to people.

4.   **(D)**   To get the right answer you must recognize that this construction is in the passive voice, which means that it's always formed with the appropriate form of "ser"—but not with the past participle (as in choice (A)) because this particular form needs the support of "haber."

5.   **(A)**   In a passive voice statement, **by** is usually translated by **por**. If the past participle expresses feeling or emotion, rather than action, **by** is translated by **de**. Therefore, choice (B) is incorrect. Because **de** is the only choice to complete this passive statement, (C) and (D) are both incorrect.

6.   **(C)**   The pronoun **se** used with the third person singular of the verb expresses an indefinite subject. This can be translated a number of ways: it is said, people say, they say, one says, etc. Choice (A) is incorrect because the verb is plural. Both (B) and (D) appear to have the literal translation needed but this type of statement is done with **se** + third person singular of the verb.

7. **(D)** If the agent (doer) is not mentioned and the subject of the statement is a thing, the reflexive construction is used for the passive. The verb will, in these cases, match the noun. In this case the actual subject ("español e inglés") is plural. Choices (A) and (C) are written in the true passive formula (**ser** + past participle) but cannot be used when the subject is a thing. Choice (B) is incorrect because the verb is singular.

8. **(A)** The indefinite **se** is used when the agent (doer) is indefinite (not mentioned or implied) and a person is being acted upon. In this case, the verb is always third person singular and the person acted upon becomes the direct object. "Los," however, is the only direct object pronoun not used and is replaced by "les." Therefore, choice (B) is incorrect because "los" has been used. Choice (C) needs the pronoun "les" and choice (D) is simply the direct object pronoun by itself.

9. **(B)** When there is a focus on the "resultant state of a previous action" and **not** on the action itself, a form of **estar** will precede the past participle. The past participle will still be used as an adjective. Therefore, choices (A) and (C) are incorrect because **ser** has been used. Choice (D) when translated (Upon entering, I saw that the windows have been opened.) is incorrect usage of the perfect tense.

10. **(D)** The focus is on the past participle and its function as an adjective in the passive voice statement. It must agree in this sample with "casas." All other answers use incorrect gender or number.

MEASURES OF TIME

The word *tiempo* in Spanish designates both "time" and "weather," as in the following examples:

*Ha pasado tanto **tiempo** desde que nos vimos.*
So much **time** has passed since we saw each other.

*¿Cómo está el **tiempo** hoy?*
How is the **weather** today?

The following are some of the expressions Spanish uses to measure or divide time.

Seasons of the Year

las estaciones – the seasons
el verano – summer   *el otoño* – fall
el invierno – winter   *la primavera* – spring

Months of the Year

el mes – the month
enero – January   *febrero* – February
marzo – March   *abril* – April
mayo – May   *junio* – June
julio – July   *agosto* – August
septiembre – September   *octubre* – October
noviembre – November   *diciembre* – December

Note: In Spanish, the names of the months are not capitalized.

Days of the Week

el día – the day   *la semana* – the week
el lunes – Monday   *el martes* – Tuesday
el miércoles – Wednesday   *el jueves* – Thursday
el viernes – Friday   *el sábado* – Saturday
el domingo – Sunday

Note: The days of the week (which are not capitalized in Spanish) are preceded by the definite article except after a form of *ser*:

el lunes – Monday; on Monday   los lunes – Mondays; on Mondays
Es lunes. – It is Monday.

Other Expressions of Time

hoy – today   ayer – yesterday
mañana – tomorrow*   anoche – last night
anteanoche – the night before   anteayer – the day before
   last   yesterday
pasado mañana – the day after   el día siguiente – the following
   tomorrow   day
la madrugada – dawn   la mañana – the morning*
el mediodía – noon   la tarde – afternoon
la noche – night (time)   la medianoche – midnight
tarde – late   pronto – soon

*Be sure to distinguish between *mañana* (tomorrow) and *la mañana* (the morning).

TELLING TIME

When telling the time of day, the word "time" is rendered as *hora*.

*¿Qué **hora** es?*   What **time** is it?

When telling the hours of the day, Spanish uses the feminine definite article before the time expression.

*Es **la** una.*   It's one o'clock.
*Son **las** dos.*   It's two o'clock.

Note: To specify A.M., Spanish uses *de la mañana* or *de la madrugada*. (The hours after midnight but before dawn.) P.M. is expressed with either *de la tarde* or *de la noche*.

*Son las tres **de la mañana.***   It's three a.m.

*Son las cinco **de la tarde.***   It's five p.m.

To render the half-hour, Spanish uses *media*. To render the quarter-hour, *cuarto* or *quince* are used.

*Son las diez y **cuarto**. Son las diez y **quince**.*
It's a **quarter** past ten. It's ten **fifteen.**

*Son las diez y **media**.*
It's **10:30.** It's **half past** ten.

*Son las once menos **cuarto**. Son las once menos **quince**.*
It's a **quarter** of eleven.

Falta un **cuarto** (Faltan **quince**) para las once.*
It's a **quarter** of eleven.

*Faltar means "to be wanting, lacking."

Note: *y* is used through the half-hour and *menos* is used after the half- hour.

Portions of time other than the half- or quarter-hour are expressed thus:

Son las seis y diez.	It's 6:10.
Son las seis y veinte.	It's 6:20.

Son las siete menos veinte. (Faltan veinte para las siete.)
It's 6:40. (It's twenty of seven.)

At plus the hour is expressed with *a* + *la/las*.

A la una/A las dos salí.   At one/at two I left.

To tell time in the past, use the imperfect tense.

Era la una/Eran las dos.   It was 1:00/2:00.

To express "a little after" the hour, use ***y pico***.

Llegó a las cinco y pico.   He arrived a little after 5:00.

To express "at about," use ***a eso de*** + the hour.

Salió a eso de las seis.   He left about 6:00.

When **no** exact hour is indicated, "in the morning/afternoon/evening" is expressed with ***por la mañana, por la tarde, por la noche***.

If using the 24-hour clock, the following applies:

1:00 p.m.	*trece horas*
2:00 p.m.	*catorce horas*
8:00 p.m.	*veinte horas*
15:30 (3:30 p.m.)	*quince horas treinta*
20:42 (8:42 p.m.)	*veinte horas cuarenta y dos*
9:10 (9:10 a.m.)	*nueve horas diez*

Note: ***Cuarto***, ***media***, and *y* are not used.

HACER WITH EXPRESSIONS OF TIME

With expressions of time, *hacer* is an impersonal verb. Only the third person singular is used.

Hace (Tiempo) Que + Present Indicative of Main Verb

This formula shows that the action is still going on in the present. Note that Spanish uses the simple present where English uses the present perfect.

Hace una semana que el prisionero no come.
The prisoner has not eaten for a week.

Hace muchos días que llueve.
It has been raining for many days.

Note: By turning the sentence around, the conjunction *que* can be suppressed. (In negative sentences, it is possible to use a compound tense.)

El prisionero no come hace una semana.
(El prisionero no ha comido hace una semana.)
The prisoner has not eaten for a week.

Llueve hace muchos días.
It has been raining for many days.

Hace (Tiempo) Que + Preterite of Main Verb

This formula designates the sense of time expressed by the English particle "ago."

Hace tres días que la vi. (La vi hace tres días.)
I saw her three days ago.

Hace años que nos dejaron. (Nos dejaron hace años.)
They left us years ago.

Hacía (Tiempo) Que + Imperfect of Main Verb

This formula shows that the action was still going on in the past.

Hacía tres días que llovía. (Llovía hacía tres días.)
It had been raining for three days.

Hacía tiempo que te esperaba. (Te esperaba hacía tiempo.)
I had been waiting for you for a while.

AGE

Cumplir años and *tener años* are the expressions most commonly used to indicate age:

Mi padre tiene cuarenta y dos años.
My father is 42 (years of age).

Hoy es mi cumpleaños. Cumplo ocho.
Today is my birthday. I turn eight.

To express "at the age of 40 (or any number)," one says "*a los cuarenta años.*"

WEATHER EXPRESSIONS

In English these weather expressions are formed with the verb "to be"; in Spanish they are formed with the verb *hacer* used impersonally.

***Hace** calor.*	It **is** hot.
***Hizo** frío.*	It **was** cold.

Hará buen tiempo.	The weather **will be** good.
Hace sol.	It **is** sunny.
Hacía viento.	It **was** windy.
¿Qué tiempo **hace***?*	What**'s** the weather like?
Hace mal tiempo.	The weather **is** bad.

With *Tener*

When the sentence is personal, Spanish uses *tener* where English uses "to be."

| *Tengo calor.* | I **am** hot. |
| *Teníamos frío.* | We **were** cold. |

With *Haber* Used Impersonally

Notice that the third person singular of the present indicative changes from *ha* to *hay* when *haber* is impersonal.

Hay neblina.	It **is** misty (foggy).
Hubo humedad.	It **was** damp.
Habrá tempestad.	It **will be** stormy.

With *Nevar* and *Llover*

"To snow" and "to rain" are rendered by the impersonal verbs *nevar* and *llover,* respectively:

| *Ayer* **nevó***.* | **It snowed** yesterday. |
| *Mañana* **lloverá***.* | Tomorrow **it will rain**. |

CARDINAL AND ORDINAL FORMS OF NUMERALS

The cardinal and ordinal forms of numbers in Spanish are as follows:

Cardinal Numbers

1	*uno/a*	11	*once*
2	*dos*	12	*doce*
3	*tres*	13	*trece*
4	*cuatro*	14	*catorce*
5	*cinco*	15	*quince*

6	seis	16	diez y seis
7	siete	17	diez y siete
8	ocho	18	diez y ocho
9	nueve	19	diez y nueve
10	diez	20	veinte
21	veinte y uno, –a	300	trescientos, –as
22	veinte y dos	400	cuatrocientos, –as
30	treinta	500	quinientos, –as
40	cuarenta	600	seiscientos, –as
50	cincuenta	700	setecientos, –as
60	sesenta	800	ochocientos, –as
70	setenta	900	novecientos, –as
80	ochenta	1,000	mil
90	noventa	1,100	mil cien(to)/a
100	cien(to)/a	2,000	dos mil
101	ciento uno, –a	1,000,000	un millón (de)
200	doscientos, –as	2,000,000	dos millones (de)

Note: The cardinal numbers from 16 to 29 may be written together: *dieciséis, diecisiete, dieciocho, diecinueve, veintiuno, veintinueve.* Beyond 30, cardinal numbers are written: *treinta y uno, treinta y dos,* etc.

Ordinal Numbers

First	primero	Sixth	sexto
Second	segundo	Seventh	séptimo
Third	tercero	Eighth	octavo
Fourth	cuarto	Ninth	noveno (nono)
Fifth	quinto	Tenth	décimo

a) Ordinal numbers are variable in gender and number:

   *Eres la **cuarta** persona que me pregunta lo mismo.*
   You are the **fourth** person to ask me the same thing.

   *Los **primeros** en irse fueron los últimos en llegar.*
   The **first** to leave were the last to arrive.

b) *Primero* and *tercero* drop their final "*o*" in front of masculine singular nouns:

   *el **tercer** ojo*   the **third** eye

c) Ordinal numbers precede the noun except when referring to kings, dukes, popes, or some other kind of succession:

*Juan Carlos **Primero** es el rey de España.*
Juan Carlos I is the king of Spain.

*Juan Pablo **Segundo** es el Papa.*
John Paul II is the pope.

d) Usage dictates that after *décimo* no more ordinal numbers are used; they are replaced by cardinal numbers situated after the noun:

*La **décima** carrera fue más emocionante que la (carrera) **once**.*
The **tenth** race was more exciting than the **eleventh** (race).

*España no tuvo un rey llamado Pedro **Quince**.*
Spain did not have a king named Pedro the Fifteenth.

Un, Una, or Uno

Un and *una* (like the indefinite articles they resemble) are used according to the gender of the noun they precede. *Uno* is used alone (i.e., not before a noun).

*un libro, **una** mujer, veinte y **uno***

Note: **un** will precede a noun that begins with a stressed *a–* or **ha–** for *pronunciation.*

el águila = *un* águila   *el* hacha = *un* hacha
the eagle = an eagle   the hatchet = a hatchet

Ciento vs. Cien

a) *Ciento* will apocopate to *cien* before any noun or a number larger than itself (i.e., *mil, millones*).

cien casas	*cien soldados*	*cien mil*	*cien millones*
100 houses	100 soldiers	100,000	100 million

But: *ciento once, ciento veinte y tres, ciento sesenta*

Note: After 100, an **y** is not placed between it and the next number.

b) ***Ciento*** and ***mil,*** when used as collective nouns, may be plural.

muchos miles de dólares   *cientos (centenares) de leguas*
many thousands of dollars   hundreds of leagues

Note: *Centenar* is preferred to *ciento* as a collective noun.

c) The multiples of 100 (200–900) have both masculine and feminine forms.

doscientas una mujeres   *quinientos un hombres*
201 women   501 men

d) Although ***ciento*** should be used when the number stands alone, in everyday speech it is apocopated as follows:

Hemos comprado cien.   *Yo vivo en el cien.*
We have bought 100.   I live in number 100.

Expressing Millions

Millón is considered a noun and therefore takes the indefinite article and is followed by the preposition *de:*

un millón de dólares   *doscientos millones de aves*
one million dollars   200 million birds

DATES

Contrary to English usage, **cardinal** numbers are used to indicate dates **except in the case of the first of the month:**

*el **primero** de mayo*   the first of May
*el **dos** de mayo*   the second of May
*el **tres** de mayo*   the third of May
*el **diez** de mayo*   the tenth of May
*el **treinta** de mayo*   the thirtieth of May

The year may be added to these dates by inserting the preposition *de:*

*el tres de octubre **de** 1951*   October 3, 1951
*el veinte de abril **de** este año*   April 20 of this year

In dating letters the definite article is omitted.

It's common to replace *de este año* by *del corriente* (of the current year):

el veintiocho de febrero del corriente.
February 28 of this year.

"What day is today?" may be rendered literally as *¿Qué día es hoy?* or idiomatically as *¿A cómo estamos (hoy)?* The latter expression implies a date as an answer, not just the day of the week:

¿A cómo estamos? Estamos a trece de junio.
What's the date? It is June 13.

¿Qué día es hoy? Hoy es lunes.
What day is today? Today is Monday.

ARITHMETIC SIGNS

+ *más*

− *menos*

× *por*

÷ *dividido por*

2 + 2 is dos **más** dos

10 ÷ 5 is *diez **dividido por** cinco*

3 × 3 is *tres **por** tres*

COLLECTIVE NUMERALS

un par	a pair
una decena	ten
una docena	a dozen
una quincena	fifteen, two weeks
una veintena	twenty
una centena (un centenar)	hundred
un millar	thousand

*Pagan cada **quincena.***
They pay every two weeks.

*El libro tiene una **centena** de poemas.*
The book has **one hundred** poems.

*Un **millar** de personas*
A **thousand** people

Note: *Quincenal* is an adjective made from *quincena*. Other similar numerical adjectives are *semanal* (weekly), *mensual* (monthly), *semestral* (half-yearly), and *anual* (yearly).

*Una publicación **quincenal***
A **biweekly** publication

*Una revista **semestral***
A **half-yearly** magazine

FRACTIONS

1/2	*un medio*		1/3	*un tercio*
1/4	*un cuarto*		1/5	*un quinto*
1/6	*un sexto*		1/7	*un séptimo*
1/8	*un octavo*		1/9	*un noveno*
1/10	*un décimo*			

Two-thirds is either *dos tercios* or *las dos terceras partes*; three-fourths is either *tres cuartos* or *las tres cuartas partes*.

Un medio is only used in arithmetical calculations; the adjective meaning "half" is *medio/a;* the noun meaning "half" is *la mitad:*

*Trabajamos sólo **medio** día hoy.*
Today we only worked **half** a day.

***La mitad** del electorado no votó.*
Half of the electorate did not vote.

➦ DRILL 16

1. ¿Cuánto tiempo _____ que esperaban el tren?

    (A) hace   (C) hacían

    (B) hizo   (D) hacía

2. _____tres horas que regresó de su viaje.

(A) Hacen

(C) Hace

(B) Ha

(D) Desde

3. Mis botas están sucias porque_____lodo afuera.

(A) hay

(C) es

(B) hace

(D) está

4. No puedo conducir bien porque_____neblina.

(A) está

(C) hace

(B) es

(D) hay

5. Había (231)_____mujeres en el estadio.

(A) doscientos treinta y uno

(C) doscientas treinta y una

(B) doscientas treinta y uno

(D) doscientas treinta y unas

6. Ganó (100 million)_____dólares en la lotería.

(A) cien millón de

(C) ciento millones de

(B) ciento millón de

(D) cien millones de

7. (The first)_____de mayo es mi cumpleaños.

(A) El primero

(C) El uno

(B) El primer

(D) Primero

8. Había (hundreds)_____de pájaros en San Juan Capistrano.

(A) cien

(C) centenares

(B) cientos

(D) un cien

9. Juan llegó un poco después de las cinco, o sea,_____.

(A) a las cinco en punto

(C) a las cinco y pico

(B) a eso de las cinco

(D) hace las cinco

10. Durante el invierno mi mamá siempre_____.

(A) está fría

(C) hace frío

(B) tiene frío

(D) es fría

Drill 16—Detailed Explanations of Answers

1.   **(D)**   In time expressions involving the verb "hacer," the form of this verb will be third person singular. To balance with "esperaban" in the other part of sentence, "hacer" will be expressed in the imperfect tense also. This renders the translation "had been + ing." Therefore, (A) the present tense and (B) the preterite are incorrect. (C) is incorrect because it is plural.

2.   **(C)**   The formula for this kind of expression is *hace* (never in the plural) + **time** + *que* + **preterite** (or **preterite** + *hace* + **time**). In English, this formula translates the particle "ago."

3.   **(A)**   Weather conditions used with *haber* are "lodo" (muddy), "neblina" (foggy), "polvo" (dusty), "luna" (moonlight), and "nieve" (snow). A good way to remember is that these conditions are visible, whereas hot and cold are not. Forms of "estar/ser" (to be) are never used to express weather.

4.   **(D)**   See the explanation given in number 3 above.

5.   **(C)**   Because "doscientos" and "uno" have gender and can be feminine, and because they precede a feminine plural noun in this sample, each must also be feminine. It should be noted that "uno" cannot be plural and still mean "one."

6.   **(D)**   "Ciento" apocopates to "cien" before nouns or numbers larger than itself. "Millón" also has a plural form. It will remain "millón" when accompanied by "un." Whenever a noun follows this number, **de** is needed.

7.   **(A)**   The first of the month is expressed with the ordinal number "primero." All other days of the month use cardinal numbers. "Primero" apocopates to "primer" before a masculine singular noun. In this case it precedes **de** (a preposition) and apocopation is not needed.

8.   **(C)**   Forms of "centenar" are preferred to forms of "ciento" when used as collective nouns.

9.   **(C)**   To express "a little after the hour," use **y pico**. "En punto" means "exactly," "A eso de" means "at about," with the hour.

10. **(B)**   To express warm or cold personally, **tener** is used. Because "frío" and "calor" are nouns, they do not change in gender to match the subject. "Hace frío" expresses the weather condition itself. Forms of **estar** with "frío/caliente" refer to the warmth or coolness of things (such as soup, tea, coffee, etc.).

VOCABULARY/IDIOMS

Idioms with *Dar*

dar a	to face, to look out upon
dar con	to come upon, to find
dar cuerda (a)	to wind
dar de beber (comer) a	to give a drink to, to feed
dar en	to strike against, to hit
dar gritos (voces)	to shout
dar la bienvenida	to welcome
dar la hora	to strike the hour
darse la mano	to shake hands
dar las gracias (a)	to thank
dar por + past part.	to consider
darse por + past part.	to consider oneself
dar recuerdos (a)	to give regards to
darse cuenta de	to realize
dar prisa	to hurry
dar un abrazo	to embrace
dar un paseo	to take a walk
dar un paseo en coche	to take a ride
dar una vuelta	to take a stroll
dar unas palmadas	to clap one's hands

Idioms with *Haber*

hay	there is, are
había	there was, were
hubo	there was, were (took place)
habrá	there will be
habría	there would be
ha habido	there has been
había habido	there had been
haya	there may be
hubiera	there might be
va a haber	there is going to be
iba a haber	there was going to be
tiene que haber	there has to be

puede haber	there can be
debe haber	there should be
haber de + infinitive	to be (supposed) to
haber sol	to be sunny
haber (mucho) polvo	to be (very) dusty
haber (mucho) lodo	to be (very) muddy
haber (mucha) neblina	to be (very) cloudy, foggy
hay luna	there is moonlight
hay que + infinitive	one must, it is necessary
hay + noun + *que* + inf.	there is/are + noun + inf.

Idioms with *Hacer*

hace poco	a little while ago
hacer buen (mal) tiempo	to be good (bad) weather
hacer (mucho) frío (calor)	to be (very) cold (hot)
hacer (mucho) viento	to be (very) windy
hacer caso de (a)	to pay attention to, to heed
hacer de	to act as, to work as
hacer falta	to be lacking
hacerle falta	to need
hacer el favor de	please + infinitive
hacer el papel de	to play the role of
hacer pedazos	to tear (to shreds)
hacer una broma	to play a joke
hacer una maleta	to pack a suitcase
hacer una pregunta	to ask a question
hacer una visita	to pay a visit
hacer un viaje	to take (make) a trip
hacerse	to become (through effort)
hacerse tarde	to become (grow) late
hacer daño (a)	to harm, to damage
hacerse daño	to hurt oneself

Idioms with *Tener*

tener (mucho) calor (frío)	to be (very) warm (cold)
tener cuidado	to be careful
tener dolor de cabeza	to have a headache,
(*de estómago,* etc.)	(stomachache, etc.)

tener éxito	to be successful
tener ganas de	to feel like doing something
tener gusto en	to be glad to
tener (mucha) hambre (sed)	to be (very) hungry (thirsty)
tener la bondad de	please + infinitive
tener la culpa (de)	to be to blame (for)
tener lugar	to take place
tener miedo de	to be afraid of
tener por + adj.	to consider
tener prisa	to be in a hurry
tener que	to have to, must
tener que ver con	to have to do with
tener razón (no tener razón)	to be right (wrong)
tener (mucho) sueño	to be (very) sleepy
tener (mucha) suerte	to be (very) lucky
tener vergüenza (de)	to be ashamed (of)

Miscellaneous Verbal Idioms

dejar caer	to drop
echar al correo	to mail
echar de menos	to miss (people)
echar la culpa (a)	to blame
encogerse de hombros	to shrug one's shoulders
estar a las anchas	to be comfortable
estar a punto de + inf.	to be about to
estar conforme (con)	to be in agreement (with)
estar de acuerdo (con)	to agree (with)
estar de pie	to be standing
estar de vuelta	to be back
estar para + inf.	to be about to
guardar cama	to stay in bed
llegar a ser	to become (through effort)
llevar a cabo	to carry out (plans, etc.)
pensar + inf.	to intend
perder cuidado	not to worry
perder de vista	to lose sight of
ponerse + adj.	to become (involuntarily)
ponerse de acuerdo	to come to an agreement

querer decir	to mean
(saber) de memoria	(to know) by heart
tocarle a uno	to be one's turn (uses I.O.)
valer la pena	to be worthwhile
volver en sí	to regain consciousness

Words with the Same English Translation

The following pairs of words cause problems because they share the same translation in English but are not interchangeable in Spanish.

To Know

a) *Conocer* is to know the sense of "being acquainted with" a person, place, or thing.

¿Conoce Ud. a Maria?	Do you know Mary?
¿Conoces bien España?	Do you know Spain well?
¿Conoce Ud. esta novela?	Do you know this novel?

Note: In the preterite, *conocer* means **met** for the first time.

La conocí ayer.	I met her yesterday.

b) *Saber* means to know a fact, know something thoroughly, or to know how (with infinitive).

¿Sabe Ud. la dirección?	Do you know the address?
¿Sabes la lección?	Do you know the lesson?
¿Sabes nadar?	Do you know how to swim?

Note: In the preterite, *saber* means **found out**.

Supiste la verdad.	You found out the truth.

To Leave

a) *Dejar* is used when you leave someone or something behind.

Dejé a María en el cine.	I left Mary at the movies.
Dejó sus libros en casa.	He left his books at home.

b) *Salir* is used in the sense of physically departing.

Salió del cuarto.	He left the room.

To Spend

Gastar refers to spending money. *Pasar* refers to spending time.

Me gusta gastar dinero.	I like to spend money.
Pasé mucho tiempo allí.	I spent a lot of time there.

To Play

Jugar refers to playing a game; *tocar* to playing an instrument.

Juego bien al tenis.	I play tennis well.
Juana toca el piano.	Juana plays the piano.

Note: **Tocar** has other uses as well:

Le toca a Juan.	It's Juan's turn.
Toqué la flor.	I touched the flower.
Alguien tocó a la puerta.	Someone knocked.

To Take

a) *Llevar* means to take in the sense of carry or transport from place to place or to take someone somewhere. It also means to wear.

José llevó la mesa a la sala.	Joe took the table to the living room.
Llevé a María al cine.	I took Mary to the movies.
¿Por qué no llevas camisa?	Why aren't you wearing a shirt?

b) *Tomar* means to grab, catch, take transportation, or take medication.

Ella tomó el libro y comenzó a leerlo.
She took the book and began to read it.

Tomé el tren hoy.
I took the train today.

¡Toma esta aspirina!
Take this aspirin!

To Ask

a) *Pedir* means to request or to ask for something. (If there is a change in subject, it will require the use of the subjunctive.)

> *Pedí el menú al entrar.*   Upon entering I asked for the menu.
> *Le pido a Juan que vaya.*   I ask Juan to go.

b) *Preguntar* means to inquire or ask a question.

> *Ella le preguntó adonde fue.*   She asked him where he went.

To Return

Volver means to come back; *devolver* to give back.

> *Volví (Regresé) tarde.*   I came back late.
> *Devolví el libro.*   I returned the book.

To Realize

Realizar means to "make real" one's dreams, ambitions, or desires. *Darse cuenta de* means to "take note."

> *Juan realizó su sueño de ser doctor.*
> Juan realized his dream to be a doctor.

> *Me di cuenta de que no tenía mis apuntes.*
> I realized that I didn't have my notes.

To Become

a) *Llegar a ser* + noun/adj. means to become something through natural developments of time/circumstance.

> *Llegó a ser capitán/poderoso.*
> He became a captain/powerful.

b) *Hacerse* + noun/adj. means to become something through personal will or effort.

> *Se hizo abogado/indispensable.*
> He became a lawyer/indispensable.

c) *Ponerse* + adj. indicates a sudden change of emotional state or change in physical appearance.

> *Ella se puso triste/gorda.*
> She became sad/fat.

d) *Convertirse* + noun often indicates a somewhat unexpected change (not a profession).

> *Hitler se convirtió en un verdadero tirano.*
> Hitler became a real tyrant.

e) *Volverse* + adj. indicates a sudden or gradual change of personality. [Only adjectives that can be used with **both** *ser* and *estar* may follow *volverse*.]

Ella se volvió loca/alegre/sarcástica.
She became mad/happy/sarcastic.

To Enjoy

a) *Gustar, gozar de, disfrutar de* = to get pleasure from.

> *Me gusta viajar.*
> *Gozo de viajar/Gozo viajando.*   } I like (enjoy) traveling
> *Disfruto de viajar/Disfruto viajando.*

b) *Divertirse* (ie, i) = have a good time, enjoy oneself.

> *Nos divertimos mucho aquí.*   We enjoy ourselves a lot here.

To Save

a) *Salvar* means to rescue from destruction.

> *Ellos le salvaron la vida a ella.*
> They saved her life.

b) *Guardar* means to keep or put aside.

> *Voy a guardar mis cuentas.*
> I am going to keep my bills.

c) *Ahorrar* means **not** to spend or waste.

> *Vamos a ahorrar agua/dinero.*
> We are going to save water/money.

d) *Conservar* means to preserve, maintain.

> *Los indios conservan sus tradiciones.*
> The Indians preserve their traditions.

To Miss

a) *Extrañar* or *echar de menos* are used when miss = feel the absence of.

   ¡Cuánto lo extraño/echo de menos!
   How much I miss you!

b) *Perder* means to miss an opportunity, deadline, or transportation.

   Perdí el autobús/la última parte de la película.
   I missed the bus/the last part of the movie.

c) *Faltar a* means to miss an appointment or fail to attend (as in a class, etc.).

   Yo perdí la clase ayer. / Yo falté a la clase ayer.
   I missed class yesterday.

To Move

a) *Mudarse* or *trasladarse* means to move from place to place (city to city, office to office, etc.)

   Cuando era joven, me mudaba mucho.
   When I was young, I moved a lot.

   La compañía le trasladó a Nueva York.
   The company transferred him to New York.

b) *Mover* means to physically move something.

   Voy a mover el sofá cerca de la ventana.
   I'm going to move the sofa near the window.

To Work

a) *Trabajar* means to work, labor, or toil.

   Juan trabaja cada día en la oficina.
   Juan works everyday in the office.

b) *Funcionar* means to work, operate, or function.

   El coche/tocadiscos no funciona.
   The car/record player doesn't work.

To Keep

a) *Quedarse con* means to keep something in one's possession.

Me quedo con la tarea hasta mañana.
I'll keep the homework until tomorrow.

b) *Guardar* means to hold or put away for safekeeping.

Voy a guardar mi dinero en la caja fuerte.
I'm going to keep my money in the safe.

False Cognates

A cognate is a word whose origin is the same as another word in other languages. Often the spelling is identical and the meanings are similar. The false cognates, however, cause the most problems, particularly in the reading comprehension passages.

actual	of the present time
antiguo, –a	former, old, ancient
la apología	eulogy, defense
la arena	sand
asistir a	to attend
atender	to take care of
el auditorio	audience
bizarro, –a	brave, generous
el campo	field, country(side)
el cargo	duty, burden, responsibility
la carta	letter
el colegio	(high) school
el collar	necklace
la complexión	temperament
la conferencia	lecture
la confidencia	secret, trust
constipado, –a	sick with a cold
la consulta	conference
la chanza	joke, fun
la decepción	disappointment
el delito	crime
la desgracia	misfortune
el desmayo	fainting

embarazada	pregnant
el éxito	success
la fábrica	factory
la firma	signature
el idioma	language
ignorar	to be unaware
intoxicar	to poison
largo, –a	long
la lectura	reading
la librería	book store
la maleta	suitcase
el mantel	tablecloth
mayor	older, greater
molestar	to bother
el oficio	trade, occupation
la pala	shovel
el partido	game (sports)
pinchar	to puncture
pretender	to attempt
recordar	to remember
ropa	clothing
sano, –a	healthy
sensible	sensitive
soportar	to tolerate
el suceso	event, happening

DRILL 17

1. El tiempo ya había pasado, pero él no _____.

   (A) los realizaba   (C) daba cuenta

   (B) lo realizó   (D) se daba cuenta

2. Me gusta juntar dinero para las necesidades del futuro, por eso tengo una cuenta de _____.

   (A) ahorros   (C) guarda

   (B) salvos   (D) salvar

3. Ramón no _____ a los padres de su novia.

    (A) muerde   (C) conoce

    (B) toca   (D) sabe

4. Ramón no _____ que los padres de su novia son inmigrantes.

    (A) conoce   (C) responde

    (B) sabe   (D) pregunta

5. Quiso abrir la puerta del auto pero en ese momento _____ de que había perdido la llave.

    (A) realizó   (C) se encerró

    (B) se repuso   (D) se dio cuenta

6. En el estadio _____ muchos espectadores ayer.

    (A) tenían   (C) hay

    (B) habían   (D) había

7. La mujer _____ su bolsa en su coche.

    (A) dejó   (C) salió

    (B) partió   (D) se quitó

8. Elena _____ los apuntes al profesor.

    (A) preguntó   (C) pidió

    (B) preguntó para   (D) pidió por

9. Juan _____ la silla de la sala a la cocina.

    (A) llevó   (C) tomó

    (B) levantó   (D) arrancó

10. Cuando vi el huracán, _____ pálida.

    (A) llegué a ser   (C) me hice

    (B) volví   (D) me puse

11. Yo sé jugar al golf y mi mejor amigo sabe _____ piano.

    (A) jugar el   (C) tocar el

    (B) jugar al   (D) tocar al

12. Este alumno no _____ estudiar bien.

    (A) conoce   (C) sabe de

    (B) sabe a   (D) sabe

13. Basta que los turistas _____ la ciudad antes de salir.

    (A) conozcan   (C) saben

    (B) sepan   (D) conocen

14. Los estudiantes _____ a la profesora cómo estaba.

    (A) pidieron   (C) preguntaron

    (B) pusieron   (D) pudieron

15. La señora Gómez _____ el cheque y se fue al banco.

    (A) vendió   (C) llevó

    (B) compró   (D) tomó

16. Mi hermano quiere _____ doctor.

    (A) llegar a ser   (C) ponerse

    (B) volverse   (D) convertirse en

17. No me encanta _____ mucho tiempo en la cárcel.

    (A) gastar   (C) pasar

    (B) gastando   (D) pasando

18. Mis amigas han _____ traer los refrescos.

    (A) de   (C) por

    (B) a   (D) nothing needed

19. Nuestro cuarto da _____ patio.

(A) por el

(B) para el

(C) al

(D) en el

20. Juan y María hablan de ganar el premio gordo y esperan tener

_____.

(A) lugar

(B) el tiempo

(C) hambre

(D) éxito

21. Ese actor sabe _____ de Sancho Panza bien.

(A) hacer caso

(B) hacer falta

(C) hacer el papel

(D) hacer un viaje

22. Tengo que _____ los libros a la biblioteca hoy.

(A) regresar

(B) dejar

(C) devolver

(D) volver

23. Yo quiero que los chicos _____ en la playa.

(A) se diviertan

(B) gocen

(C) gozan

(D) se divierten

24. Cuando me levanto tarde, siempre _____ el autobús.

(A) falto a

(B) pierdo

(C) echo de menos

(D) extraño

25. _____ de Los Ángeles hace cinco años.

(A) Moví

(B) Movía

(C) Me mudé

(D) Me mudaría

26. Por ser tan viejo mi coche rehusa _____.

(A) trabajar

(B) tejer

(C) empezar

(D) funcionar

27. La profesora me dijo, –¡ _____ la tarea para mañana!

    (A) quédese con   (C) salve

    (B) guarde   (D) gaste

28. Murió sin_____ su sueño de ser doctor famoso.

    (A) darse cuenta de   (C) saber

    (B) realizar   (D) ponerse

29. _____ mucha tarea_____ hacer esta noche.

    (A) Hay...para   (C) Hay...que

    (B) Hay...(nothing needed)   (D) Hay...por

30. Tiene que_____ una razón por sus acciones.

    (A) haber   (C) ser

    (B) estar   (D) pensar

Drill 17—Detailed Explanations of Answers

1. **(D)** **Darse cuenta** must be used here for "to realize." **Realizar** means "to realize" in the sense of gaining or resulting in. (C) would be correct if it were reflexive.

2. **(A)** A "savings account" (**ahorros**) is the only correct answer. None of the other answers indicates this. **Salvar** is "to save," but in the sense of rescuing, not in the banking sense, and **guardar** might mean "to save," but only in the sense "to keep from harm" or "to keep back."

3. **(C)** The correct answer comes down to a choice between "conoce" and "sabe," both modalities of "to know." (The first two choices don't make much sense.)

4. **(B)** Again, an exercise to distinguish between "saber" and "conocer" (and again, the last two choices don't fit semantically or grammatically). When it's a matter of knowing information (as in this case), the correct choice is "saber."

5. **(D)**   Choices (B) and (C) simply make no sense in the context. You may think that (A) is the obvious choice since it sounds like it means "realized." It does, but not in the sense demanded by the question, which can only be rendered by (D). ("Realizar" means "to realize" a project or a plan, to make something real.)

6. **(D)**   Choice (B) is incorrect because the verb "haber" is impersonal when it translates "there is," "there are," etc. (i.e., when not used in an auxiliary capacity). Choice (C) contradicts the adverb of time in the question ("ayer"), and choice (A) could only be the product of confusion between the meaning and use of "haber" and "tener."

7. **(A)**   "Dejar" means to leave something behind. "Salir" means to physically leave a place. "Partir" means to depart, and "quitarse" means to remove (as in clothing).

8. **(C)**   "Pedir" means to ask for something or to request, while "preguntar" means to inquire or ask a question. Neither needs "por" nor "para" in this sample.

9. **(A)**   "Llevar" means to carry or transport from one place to another or to take someone somewhere. "Tomar" means to take, in the sense of grab or catch. "Levantar" means to lift and "arrancar" means to start, as in an engine.

10. **(D)**   "Ponerse" is used with adjectives to indicate a sudden change of emotional state or physical appearance. "Llegar a ser" is used with adjectives/nouns and means to become something through natural developments of time/circumstance. "Hacerse" also used with adjectives/nouns means to become something through effort. "Volverse" is used with adjectives to indicate a sudden or gradual change of personality.

11. **(C)**   "Jugar a" is used in connection with sports. "Tocar" is used in connection with instruments.

12. **(D)**   "Conocer" means to know or be acquainted with people, places, or things. "Saber" is to know facts or know "how" to do something (when followed by an infinitive).

13. **(A)**   The difference between "saber" and "conocer" is given in number 12. One also needs to recognize that the subjunctive is required in this sample. The sentence begins with an impersonal expression ("it is enough") and there is a change in subject.

14. **(C)** "Preguntar" is used to inquire or ask a question. "Pusieron" from "poner" means "they put" and "pudieron" from "poder" means "they were able/managed." (A) pidieron means "to ask for" and "to order."

15. **(D)** "Tomar" means to take in the sense of grab or catch. In this sample Mrs. Gomez is "grabbing" the check to take it to the bank. "Vendió" from "vender" means "she sold," and "compró" from "comprar" means "she bought."

16. **(A)** To become something through the natural development of time/circumstance is "llegar a ser." "Ponerse" and "volverse" must be followed by adjectives. "Convertirse en" is used with nouns but indicates a somewhat unexpected change (not a profession).

17. **(C)** To spend **time** is "pasar." "Gastar" means to spend money. Because this verb is the subject of "me encanta," it is a gerund and must be in the infinitive form in Spanish. In Spanish a present participle may not be treated as a noun.

18. **(A)** The idiom "haber de" means to be (supposed) to. Neither "a" nor "por" is used with this verb. "Han" cannot be used alone.

19. **(C)** "Dar a" means to face. "Dar en" means to hit or strike against, which makes no sense in this sentence.

20. **(D)** "Tener éxito" means to be successful. "Tener lugar" means to take place. "Tener el tiempo" means to have the time, and "tener hambre" means to be hungry.

21. **(C)** "Hacer el papel de" means to play a part or role. "Hacer caso de" means to notice. "Hacer falta" means to need and is used like *gustar*. "Hacer un viaje" means to take a trip.

22. **(C)** To return objects/things, one uses the verb "devolver." Both "regresar" and "volver" are intransitive verbs (cannot take direct objects) and are used to indicate a physical return. "Dejar" means to allow/let.

23. **(A)** "Divertirse" means to enjoy oneself. "Gozar" followed by a present participle or "gozar de" followed by a noun means to get pleasure from. Also, one needs the subjunctive here since there is a verb of volition and a change in subject.

24. **(B)** "Perder" means to miss a deadline or transportation. "Echar de menos" and "extrañar" mean to feel the absence of (as in people). "Faltar a" means to miss an appointment or a class, for example.

25. **(C)** To move from place to place is "mudarse." "Mover" is to move objects. The preterite is needed here since this is an "hace" statement meaning **ago**.

26. **(D)** "Funcionar" means to work/operate/function (as in things). "Trabajar" is for people. "Tejer" means to weave, and "empezar" means to begin or start. To start a car, however, is "arrancar."

27. **(A)** "Quedarse con" means to keep in one's possession. "Guardar" means to put away for safe keeping (as in money or jewelry). "Salvar" means to save lives and "gastar" means to spend money.

28. **(B)** "Realizar" means to realize one's dreams, hopes, or ambitions. "Darse cuenta de" means to take note. "Saber" is to know facts or how to do something and "ponerse" means to become something unexpectedly (as in pale, sick, angry, etc.).

29. **(C)** These are the missing parts of the idiom "*hay* + noun + *que* + infinitive" which is translated: There is a lot of homework to do tonight.

30. **(A)** Through translation, "haber" is the logical choice: There has to be a reason for his actions.

In addition to vocabulary, spelling, and grammar, Part C of the Reading portion of the CLEP Spanish Language exam provides students with an "original document." Students will be asked to read the short passage and answer two to three questions based on what they have read. A sample document and two practice questions follow.

INSTRUCCIONES PARA INDIVIDUOS QUE DESEAN REGISTRARSE PARA VOTAR.

- Usted tiene derecho de registrarse para votar sí;
  - Usted es un ciudadano de los Estados Unidos.
  - Usted tendrá 18 años de edad o más para el tiempo de la próxima elección.
  - Usted tiene que haber vivido en New Jersey y en su condado por lo menos 30 días antes de las próximas elecciones.

- Formularios de registración para el votante debe ser completado en tinta oscura y en letra clara de imprenta (excepción las firmas).

- Si usted necesita alguna asistencia en completar el formulario, incluyendo la necesidad de un testigo, requiera ayuda en esta oficina.

- Usted no será considerado un votante certificado válido hasta que su formulario sea recibido y aprobado por el Comisionado Certificado del Condado. El Comisionado lo notificará por correo si aceptaron o rechazaron su formulario.

- Para usted poder votar en cualquier elección, usted debe registrarse para el 29 día antes de la elección.

- Si usted tiene alguna pregunta en respecto a su registración por correo, usted debe comunicarse con el Comisionado Certificado del Condado. Las direcciones y teléfonos de los Comisionados Certificados del Condado están listados en la parte inversa de este formulario.

- Usted no podrá registrarse para votar si usted tiene alguna de las siguientes descalificaciones establecidas;
  - Un tribunal de jurisdicción competente lo ha determinado a usted ser "demente" o un "idiota".
  - Usted está o será condenado de haber violado el Título 19, Leyes de Elección, por el cual, privarse de derechos civiles es parte del castigo a menos perdonar o devolver por ley al derecho de sufragio.
  - Usted está sirviendo una sentencia o en libertad condicional o en un período de prueba como resultado de una condena por una ofensa encausable bajo las leyes de ésta u otro estado o de los Estados Unidos.

1. ¿Qué no se permite cuando uno se registra para votar?

    (A)   tener menos de 18 años antes de registrarse

    (B)   completar el formulario con bolígrafo

    (C)   completar el formulario con la ayuda de otro

    (D)   firmar el formulario sin testigo certificado

2. No se puede registrar si

    (A)   ha sido condenado por la corte.

    (B)   ha estado en su condado

    (C)   un psiquiatra ha determinado que Ud. es demente

    (D)   ha cometido un delito o crímen

Answers to Practice Questions

1.   **(D)**   The correct answer is (D). It is not permitted to sign a voter registration form without the presence of a witness who is registered to vote in the state. (A) is incorrect since you may be younger than 18 years of age at the time of registration as long as you will be 18 years of age at the time of the next election. The form should be completed with an ink pen only, and if needed, the assistance of another person. Therefore, (C) and (B) are incorrect.

2.   **(A)**   The correct answer is (A). You may not register to vote if you have been convicted of an offense. (D) is incorrect since you may have committed a crime without conviction, in which case you would not lose your right to vote. (B) simply means that you have been in your county. The determination of "demented" is made by a court of law, not a psychiatrist (C).

PRACTICE TEST 1

CLEP Spanish Language

Also available at the REA Study Center (*www.rea.com/studycenter*)

This practice test is also offered online at the REA Study Center. Since all CLEP exams are administered on computer, we recommend that you take the online version of the test to receive these added benefits:

- **Timed testing conditions** – Gauge how much time you can spend on each question.
- **Automatic scoring** – Find out how you did on the test, instantly.
- **On-screen detailed explanations of answers** – Learn not just the correct answer, but also why the other answer choices are incorrect.
- **Diagnostic score reports** – Pinpoint where you're strongest and where you need to focus your study.

PRACTICE TEST 1

CLEP Spanish Language

PRACTICE TEST 1

SECTION I

Listening: Rejoinders

(Answer sheets appear in the back of the book.)

TIME: 30 Minutes
50 Questions

DIRECTIONS: For this section of the test, you will hear a number of conversations or parts of conversations. After each dialogue, you will hear four answer choices, identified as (A), (B), (C), and (D). When you have heard all four answer choices, choose the one that best completes or continues the conversation. Fill in the corresponding oval on your answer sheet. Neither the answer choices nor the conversations will be printed in your test booklet, so you must listen very carefully.

1.– 18. Mark your answers on your answer sheet.

SECTION II

Listening: Dialogues and Narratives

DIRECTIONS: You will hear a series of selections, including narratives, news reports, announcements, and dialogues. A graphic or a picture accompanies each selection. Listen very carefully to each selection, as they are spoken only once. For each selection, one or more questions will be printed in your test booklet, each with four answer choices. The questions and answers will not be spoken. Choose the best answer to each question and fill in the corresponding oval on your answer sheet. You are given 12 seconds to answer each question.

Selección 1

Vuelo	Destino	Fecha	Partida	Estado
19	Bogotá	6 de marzo	4:15	Salió a tiempo
914	Bogotá	7 de marzo	20	
755	Bogotá	7 de marzo	4:15	

19. Mira la pantalla y escoge el número del vuelo que debe estar en el espacio 19.

    (A) 495
    (B) 914
    (C) 517
    (D) 757

20. Mira la pantalla y escoge la hora de salida que debe estar en el espacio 20.

    (A) 4:15
    (B) 8:00
    (C) 9:14
    (D) 5:30

21. ¿Cuándo llegará el señor a Bogotá?

    (A) Esa noche
    (B) Dentro de cinco horas
    (C) Al día siguiente
    (D) La semana próxima

Selección 2

22. ¿Por qué tiene prisa Santiago?

(A) Quiere comer.
(B) Quiere algo de beber.
(C) Tiene que dar un examen.
(D) Quiere hablar con Viviana.

23. ¿Qué va a hacer Viviana?

(A) Va a la cafetería con Santiago.
(B) Va a volver a tomar su examen.
(C) Va a otra clase.
(D) Va a casa con Santiago.

Selección 3

Manuel Ávila Camacho	1940-46
24.	1946-52
Adolfo Ruíz Cortines	1952-58
25.	1958-64

24. Mira la tabla de arriba. ¿Qué presidente debe estar en el espacio 24?

(A) Gustavo Díaz Ordaz
(B) Manuel Ávila Camacho
(C) Miguel Alemán Valdés
(D) Adolfo López Mateos

25. Mira la tabla de arriba. ¿Qué presidente debe estar en el espacio 25?

(A) Gustavo Díaz Ordaz
(B) Manuel Ávila Camacho
(C) Miguel Alemán Valdés
(D) Adolfo López Mateos

26. ¿Ninguno puede pensar en cómo se llamaba quién?

(A) el padre del candidato
(B) el que no ganó la presidencia
(C) el presidente después de López Mateos
(D) López Mateos

Selección 4

27. ¿Qué hizo el hombre para preparar su tarea?

    (A) Contestó todas las preguntas.
    (B) Repasó con otros compañeros de su clase
    (C) Habló con el profesor
    (D) Le pidió más tiempo al profesor

28. La mujer está muy angustiada porque no tuvo tiempo para _____.

    (A) repasar la tarea
    (B) completar sus respuestas
    (C) consultar con un experto
    (D) repasar con sus compañeros

29. Los estudiantes van a pedirle al profesor que les_____.

    (A) dé más tiempo
    (B) suba la calificación
    (C) explique sus dudas
    (D) cambie de grupo

Selección 5

30. ¿Por qué tienen dificultades en encontrarle un regalo a Ricardo?

    (A) es muy lindo
    (B) no le interesa mucho
    (C) tiene muchas cosas
    (D) tiene cuarenta años

31. ¿Qué deciden regalarle a Ricardo?

    (A) un carro a control remoto
    (B) un postre cocinado por la mujer
    (C) una camiseta autografiada
    (D) una canción cantada por el hombre

Selección 6

Para hacer antes del viaje:	el/la encargado/a:
Arreglar transportación desde el aeropuerto	32.
Pagar el pasaje	33.
Hacer las maletas	34.
Confirmar el vuelo	35.

32. – 35. Empareja la persona con su trabajo en la lista de arriba. Escoge la letra de la persona que debe estar en lugar de cada número.

(A) Papá

(B) Mimi

(C) Mamá

(D) Pepe

Selección 7

36. Escoge la línea que mejor indica la temperatura de Miguelito durante el día.

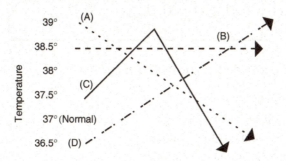

37. ¿Quién propuso que Miguelito fuera al médico?

(A) su mamá
(B) el Dr. Ponce
(C) Miguelito mismo
(D) la enfermera

38. ¿Qué le recomendó el médico al niño?

(A) que no comiera
(B) que fuera al hospital
(C) que tomara medicina
(D) que tragara agua con sal

Selección 8

39. ¿Qué les pasó a las indígenas de Ushauaia?

(A) fueron encarcelados
(B) se cambiaron a buscafortunas
(C) salieron para Tierra del Fuego
(D) se murieron de una enfermedad

40. ¿Qué se puede decir de la capital de Tierra del Fuego?

    (A) nadie vive allí ahora
    (B) está llena de prisioneros
    (C) se quedó igual por muchos años
    (D) ha cambiado mucho a través de los años

Selección 9

41. ¿Qué quiere la mujer?

    (A) beber sangre
    (B) atacar al enemigo
    (C) vivir en paz
    (D) cambiar las leyes

42. ¿Contra quiénes habla ella?

    (A) los seres pacíficos
    (B) sus vecinos
    (C) los policías
    (D) la gente violenta

43. ¿Cuál será el tema del discurso de la mujer?

    (A) ojo por ojo
    (B) la violencia no es la respuesta
    (C) la justicia racial
    (D) la pena de muerte

Selección 10

Restaurante	Bebidas alcohólicas	Carne	Postres
Girasol	44	sí	no
La Esperanza	no	45	sí
El Palenque	46	no	sí
Sabor de México	sí	no	47

44. – 47. Mira la tabla de arriba. Para cada número, escoge "A" si el restaurante indicado sí sirve algo de la categoría o "B" si no.

48. ¿Cuál será un restaurante para una familia grande con poco dinero?

    (A) Girasol
    (B) La Esperanza
    (C) El Palenque
    (D) Sabor de México

Selección 11

49. Esta noche probablemente va a _____.

    (A) nevar
    (B) caer granizo
    (C) hacer calor
    (D) llover

50. ¿Qué tiempo hará esta noche?

    (A) más frío de lo normal
    (B) igual a lo normal
    (C) más calor de lo normal
    (D) no hará tiempo esta noche

**This is the end of the audio section of Practice Test 1.
Please go to the Reading section on the next page.**

SECTION III

Reading

TIME: 60 Minutes
70 Questions

Part A

DIRECTIONS: This section contains several incomplete statements, each having four completion choices. Select the most appropriate answer and fill in the corresponding oval on your answer sheet.

51. El taxi se encuentra en _____ de aquellas dos calles.

    (A) la esquina
    (B) el techo
    (C) la alfombra
    (D) el rincón

52. El hombre que nos atiende en una tienda se llama _____.

    (A) mercancía
    (B) dependiente
    (C) cliente
    (D) parroquiano

53. ¿Cuándo vas a _____ este libro a la biblioteca?

    (A) regresar
    (B) devolver
    (C) retornar
    (D) volver

54. Voy a acostarme porque tengo _____.

    (A) sed
    (B) hambre
    (C) calor
    (D) sueño

55. Cuando el autobús llegó al fin de la trayectoria, _____ delante del Museo Arqueológico.

(A) dejó de
(B) cesó
(C) paró
(D) terminó

56. Julio dijo que _____ ayudarnos con la tarea.

(A) ensayaría
(B) trataría de
(C) probaría
(D) se quedaría

57. Mañana voy a pagar _____ de la casa.

(A) los cuentos
(B) los boletos
(C) las cuentas
(D) los billetes

58. ¿Qué piensas _____ estas pinturas?

(A) de
(B) en
(C) a
(D) con

59. Hoy he estudiado demasiado y _____ la cabeza.

(A) me hace daño
(B) me hiere
(C) me daña
(D) me duele

60. Mucha gente lleva abrigo cuando _____.

(A) hace calor
(B) está nublado
(C) corre
(D) hace frío

61. Antes de hacer el viaje voy a comprar_____.

    (A) una maleta
    (B) una máquina de coser
    (C) una multa
    (D) una muñeca

62. _____ es un lugar, muchas veces en el campo, donde hay muchos árboles.

    (A) Una verdulería
    (B) Una madera
    (C) Una leña
    (D) Un bosque

63. Felipe se cortó con el cuchillo y tiene _____ en el dedo.

    (A) un anillo
    (B) una uña
    (C) una herida
    (D) una oreja

64. ¿Cuál es tu _____ favorita? ¿El otoño o la primavera?

    (A) actividad
    (B) estación
    (C) sazón
    (D) lluvia

65. La tarea de historia fue _____, pero Rosalía me ayudó a entenderla.

    (A) comprada
    (B) complacida
    (C) compartida
    (D) complicada

Part B

     Alrededor de 8.500 personas visitan la Biblioteca Nacional de Buenos Aires todos los meses. __(66)__ no todos quedan __(67)__ con __(68)__ encuentran en el enorme edificio ubicado en Agüero y Libertador, y __(69)__ decepcionados. Aunque los archivos __(70)__ algo más de __(71)__ millón de ejemplares, casi todos son libros editados __(72)__ más de una década. Por eso, __(73)__ buscan información actualizada se ven totalmente frustrados. Por ejemplo, si alguien quiere consultar __(74)__ sobre el conflicto por las Islas Malvinas, no hay nada.

66. (A) Sin embargo
    (B) Sin novedad
    (C) Sin par
    (D) Sin recurso

67. (A) satisfecho
    (B) satisfaces
    (C) satisfechos
    (D) satisfacer

68. (A) lo que
    (B) lo cual
    (C) el cual
    (D) los que

69. (A) se irán
    (B) se vayan
    (C) se fueron
    (D) se van

70. (A) cuentan con
    (B) cuenten con
    (C) contar con
    (D) contaron con

71. (A) uno
    (B) unos
    (C) una
    (D) un

72. (A) hacía
    (B) hace
    (C) hacen
    (D) hizo

73. (A) los que
    (B) quiénes
    (C) ellos que
    (D) esos que

74. (A) obsecuencias
    (B) obras
    (C) obradas
    (D) obradoras

Al día siguiente Juan __(75)__ a hablar con el Obispo, y este le dijo que le __(76)__ __(77)__ evidencia de la aparición. Juan __(78)__ comunicó __(79)__ a la Señora, __(80)__ le dijo que __(81)__ por la mañana y le daría evidencias que __(82)__ al Obispo.

75. (A) volvió
    (B) volve
    (C) volviera
    (D) volver

76. (A) trajo
    (B) trajera
    (C) traiga
    (D) traerá

77. (A) algún
    (B) ninguna
    (C) ningún
    (D) alguna

78. (A) la
    (B) le
    (C) les
    (D) lo

79. (A) eso
    (B) ese
    (C) esos
    (D) esas

80. (A) quién
    (B) a quien
    (C) quien
    (D) de quien

81. (A) regrese
    (B) regresara
    (C) regresar
    (D) regresa

82. (A) convencerían
    (B) convenzan
    (C) convencieron
    (D) convencieran

Las reformas sociales en beneficio de los zapateros fueron __(83)__ tema central de los cinco años que fue Gobernador de Oaxaca. Abrió cincuenta escuelas nuevas y abogó por la educación de las mujeres. Construyó caminos y abrió un puerto en la costa pacífica que había __(84)__ __(85)__ durante muchos años. Logró __(86)__ las deudas del Estado y dejó la tesorería estatal en __(87)__ condiciones cuando terminó su mandato. Jamás se aprovechó del cargo público __(88)__ sacar beneficio propio.

83. (A) el
    (B) la
    (C) una
    (D) otra

84. (A) permanecida
    (B) permanecido
    (C) permaneciendo
    (D) permanecer

85. (A) cerrado
    (B) cerrada
    (C) cerrando
    (D) cerrar

86. (A) pagar
    (B) pagando
    (C) pagado
    (D) pagadas

87. (A) buenos
    (B) buen
    (C) buenas
    (D) buena

88. (A) por
    (B) para que
    (C) porque
    (D) para

Part C

La casita de Lencho estaba en el cerro. Desde allí se veía el campo de maíz y el frijol en flor. Todo prometía una buena cosecha. Pero para ello se necesitaba mucha lluvia. Desde temprano por la mañana Lencho examinaba el cielo hacia el noreste.

—¡Ahora sí que lloverá!

Su esposa asintió:

—Lloverá si Dios quiere.

Al mediodía, mientras la familia comía, grandes gotas de lluvia comenzaron a caer. Enormes nubes negras avanzaban hacia el noreste. El aire estaba cada vez más fresco y dulce, y Lencho observaba sus campos con placer. Pero, de pronto, sopló un viento fuerte y comenzó a granizar.

Durante una hora cayó el granizo sobre todo el valle. Lencho se iba angustiado cada vez más y cuando la tempestad pasó dijo con voz triste a sus hijos:

—Esto fue peor que las langostas; el granizo no ha dejado nada. No tendremos ni maíz ni frijoles este año.

Sólo guardaban una esperanza en el corazón los habitantes del valle: la ayuda de Dios.

Lencho pensaba en el futuro. Aunque era un hombre rudo, él sabía escribir. Así es que decidió escribir una carta a Dios:

"Dios, si no me ayudas, pasaré hambre con toda mi familia durante este año. Necesito cien pesos para volver a sembrar y vivir mientras viene la cosecha, porque el granizo…"

[1] <u>Escribió "A Dios" en el sobre</u>. Le puso un sello a la cara y la echó en el buzón.

[2] <u>Un empleado de correo la recogió más tarde, la abrió y la leyó, y, riéndose, se la mostró al jefe de correos</u>. El jefe también se rió al leerla, pero muy pronto se puso serio y exclamó:

—¡La fe! ¡Qué fe tan pura! [3] <u>Este hombre cree de veras y por eso le escribe a Dios</u>.

Y para no desilusionar a un hombre tan puro, el jefe de correos decidió contestar la carta.

El jefe pudo reunir sólo un poco más de la mitad del dinero pedido por Lencho. Metió los billetes en un sobre dirigido a Lencho y con ellos una carta que consistía en una palabra: DIOS.

Una semana más tarde Lencho entró en el correo y preguntó si había carta para él. Sí, había, pero Lencho no mostró la menor sorpresa.

Tampoco se sorprendió al ver los billetes, pues él tenía fe en Dios y los esperaba. [4] <u>Pero al contar el dinero se enfadó</u>. En seguida se acercó a la ventanilla, pidió papel y tinta, y se fue a una mesa a escribir:

"Dios, del dinero que te pedí sólo llegaron a mis manos sesenta pesos. Mándame el resto, porque lo necesito mucho, pero no me lo mandes por correo porque todos los empleados de correo son ladrones.

Tuyo, LENCHO."

[Adapted from: "Carta a Dios," by Gregorio López y Fuentes, in Selecciones Españolas, A Basic Spanish Reader, ed. Angel Flores (1967: Bantam Books, Inc., 271 Madison Ave., New York, NY 10016), pp. 26-30.]

89. ¿Por qué se entristeció Lencho?

    (A) Sus hijos se murieron.
    (B) Llovió demasiado.
    (C) Las langostas destruyeron su sembrado.
    (D) El granizo arrasó su cultivo.

90. ¿Qué trabajo hacía Lencho?

    (A) Era cura.
    (B) Era agricultor.
    (C) Era cartero.
    (D) Era escribano.

91. ¿Por qué escribió Lencho su primera carta a Dios?

    (A) Para pedirle que le ayudara.
    (B) Para quejarse de su mala suerte.
    (C) Para denunciar irregularidades en el correo.
    (D) Para rogarle que le diera una buena cosecha.

92. Luego de leer la carta de Lencho, ¿qué hizo el jefe de correos?

    (A) Se rió nada más.
    (B) Regañó al empleado por abrir una carta.
    (C) Juntó dinero para ayudarle a Lencho.
    (D) Le devolvió la carta a Lencho sin dinero.

93. (To answer question 93, choose the sentence from the reading selection that best answers the question.)

Escoge y haz clic en la frase de la selección que explica por qué no mostró ninguna sorpresa Lencho al recibir la respuesta a su carta.

    (A) Sentence 1
    (B) Sentence 2
    (C) Sentence 3
    (D) Sentence 4

94. ¿Qué pensaba Lencho de los empleados de correo?

   (A) Que eran hombres honrados.
   (B) Que eran deshonestos.
   (C) Que eran muy generosos.
   (D) Que eran muy bondadosos.

95. ¿Qué sintió Lencho al ver la lluvia en sus campos?

   (A) Placer
   (B) Desesperación
   (C) Enojo
   (D) Angustia

El cacao no debe confundirse ni con el coco ni con la coca, fuente de la cocaína. Los árboles crecen en los trópicos, y por eso no pueden ser cultivados en los Estados Unidos. El cacao y su derivado, el chocolate, pueden ser auxiliares digestivos, estimular el flujo sanguíneo al corazón y ayudar a las personas con pecho congestionado a respirar mejor.

Una vez recolectados los granos del cacao, se tuestan y muelen para producir el licor de cacao. A ese líquido se le agrega cantidades minúsculas de lejía para intensificar su sabor. Se continúa el proceso para eliminar su grasa, conocida como manteca de cacao. El producto final, el chocolate, es una combinación del polvo de cacao desgrasado con un poco de su misma manteca que se le vuelve a añadir.

El polvo al que llamamos cocoa es simplemente licor de cacao seco, quizás con un poco de azúcar. El chocolate de pastelería es licor de cacao procesado sin azúcar. Al chocolate amargo se le añade un poco de azúcar; al chocolate semidulce un poco más, y al chocolate de leche todavía más—además la leche para hacerlos cremoso.

Los europeos desconocían la existencia del cacao hasta 1519, cuando el conquistador español Hernán Cortés vio al emperador azteca Moctezuma tomar una bebida llamada *chocolatl* en un tazón de oro. Cortés se interesó más en el tazón que en su contenido, hasta que los aztecas le informaron que la bebida se elaboraba de granos tan valiosos que cien podían comprar un esclavo en buen estado de salud.

Cortés introdujo el agasajo azteca a la corte española, donde resultó una sensación. Los españoles trataron de mantener el chocolate en secreto y lo lograron por más de cien años, pero para 1660 se había extendido por toda Europa. El chocolate adquirió especial popularidad en Inglaterra y Holanda, donde la amarga bebida se enriqueció y endulzó con azúcar. Por extraño que parezca, hasta el siglo XIX el chocolate era sólo una bebida, en ocasiones amarga, a veces dulce, pero siempre líquida. No fue hasta hace unos 150 años que se elaboró en las barras y dulces que nos gustan tanto.

Hoy en día, el chocolate es una bebida moderna que caliente o fría, es muy popular y además tiene muchos beneficios para la salud. Estudios realizados han descubierto que comer chocolate regularmente puede disminuir el colesterol malo, la presión arterial y el riesgo de contraer enfermedades del corazón.

[Adapted from: Las Hierbas que Curan, por Michael Castelman (1991, Rodale Press, 33 East Minor St., Emmaus, PA), pp. 123,124,127.]

96. ¿A qué se refiere "el agasajo azteca"?

(A) A la actitud del emperador Moctezuma con respecto a los conquistadores.
(B) Al tazón de oro del cual bebía Moctezuma.
(C) A la bebida *chocolatl* que Cortés llevó a España.
(D) A la destrucción del Imperio Azteca por los españoles.

97. ¿Dónde se cultivan los árboles de cacao?

(A) En los Estados Unidos.
(B) En las zonas tropicales.
(C) En España.
(D) En Inglaterra y Holanda.

98. ¿Qué hizo la corte española cuando supo del cacao?

(A) Difundió las noticias de inmediato al resto de Europa.
(B) Armó un escándalo, pues no le gustó la bebida amarga.
(C) Empezó a hacer chocolate en barra para exportar.
(D) Procuró que nadie más se enterara.

99. ¿De qué forma mejoraron la bebida de cacao los ingleses y los holandeses?

(A) Le echaron azúcar y leche.
(B) La sirvieron helada en vez de caliente.
(C) Le agregaron lejía para intensificar su sabor.
(D) Le quitaron toda la grasa.

100. Además de molerlos para elaborar una bebida, ¿qué otro uso les daban a los granos de cacao los aztecas?

(A) Los usaban como armas para hacer la guerra.
(B) Los echaban al mar para tener buena suerte.
(C) Los utilizaban para envenenar a sus enemigos.
(D) Los empleaban como dinero.

101. Según este pasaje, el chocolate_____.

(A) no tenía éxito fuera de México
(B) tiene valor medicinal
(C) tiene mucho valor nutritivo
(D) se parece al coco y a la coca

   A Rafael López, vecina del barrio de Santa Cruz, le ha tocado el Gordo de la lotería de Navidad. Antes, la joven sevillana soñaba con ser cantante de música folclórica y hacerse rica y famosa. Mientras tanto, según nos ha contado la misma López, para ganarse la vida, pertenecía a un conjunto musical en el cual tocaba el tambor, pero sólo cuando faltaba alguien. Ahora ya no está apurada y por encima de todo no hay nadie que le desconozca en toda España.

102. ¿Cuál de las oraciones a continuación resulta verdadera?

   (A) El joven se hizo cantante popular.
   (B) El sevillao fingía ser cantante popular.
   (C) Ahora, al joven le hace falta dinero para vivir.
   (D) El joven sevillano quería ser cantante.

103. Rafael_____.

    (A) ganó un premio musical
    (B) servía de sustituto en una banda
    (C) era pertinente
    (D) tenía su propio conjunto

104. Rafael ganó_____.

    (A) un viaje
    (B) un conjunto musical
    (C) mucho dinero
    (D) un tambor

105. El joven sevillano_____.

    (A) es célebre ahora
    (B) tiene por qué llorar
    (C) sigue careciendo de dinero
    (D) tiene prisa

Ayer por la tarde hubo un atraco en una sucursal del Banco Nacional situado en las afueras de la capital. Los reos enmascarados huyeron del lugar del crimen llevándose una cantidad de dinero todavía por determinar y sin ser identificados. Los agentes de la policía armada, rodearon el barrio, hicieron una redada y, a las cinco de la tarde, tuvieron éxito en su búsqueda. Se enteraron de que se trataba de una pareja campesina temporalmente radicada en la capital.

106. ¿Cuál de las contestaciones está bien?

   (A) Los policías salieron del barrio a las cinco de la tarde.
   (B) Los criminales todavía quedan libres.
   (C) Se sabe cuánto dinero fue robado.
   (D) La policía ha encontrado a los ladrones.

107. El asalto del banco fue llevado a cabo por_____.

   (A) la mañana
   (B) el centro de la ciudad
   (C) la policía armada
   (D) dos campesinos

108. El Banco Nacional_____.

   (A) cierra a las cinco de la tarde
   (B) está situado en el centro de la capital
   (C) fue robado ayer por la tarde
   (D) es el banco más grande de la ciudad

109. Los guardias_____.

   (A) trataron de impedir una rebelión
   (B) tuvieron que perseguir a los criminales al campo
   (C) supieron quiénes eran los reos
   (D) llegaron sin fusiles

110. Los criminales eran_____.

   (A) dos chicos del pueblo vecino
   (B) dos personas del extranjero
   (C) disfrazados
   (D) los policías armados

En algunas partes de la América Latina la situación económica va de mal en peor a causa de las deudas internacionales que no pueden pagar muchos gobiernos. A esto hay que agregar el aumento del costo de vida y el paro forzoso.

Teniendo en cuenta la situación inestable de las bolsas internacionales, la bajada del valor del dólar y el desequilibrio de la balanza de pagos, se han reunido los representantes de los poderes más influyentes del mundo económico a fin de llegar a un acuerdo que evite un posible derrumbamiento financiero, para cuyo efecto habrá que obrar con cautela.

111. ¿Cuál de las frases describe mejor la situación?

    (A) Suben los precios, hay bastante trabajo y a los gobiernos les falta dinero.

    (B) Bajan los precios, hay demasiado trabajo y a los gobiernos les sobra dinero.

    (C) Suben los precios, hay mucho desempleo y a los gobiernos les falta suficiente dinero.

    (D) Suben los precios, hay mucho paro y los gobiernos consiguen pagar sus deudas.

112. Los delegados de las varias naciones_____.

    (A) quieren estabilizar la economía internacional

    (B) apenas se dan cuenta de la seriedad del problema

    (C) niegan la gravedad de la situación

    (D) van a bajar el valor de la moneda

113. Se entiende que _____.

    (A) el resultado será eficaz

    (B) será necesario proceder con cuidado

    (C) se efectuará el fin deseado

    (D) se logrará el propósito de la conferencia

Blas de Santillana, mi padre, después de haber servido muchos años en los ejércitos de España, se volvió al pueblo donde había nacido. Allí se casó con una aldeana, y yo nací al mundo diez meses después de que se habían casado.

De Santillana pasaron mis padres a vivir a Oviedo donde ambos encontraron trabajo. En Oviedo vivía un hermano mayor de mi madre, llamado Gil Pérez, el cual era sacerdote. [1] <u>Éste me llevó a su casa cuando yo era niño, y me enseñó a leer; más tarde me envió a la escuela del doctor Godínes, el maestro más hábil que había en Oviedo, para estudiar la lengua latina</u>.

Aprendí tanto en esta escuela, que al cabo de cinco o seis años entendía un poco los autores griegos, y bastante bien los autores latinos. Estudié además, la lógica, que me enseñó a pensar y argumentar sin término. Me gustaban mucho las disputas y detenía a los que encontraba por la calle, conocidos o desconocidos, para proponerles cuestiones y argumentos.

De esta manera me hice famoso en toda la ciudad, y mi tío estaba muy orgulloso de mí. Un día me dijo:

—Gil Blas, ya no eres niño; tienes diecisiete años, y Dios te ha dado habilidad. Voy a enviarte a la universidad de Salamanca, donde con tu clara inteligencia llegarás a ser un hombre de importancia. Para tu viaje te daré dinero y una buena mula que podrás vender en Salamanca.

[2] <u>Mi tío no podía proponerme cosa más de mi gusto, porque yo tenía ganas de ver el mundo; pero no mostré mi gran alegría</u>. Al contrario, cuando llegó la hora de partir, puse una cara tan triste que mi tío me dio más dinero del que me habría dado si hubiese mostrado alegría.

Antes de montar en mi mula fui a dar un abrazo a mi padre y a mi madre, los cuales me dieron no pocos consejos. [3] <u>Me repitieron muchas veces que viviese cristianamente, y sobre todo no tomase jamás lo ajeno contra la voluntad de su dueño, y que no engañase a nadie</u>. Después de haberme hablado largamente, me dieron la única cosa que podía esperar de ellos: su bendición. [4] <u>Inmediatamente monté en mi mula y salí de la ciudad</u>.

[From: Aventuras de Gil Blas, retold and edited by Carlos Castillo and Colley F. Sparkman, graded Spanish readers, book Four (New York: D.C. Heath and Company, 1936 and 1937), pp. 1–2.]

114. ¿Cómo se llama el narrador del relato?

    (A) Blas de Santillana
    (B) Gil Blas
    (C) Gil Pérez
    (D) el doctor Godínez

115. ¿Cómo aprendió a leer Gil Blas?

    (A) su tío le enseñó
    (B) en la escuela del doctor Godínez
    (C) se lo enseñaron en la universidad
    (D) sus padres se lo enseñaron

116. ¿Por qué Gil Blas abandonó Oviedo?

    (A) quería ir a vivir con su tío.
    (B) pensaba volver a su pueblo natal.
    (C) sus padres lo echaron de la casa.
    (D) iba a estudiar en la universidad.

117. ¿De quién fue la idea de que Gil Blas fuera a Salamanca?

    (A) Gil Pérez

    (B) el doctor Godínez

    (C) sus padres

    (D) Gil Blas

118. Antes de que Gil Blas se fuera a Salamanca, sus padres le dieron_____.

    (A) una mula y dinero para el viaje

    (B) un abrazo y muchos consejos

    (C) un caballo nuevo y una espada

    (D) un traje nuevo y varios libros.

Registro del Vehículo de Motor

Los residentes tienen que titular y registrar sus vehículos antes de conducir en las vías públicas.

Los residentes nuevos tienen que titular y registrar su vehículo dentro de un término de 60 días (o antes de que se venza el registro de otro estado, lo que ocurra primero).

Este capítulo cubre el registro de su vehículo.

También discute las tablillas o placas, las inspecciones de seguridad del vehículo, y el seguro de responsabilidad civil.

Tablillas o Placas

En el momento en que usted registre su vehículo, usted recibirá dos tablillas (una para los vehículos remolcados o trailers, bicicletas motorizadas y motocicletas).

Hay que fijar una de las tablillas en la parte delantera y la otra en la parte trasera del vehículo.

Deben colocarse por lo menos a 12 pulgadas, pero a menos de 48 pulgadas, sobre el suelo.

Ambas tablillas tienen que ser limpias y visibles.

La tablilla de la parte posterior tiene que estar alumbrada para poder verse de noche a una distancia de 50 pies, aunque tenga tablillas reflectores.

119. Para conducir en las vías públicas, hay que _____.

    (A) vivir en el estado por lo menos 60 días

    (B) tener menos de 17 años de edad

    (C) titular y registrar el vehículo con seguro

    (D) tener el vehículo titulado y registrado con seguridad

120. Es muy importante que las tablillas _____.

    (A) estén colocadas en la parte de enfrente y delantera

    (B) sean visibles con tablillas reflectores

    (C) estén no sólo visibles sino bien colocadas

    (D) se remplacen cuando se compra un nuevo vehículo

PRACTICE TEST 1

Answer Key

Listening Comprehension

1.	(B)	14.	(C)	27.	(B)	40.	(D)
2.	(C)	15.	(B)	28.	(B)	41.	(C)
3.	(D)	16.	(C)	29.	(A)	42.	(D)
4.	(C)	17.	(D)	30.	(C)	43.	(B)
5.	(C)	18.	(A)	31.	(B)	44.	(A)
6.	(C)	19.	(C)	32.	(C)	45.	(B)
7.	(C)	20.	(C)	33.	(A)	46.	(B)
8.	(C)	21.	(C)	34.	(C)	47.	(A)
9.	(C)	22.	(B)	35.	(B)	48.	(D)
10.	(D)	23.	(A)	36.	(B)	49.	(D)
11.	(A)	24.	(C)	37.	(D)	50.	(A)
12.	(C)	25.	(D)	38.	(C)		
13.	(B)	26.	(B)	39.	(D)		

Reading

51.	(A)	70.	(A)	88.	(D)	106.	(D)
52.	(B)	71.	(D)	89.	(D)	107.	(D)
53.	(B)	72.	(B)	90.	(B)	108.	(C)
54.	(D)	73.	(A)	91.	(A)	109.	(C)
55.	(C)	74.	(B)	92.	(C)	110.	(C)
56.	(B)	75.	(A)	93.	(C)	111.	(C)
57.	(C)	76.	(B)	94.	(B)	112.	(A)
58.	(A)	77.	(D)	95.	(A)	113.	(B)
59.	(D)	78.	(B)	96.	(C)	114.	(B)
60.	(D)	79.	(A)	97.	(B)	115.	(A)
61.	(A)	80.	(C)	98.	(D)	116.	(D)
62.	(D)	81.	(B)	99.	(A)	117.	(A)
63.	(C)	82.	(D)	100.	(D)	118.	(B)
64.	(B)	83.	(A)	101.	(B)	119.	(C)
65.	(D)	84.	(B)	102.	(D)	120.	(C)
66.	(A)	85.	(A)	103.	(B)		
67.	(C)	86.	(A)	104.	(C)		
68.	(A)	87.	(C)	105.	(A)		
69.	(D)						

PRACTICE TEST 1

Detailed Explanations of Answers

Section I

1. **(B)** The correct answer is (B) since *Bastante cansada, gracias* (Quite tired, thanks) is the only logical answer since neither (A), (C) or (D) answer the question "How are you, Mrs. Torres?"

2. **(C)** The correct answer is (C). The verb venir (to come) is shown in answers (C) or (D) but only (C) answer the question "How did Pepe arrive?" Answers (A) and (B) refer to vino = wine. (D) answers the question of *when* rather than *how* with, "He came in the summer time." Therefore, (C) "He came by plane," is the correct answer.

3. **(D)** The correct answer is (D). The question is "Who called last night?" Option (A) cannot be correct since the verb "llama" is in the present tense. Option (B) "I will call you later" does not answer the question. Option (C) "You come tonight" cannot be correct. (D) says, "It was my brother Carlos."

4. **(C)** The correct answer is (C). "What are they putting inside the recipient?" Option (A) "I am putting some strawberries can be an option, however, the verb is conjugated in the *yo* form and does not answer the question. Option (B) "Is not set properly" cannot be the answer since it does not make any sense. Option (C) "They are filling it up with water" answers the question properly. Option (D) "We are working in the kitchen" can't be the correct answer.

5. **(C)** The correct answer is (C). The question is "If I continue on this street, do I arrive to the President's House? (C) "No sir, it takes you to the Paseo Colón" is the only answer that answers the question correctly. Answers (A), and (B), talk about the president. Answer (D) "No sir, stop saying absurd things" cannot be the correct answer.

6. **(C)** The correct answer is (C). The question is "Waiter, how much do we owe you?" Option (A) "I will help you with your luggage right away" does not answer the question. Option (B) "You must leave right away" cannot be the right answer. Option (D) "I will bring you the dessert menu" cannot be right. (C) says, "I'll bring you the bill right away."

7. **(C)** The correct answer is (C). "Where does your cousin Celeste work?" Answer (A) "She is a Spanish teacher" does not answer the question. Option (B) "She works from eight until two" cannot be the correct answer. Option (D) "She works hard and she likes what she does." does not answer the question. Therefore, option (C) "She is an employee in a school" is the only answer that is correct.

8. **(C)** The correct answer is (C). The question is "Why did you buy so many apples?" Option (A) "I bought them in the supermarket yesterday" does not answer the question "why?" Option (B) "I like orange marmalade" is completely unrelated to the question. Option (D) "I have too many apples at home" is illogical. Option (C) "I am going to make a delicious cake" is the only answer that is logical.

9. **(C)** The correct answer is (C). "Where can one buy cheap make up?" Option (A) could be a possible answer, however the direct object pronoun *las* does not match the noun *cosméticos*, therefore option (A) has to be eliminated. Option (B) "One can find them easily" does not answer the question. Option (D) "One can buy them at a good price" does not answer the question and cannot be the right answer. (C) says that they can be bought at any pharmacy or department store.

10. **(D)** The correct answer is (D) since it answers the question "When are we going to leave?" (D) says that we are going to leave in a moment. Option (A) "We went to the supermarket yesterday" cannot be the right answer. Option (B) "It is four o'clock" does not answer the question. Option (C) "We always go to the movies" does not answer the question when.

11. **(A)** The correct answer is (A). The question asks when the train to Guanajuato is leaving. (A) says, "At exactly 6:00." (B), "At the station," and (C), "Toward the next town," do not answer the question. (D) refers to an arriving train, rather than a departure.

12. **(C)** The correct answer is (C). The question asks who is sending a letter, not where it was sent, so (A) cannot be the correct answer. (B) and (D) answer how it was sent (in an envelope or without stamps). (C) indicates that it was sent to the girlfriend of the speaker.

13. **(B)** The correct answer is (B). The question asks why they were running so fast. (A) says that they were walking, not running. (B) says that there was a fire, which would cause people to run and is the correct answer. (C) says that they were paralyzed (not running) and (D) says that they didn't like the bullfight, which doesn't address the question.

14. **(C)** The correct answer is (C). The question asks Juan Carlos to reach a book. (C) says that it is too high. The other excuses don't make sense. (A) having no money would not make him unable to reach the book. (B) says it is too hot and (D) says that it's Quantum Physics, neither of which would make one unable to reach the book.

15. **(B)** The correct answer is (B). The speaker tells him to put on a sweater because it is cold. (A) indicates that the summer is long, which would not be an appropriate response. (B) states that the speaker doesn't want to, since it is a spring day. (C) says that he won't do it because it's snowing too much, which would not be a logical argument. (D) says that he is going to buy them, which does not relate to the question.

16. **(C)** The correct answer is (C). The question asks, "Isn't Julio precious?" This most likely refers to a child named Julio, rather than the month of July. Regardless, (A) doesn't make sense, since it states that it is after August, which the month is not. (B) says, "Too expensive," and (D) says that it costs a lot, neither of which answer the question. (C) says that especially his little face (*carita*) is cute.

17. **(D)** The correct answer is (D). The question asks why he didn't give you a ticket (*multa*). (A) says that her leg isn't broken, which would indicate a need for a *muleta*, or crutch. (B) says, "I'm not going on vacation." A *maleta* is a suitcase and might be needed for a vacation, but a *multa* is a ticket as in a fine given by the police, not a ticket to go on a trip. (D) says, "I cried and asked him to pardon me." This could result in the officer not issuing a ticket.

18. **(A)** The correct answer is (A). The question asks, "Aren't you going to wash your hands?" (A) says, "Of course, but I need soap." (B) indicates that a place called *Las Manos* is far away and does not address the question. (C) indicates that they cannot be found and (D) says "I don't want to carry them," neither of which would make sense referring to one's hands.

Section II

19. **(C)** The correct answer is (C). The man asks when flight 517 leaves for Bogotá and is told that it has already left, so the flight that *salió a tiempo* (left on time) is 517. (B) is tomorrow's flight number. (A) 495 is the cost of the flight (*el pasaje*) and (D) 757 was never mentioned.

20. **(C)**   The correct answer is (C). The flight leaves tomorrow morning at 5:30 (*las cinco y media*). (A) 4:15 is the time of the afternoon flight both days. (B) 8:00 is when the man should arrive in Bogotá. (C) 914 is a flight number, not a departure time.

21. **(C)**   The correct answer is (C), the next day. Since he can't leave until tomorrow morning, he won't arrive (A) that evening or (B) within 5 hours. He's leaving in the morning and arriving at 8:00, so he will be there before next week (D).

22. **(B)**   The correct answer is (B). Santiago says that he is dying of thirst (*me muero de sed*) after his test, so he is headed to the cafeteria for a drink (B). He doesn't mention eating (A). He is already talking to Viviana (D) and has already taken the test (C), so he would not need to hurry to do these things.

23. **(A)**   The correct answer is (A). Viviana mentions that she is hungry and that she will go with him (*te acompaño*). Since he is headed to the cafeteria, that's where she will go also. She's not going to (B) take another test, (C) go to another class or (D) go home with Santiago.

24. **(C)**   The correct answer is (C). The woman mentions Ávila Camacho was president before Ruíz Cortines, but that in between (*entre ellos sirvió de presidente*) them, the president was Alemán Valdés. The others were president at different times.

25. **(D)**   The correct answer is (D). The man remembers that his dad voted for Adolfo López Mateos when he won in 1958 (*pero mi padre me dijo que votó por él cuando ganó en el año 1958.*) The others were president at different times.

26. **(B)**   The correct answer is (B). The woman says that her dad voted for the man who ran against López Mateos, but she can't remember his name (*Prefirió el otro candidato popular, pero no me acuerdo de su nombre.*) Therefore, they couldn't think of the name of the one who did not win the presidency (B), not the candidate's father (A), the president after López Mateos (C), or (D) López Mateos, who is mentioned by name.

27. **(B)**   The correct answer is (B). The question asks what the man did to prepare his work. He mentions several things, among which was reviewing with his classmates (*Estudié con Pedro y Marta*). He was unable to answer all of the questions on his test (A), so he wants to speak with the professor (C) to ask for more time (D), but he did not already do these things in preparation.

28. **(B)** The correct answer is (B). When the man states that he wasn't able to answer all of the questions (*no alcancé a contestar todas las preguntas*), the woman says that she couldn't either (*yo tampoco*). She doesn't mention being anguished or worried (*angustiada-preocupada*) about anything else, so (A), (C), and (D) are not correct.

29. **(A)** The correct answer is (A). Since the students did not have enough time to complete their assignment, they are planning to talk to the teacher and ask him for more time so they can finish the assignment. Options (B) raise their grade, (C) explain their doubts and (D) change their group, are not mentioned, and therefore cannot be correct.

30. **(C)** The correct answer is (C). When discussing what to get Ricardo, the man mentions that he already has everything (*tiene todo*), which implies that he has many things. The woman was referring to a little car when she said something was (A) *lindo* (cute). Since he has so many things, it would not make sense for him to not be interested in much (B). (C) 40 was the number of cars the man thought Ricardo had, not his age.

31. **(B)** The correct answer is (B). He already has remote control cars (A) and autographed t-shirts (C), so the woman decides to bake him a cake (*pastel*), which is a (B) dessert (*postre*). She asks the man to please not sing, so (D) a song would not be the correct choice.

32. **(C)** The correct answer is (C). When discussing how much to pack, the father tells Pepe not to bring too much or mom will have to call 2 taxis to take them to the hotel when they arrive (*no traigas demasiado o mamá va a tener que llamar a dos taxis para llevarnos al hotel cuando llegamos*), which indicates that mom (C) will be arranging the transportation from the airport rather than someone else.

33. **(A)** The correct answer is (A). The father states that he has to use the computer to give the airline his credit card number (*tengo que usar la computadora para enviarle el número de la tarjeta de crédito al aerolínea*), indicating that he is paying the fare (*pagar el pasaje*).

34. **(C)** The correct answer is (C). The father tells the children to bring their clean clothes to mom so she can put them in the luggage (*le traigan a mamá su ropa limpia para que ella pueda poner todo en el equipaje*), which means that mom is packing the suitcases (*hacer las maletas*).

35. **(B)** The correct answer is (B). The father asks Mimi to call and make sure everything is going fine and that they will be able to leave on time

(*llama por favor al aeropuerto a ver si todo va bien y vamos a poder salir a tiempo*), so Mimi is confirming the flight (*confirmar el vuelo*).

36. **(B)**   The correct answer is (B). The mother says that the boy had a high fever (*tenía fiebre muy alta*) and the father asks at the end of the conversation if his fever is better, but she says it is the same (*igual*). Choice (B) is the only line in which the fever starts high and remains that way, so it is the correct choice.

37. **(D)**   The correct answer is (D). It is the nurse the one who suggests the mom to take her son to see the doctor. Choices (A), (B), and (C) cannot be right.

38. **(C)**   The correct answer is (C). The doctor prescribed the boy antibiotics, so he wants him to take medicine. Choices (A) not eating, (B) going to the hospital, and (D) swallowing salt water are not mentioned.

39. **(D)**   The correct answer is (D). The indigenous people died of illness. The speaker states that they were devastated by tuberculosis (*fue devastada por la tuberculosis*). The indigenous people were not incarcerated (A) or turned into fortune hunters (B), although it was mentioned that, in later years, fortune hunters came there and a prison was later built. (C) is incorrect since the natives died and were not able to leave Tierra del Fuego.

40. **(D)**   The correct answer is (D). The speaker explains that Ushauaia was first an evangelical spot for the natives (*puesto de evangelización de indígenas*), then a stop for fortune hunters and adventurers. Later a prison was built, which was turned into a naval base. Currently, it is a center for fishing, tourism, and the technology industry (*centro de pesca, turismo, y fabricación de tecnología*). All of these changes through the years cause (D) to be the correct answer. (A) says that no one lives there now, which would not allow for it to be a center for tourism. (B) states that it is full of prisoners, but the prison has been turned into a naval base, so there are no more prisoners. (C) says that the city has stayed the same for many years, which is the opposite of what was expressed.

41. **(C)**   The correct answer is (C). The woman is speaking out against violence in the neighborhood and encouraging the crowd to work together to stop the acts of violence that have been occurring, but to do so in a peaceful way. She asks that everyone fight against these disgraceful acts, put with conviction and peace (*pero con la fuerza de la convicción y la paz*). At one point, she talks about not reacting with a metaphorical "thirst for blood"

(*sed de sangre*), but this does not indicate that she wants to drink blood (A). Since she is speaking against violence, she does not want to attack the enemy (B). She does not mention any laws that need to be changed (D).

42. **(D)**   The correct answer is (D). The woman starts her speech by saying that she has been asked why she does not seek revenge against the people that committed those acts of violence (*la gente que realizó esos actos de violencia*) and continues to speak about how to fight them without submitting to acts of violence in return. She does not mention peaceful people (A) or the police (C) and is speaking *to*, rather than *against*, her neighbors (B).

43. **(B)**   The correct answer is (B). Since she is speaking about ending the problems in a peaceful way, the best topic or theme for her speech would be (B), violence is not the answer. Both (A), an eye for an eye, and (D), the death penalty or pain of death, suggest condoning violence. There was no discussion of race playing a part in the problem, so racial justice (C) would not be correct.

44. **(A)**   The correct answer is (A)—sí. When the woman said that she wanted either sangria (wine with fruit added) or beer (*cerveza*), she was told that Girasol and Sabor de México served alcohol, but that El Palenque did not.

45. **(B)**   The correct answer is (B)—no. When suggesting the restaurant for the evening, the man referred to La Esperanza as a *restaurante vegetariano*, or vegetarian restaurant, which would not serve meat.

46. **(B)**   The correct answer is (B)—no. When the woman said that she wanted either sangria (wine with fruit added) or beer (*cerveza*), she was told that Girasol and Sabor de México served alcohol, but that El Palenque did not.

47. **(A)**   The correct answer is (A)—sí. When the woman asked about something sweet after dinner, the man said that Sabor de México was famous for their *tres leches* cake (*pastel de tres leches*), which is a dessert (*postre*).

48. **(D)**   The correct answer is (D). They reference the fact that many children go to Sabor de México and that the prices are good and they have something for everyone (*Los precios son muy buenos y tienen algo para todos*), so Sabor de México would be a place for a big family with little money. The prices at the other restaurants were not mentioned.

49. **(D)**   The correct answer is (D). The forecast begins by saying "probably light rain showers toward evening . . ." (*probables lluvias ligeras hacia el anochecer*), indicating that it will rain (D). There is mention later of the

cold coming in so it would feel like a springtime winter (*invierno prima-veral*), so it would not be warm (C), but there is also no mention of snow (A) or hail (B).

50. **(A)** The correct answer is (A). With cold air coming, it will feel like a springtime winter (*invierno primaveral*), with unheard of temperatures for this time of year (*registremos una temperatura inédita para esta época del año*), indicating that it will be colder than normal (A), not the same (B) or warmer (C). (D) does not make sense because it says that there will be no weather tonight.

Section III – Part A

51. **(A)** *Esquina* means "the corner or outer side of an angle formed, for example, by two streets which meet or intersect each other." In the list of choices there appears the word *rincón*, which is not appropriate in this case, although it does mean "corner," but in another sense: the inner side of an angle such as that formed by two walls which meet to form a corner of a room. The other two possible answers given (*techo* = "roof" and *escalera* = "staircase") would not logically be used when talking about streets.

52. **(B)** *Dependiente* means clerk. This word also has feminine form which is *dependienta*. *Atender* (*ie*) means "to wait on." *Mercancía* means "merchandise." *Cliente* and *parroquiano* both signify "customer."

53. **(B)** *Devolver* means "to return" in the sense of "to give back." The other three possible choices also mean "to return," but only in the sense of "to come or go back." Of these three, *retornar* is the least frequently used.

54. **(D)** *Tengo sueño* signifies "I am sleepy." The verb *acostarse* means "to go to bed." Hence, the other three answers would not apply. Notice how the verb *tener* is frequently used in Spanish to form idiomatic expressions: *tener sed* (to be thirsty), *tener hambre* (to be hungry), *tener calor* (to be hot). To this list, we might add other expressions such as *tener frío* (to be cold), *tener razón* (to be right), *no tener razón* (to be wrong), *tener vergüenza* (to be ashamed), *tener ganas de* +infinitive (to feel like doing something), *tener celos* (to be jealous), etc.

55. **(C)** All four of the answers mean "stopped," but the verb *parar* refers to a moving object which comes to a physical halt and *movement* ceases. *Dejar de* means to stop doing something (*Dejé de estudiar a las once* = I stopped studying at 11:00). Observe that this expression is always followed

by an infinitive. *Cesar* and *terminar* also have this meaning. (*Cesó la lluvia a las nueve* = the rain stopped at 9:00. *La fiesta terminó a la medianoche* = the party ended/stopped at midnight.) The word *trayectoria*, in this case, means "route."

56. **(B)** The first three verbs all have to do with the idea of "try," but each is used under very particular circumstances. *Tratar de* + infinitive is used when we want to say "to try to do something." *Ensayar* and *probar* mean "to try" or "to try out," but they are generally not followed by infinitives, but rather by nouns. For example, *Voy a probar el agua* (I'm going to try out the water). *Ensayar* can also be used to mean "to rehearse," as for a play. In addition, it can occasionally mean to try on, as with clothing, but the most common verb we use in this instance is the reflexive form of *probar*, i.e., *probarse*: *Voy a probarme esta blusa* (I am going to try on this blouse). Remember that *probar* can also mean "to prove": *Me probaron que no tenía razón* (They proved to me that I was wrong). *Quedarse* (to remain) would be entirely illogical syntactically in this case because it would have to be followed by the preposition *para* (in order to), which would be obligatory in front of the infinitive.

57. **(C)** Both *boletos* and *billetes* are tickets, for the theater or the train, for example, and would not fit in here with the word *casa* (house). *Cuentos* and *cuentas* look rather alike except for the difference in gender. The first means "story," or in a literary sense, "short story"; the second means "bills," and would therefore make sense within the context of the sentence.

58. **(A)** Normally, the only two prepositions which appear directly after *pensar* are *de* and *en*. *Pensar de* is most often used in questions to ask for an opinion: *¿Qué piensas de este examen?* (What do you think about this test?). *Pensar en* means "to think about" in the sense of concentrating or meditating upon something or someone: *Pienso mucho en mi familia* (I think about my family a lot, i.e., my family is often on my mind). Remember that when *pensar* is followed directly by an infinitive (with no intervening preposition), the meaning is "to intend" or "to plan on" doing something: *Pienso ir al cine mañana* (I intend to go to the movies tomorrow).

59. **(D)** When a part of the body is causing pain, we use the verb *doler* (*ue*) preceded by the proper form of the indirect object pronoun (*me, te, le, nos, os, les*), which refers to the person feeling the pain. The subject of the verb *doler* is the part(s) of the body mentioned. Consequently, *doler*, in any tense, will normally be used only in the third person singular and the

third person plural. Compare the following sentences: *Le duelen los ojos* (His eyes hurt him), *Te dolía una muela* (Your tooth was hurting you, i.e., you had a toothache). *Dañar* and *hacer daño* mean "to hurt" in the sense of "to damage" or "harm": *El gato dañó las cortinas* (The cat damaged the curtains). *Herir* (*ie,i*) is related to the noun *herida* (wound), and means "to wound."

60. **(D)** To answer properly here, it is important to know the meaning of *abrigo* (overcoat). This helps us associate the sentence with cold weather and the word *frío* (cold) in the correct answer. One would not wear a coat when it is warm (A) or cloudy (B) or when running (C).

61. **(A)** Choosing the right answer here depends first on understanding the expression *hacer un viaje* which means "to take a trip." Of the four possibilities suggested, only *una maleta* (a suitcase) has a direct bearing on travel. *Una máquina de coser* is a sewing machine. *Una multa* means "a fine." *Una muñeca* signifies either "a wrist" or "a doll."

62. **(D)** Answering correctly in this case can be aided if you recognize the words *lugar* (place), *árboles* (trees), and *campo* (countryside). A place in the countryside where there are many trees is logically a woods. A stand of trees is a *bosque*. The word *madera* means "wood" as a building material, for example. *Leña* has a very specific meaning: "firewood" or "kindling wood." *Verdulería*, although it suggests the idea of *verde* (green), actually means "green grocery," a place where one can buy green vegetables.

63. **(C)** Key words in the statement are *se cortó* (cut himself), *cuchillo* (knife), and *dedo* (finger). *Anillo* (ring) and *uña* (fingernail) can be related to finger, but they seem to have no relationship to the idea of Felipe's cutting himself. *Oreja* (ear) would also be out of place here. *Herida* (wound), on the other hand, can be related to the idea of cutting oneself. Notice how, in this case, the verb *cortar* is used in its reflexive form *cortarse*. Reflexive verbs can often be used to show an action which the subject does to itself: *Se sentó*: (He sat down, i.e., he sat himself down) and *Me miré en el espejo* (I looked at myself in the mirror). In our sentence we did not use the possessive adjective *su* in front of the word *dedo* because in most cases we simply use the definite articles (*el, la , los, las*) with the parts of the body and clothing.

64. **(B)** The options are *otoño* (fall) or *primavera* (spring), so the correct choice is the word *estación*, in this case referring to the season. However, the word *estación* can mean channel or station. The options *actividad*

(activity) and *lluvia* (rain) do not make sense. (C) *sazón*, refers to a seasoning or flavor, not a season of the year.

65. **(D)** The correct answer is *complicada* (complicated or difficult). All the other options look similar but are definitely not related. The word *comprada* (bought), *complacida* (pleased), or *compartida* (shared), are options that have a very different meaning that cannot be used as answers.

Part B

66. **(A)** *Sin embargo* is correct. It means nevertheless and makes sense in this context. (B) means "as usual," (C) means "without equal," and (D) means "without remedy."

67. **(C)** *Satisfechos* is correct. The masculine plural adjective form of *satisfacer* (to satisfy) is needed to match the noun *todos*. (A) is incorrect because it isn't plural. (B) is conjugated in the present tense (he satisfies), and (D) is the infinitive (to satisfy).

68. **(A)** *Lo que* is correct. In context the translation needed here is "that which" or "what." *Lo cual* does not share this same translation, which makes (B) incorrect. Response (C) is incorrect because it is the masculine relative pronoun that could mean "who," "which," or "he who." Choice (D) is the plural relative pronoun meaning "those who."

69. **(D)** *Se van* is correct. The present tense predominates throughout this paragraph. Therefore, choices (A) the future tense ("they will go"), (B) the present subjunctive ("they may go"), and (C) the preterit tense ("they went") are incorrect.

70. **(A)** *Cuentan con* is correct. Again, the present tense is called for in keeping with the meaning of this paragraph. (B) is incorrect because there is no reason for a subjunctive in this statement. (C) is the infinitive. (D) is the preterit form of the verb.

71. **(D)** *Un millón de* is correct. (A) is incorrect because the word *uno* must be apocopated before a masculine singular noun, in this case *millón*. (B) *Unos* is plural. (C) *Una* is feminine.

72. **(B)** *Hace* is incorrect. *Hace* followed by a period of time means "ago." No other tense will render this meaning, which makes (A) the imperfect and (D) the preterit incorrect. (C) is incorrect because it is plural.

73. **(A)** *Los que* is correct. The translation "those who" is required in this context. (B) would also mean "those who" if it weren't accented. (C) and (D) are written incorrectly.

74. **(B)** *Obras* is correct. *Obras* are written works. (A) means "compliances," (C) refers to physical work (in farming), and (D) means "female workers."

75. **(A)** *Volvió* is correct. In the context of this paragraph, the preterit is required. Therefore, choices (B) the present tense and (C) the past subjunctive are incorrect. Choice (D) is the infinitive and a conjugated verb is required here.

76. **(B)** *Trajera* is correct. The subjunctive is required as part of the noun clause introduced by a form of *decir (dijo)*, an indirect command verb. The past subjunctive is required to follow the sequence. (A) the preterit, (C) the present subjunctive, and (D) the future are, therefore, incorrect.

77. **(D)** *Alguna* is correct. *Alguna* is the feminine singular adjective meaning "some," which matches the noun *evidencia*. No negatives are called for since this statement is affirmative. Therefore, (B) and (C) are incorrect. (A) is incorrect because it is the masculine singular form that would precede a masculine singular noun.

78. **(B)** *Le* is correct. The verb *comunicó* would require an indirect object pronoun, in this case, to match up with *a la Señora*. Choices (A) and (D) are direct object pronouns. Choice (C) is the plural indirect object pronoun.

79. **(A)** *Eso* is correct. The neuter form of the demonstrative is used to refer to previously mentioned events, occurrences, or happenings. In this case, Juan is communicating to the Virgen the information given to him by the Bishop. Because both (B) and (C) have gender, they are incorrect. Choice (D) is incorrect since it is feminine plural.

80. **(C)** *Quien* is correct. *Quien* is the relative pronoun referring to *Señora*. No accent is required, which would make (A) incorrect. (B) "whom" and (D) "of whom" are incorrect translations in this context.

81. **(B)** *Regresara* is correct. Again, subjunctive is required in this noun clause prompted by the verb *dijo*. To follow sequence, the past subjunctive is used. (A) is the present subjunctive, (C) is the infinitive, and (D) is the present indicative.

82. **(D)** *Convencieran* is correct. This adjective clause requires a subjunctive because its antecedent *evidencias* is indefinite. To follow sequence, the past

subjunctive is required. (A) the conditional, (B) the present subjunctive, and (C) the preterit are incorrect.

83. **(A)** *El* is correct. *Tema*, although it ends in "a," is masculine and would require a masculine singular article. Therefore, (B) and (D), which are feminine are incorrect. Since an article is needed, choice (C) is incorrect.

84. **(B)** *Permanecido* is correct. The past participle is required after the form of *haber* and is invariable. (A) is incorrect because it is feminine. (C) is the present participle and (D) is the infinitive.

85. **(A)** *Cerrado* is correct. *Cerrado* is the past participle used here as an adjective modifying *Puerto*. Therefore, (B) the feminine participle, (C) the present participle, and (D) the infinitive are incorrect.

86. **(A)** *Pagar* is correct. After the conjugated verb *logró* an infinitive is required. (B) is the present participle, (C) is the past participle, and (D) is the feminine plural form of the past participle which is used as an adjective.

87. **(C)** *Buenas* is correct. The feminine plural form is required here to match the nouns *condiciones*. (A) is the masculine plural form, (B) is the masculine singular shortened form, and (D) is the feminine singular form.

88. **(D)** *Para* is correct. "In order to" is expressed by *para* before an infinitive. Therefore, (A), which does not have this translation, and (C), which means "because," are incorrect. (B) is incorrect because the word *que* is not necessary.

Part C

89. **(D)** Choice (D) is the correct answer. Lencho became sad because a hailstorm had destroyed his crop of beans and corn. The story tells us: "… *cuando la tempestad pasó dijo con voz triste a sus hijos…el granizo no ha dejado nada*" (when the hailstorm was over he told his children with a sad voice… the hail has left nothing). (A) is not a good choice, since nothing is said in the narrative about his children dying. (B) is not correct; we are told that a lot of rain was needed to ensure a good harvest. What saddened Lencho was not too muh rain, but that the storm also brought hail. (C) is not the best choice. Lencho mentions the locusts (*langostas*) only to say that the damage done by the hail was much worse than what a cloud of locusts might have caused.

90. **(B)** Choice (B) is the best answer. In the letter he wrote to God, he said, *"Necesito cien pesos para volver a sembrar y vivir mientras viene la cosecha, porque el granizo. . ."* This, as well as other statements in the text, makes it clear that he was a farmer (*agricultor*). That means (A) priest (*cura*), (C) postman (*cartero*), and (D) notary, court clerk (*escribano*) are all incorrect.

91. **(A)** Choice (A) is the correct answer. The story tells us that Lencho had faith in God, so he wrote him a letter asking for 100 pesos to replant his crop and to live on until harvest time. (B) is incorrect, because Lencho never complained about his bad luck. (C) is not the best answer, because in his first letter to God, he does not mention any irregularities in the post office. In his second letter, at the end of the narrative, he indicates that he thinks the postal workers stole part of the money God sent him. (D) is not a good choice; in his letter Lencho does not ask God to give him a good harvest.

92. **(C)** Choice (C) is correct. After reading Lencho's letter, the postmaster was impressed by Lencho's faith, so he decided to collect some money to help him. (A) is not a good choice; while the postmaster's initial reaction to the letter was laughter, he did not "just laugh," but rather took steps to help Lencho. (B) is not right, because in the story the postmaster does not scold the employee for opening someone else's mail. (D) cannot be correct, because we are told that the postmaster collected money and answered Lencho's letter; he did not simply give the letter back to him without any money.

93. **(C)** Sentence 3 (C) says that he truly believes (in God) and that's why he wrote the letter. Lencho showed no surprise at all when he received the letter from God because he had faith and was expecting it. (A) is not correct, since it simply states that he wrote "To God" on the envelope. (B) is not a good choice because it explains the postal employee's reaction upon reading the letter Lencho sent. (D) is incorrect also because it explains that Lencho got angry when he counted the money.

94. **(B)** Choice (B), "dishonest," is the correct answer. When Lencho got the money "from God," there was only 60 pesos in the envelope, and he had asked for 100. Lencho assumed that God had sent the 100 pesos as requested, and that the postal workers had stolen some of it. In his second letter, he asks God to send the rest of the money, but advises him not to send it through the post office, because "all the postal employees are

thieves" (*todos los empleados del correo son ladrones*). (A) is incorrect, because Lencho did not believe the postal workers were "honest" (*honrados*), but rather dishonest. (C) is not a good choice; although the postmaster was very generous. Lencho did not know it, and in fact suspected that the postal workers had stolen part of the money God had sent for him. (D) is not the best choice, since there is no information in the narrative that would indicate that Lencho thought the post office employees were *bondadosos* (kind, good-natured).

95. **(A)** Choice (A) is the best answer. Since a lot of rain was necessary for a good harvest, Lencho was pleased that it was raining. The story tells us: ... *Lencho observaba sus campos con placer* (Lencho watched his fields with pleasure). (B) is not a good choice, because his reaction to the rain was not "despair (or desperation)." (C) "Anger" does not accurately express what Lencho felt when he saw the rain falling on his crops, so it is not the best choice. (D) cannot be correct; Lencho did not feel "anxiety" (*angustia*) when the rain came. The story indicates that he began to feel that way when it started hailing.

96. **(C)** (C) is the correct answer. In the context in which it is used in the passage, *agasajo* means "gift" or "present," and clearly refers to *chocolatl*, the drink the Aztecs made from ground cacao beans. (A) is not an appropriate answer, since Moctezuma's attitude toward the conquistadors is not mentioned in the selection. Although (B) fits in with the concept of a gift, the *tazón de oro* (large golden cup) from which Moctezuma drank the *chocolatl* is only mentioned in passing, and the context excludes it as the antecedent of *agasajo*. Since the destruction of the Aztec Empire by the Spaniards is not dealt with in this passage, (D) is not a good choice.

97. **(B)** Choice (B) correctly answers the question, "Where are the cacao trees cultivated?" The text states that they grow in the tropics. (A) is not a good choice, because the information given in the passage indicates that cacao trees do not grow in the U.S. (C) is incorrect; since cacao was unknown in Europe until Cortés brought it from Mexico, and Spain is not in the tropics, it is logical to conclude that cacao trees are not cultivated in Spain. (D) is not a logical choice; while England and Holland are mentioned as having made improvements on the cacao drink, the European climate precludes the cultivation of cacao trees in those countries.

98. **(D)** Choice (D) is the best answer, since the passage reveals that the Spanish court tried to keep cacao, and the drink made from it, a secret,

and managed to, for more than 100 years. (A) is not a good choice, since Spain did not immediately spread the news to the rest of Europe. (B) is not correct, because although the passage relates that *chocolatl* caused a sensation in the Spanish court, it mentions nothing of the members of the court kicking up a scandal because they did not like the bitter drink. Choice (C) cannot be right; we are told in the reading that chocolate was only a drink up until 150 years ago when the process for making solid bar chocolate was developed.

99. **(A)** Choice (A) is correct, since the passage tells us that they sweetened it and made it richer by adding sugar and milk to it. (B) is not a good choice, since the text mentions nothing at all about whether the cacao drink was served hot or cold. (C) is incorrect; the passage states that a miniscule amount of lye (*lejía*) is added to the liquid cacao during processing to intensify its flavor, but that has nothing to do with making the drink. (D) makes reference to another step in the refining process, the removal of cacao butter, which has no connection with the early improvements made to the cacao drink by the English and Dutch.

100. **(D)** Choice (D) is the correct answer. Besides grinding the cacao beans to make the drink *chocolatl*, the Aztecs used cacao beans as a form of money. The passage reveals that 100 beans could buy a healthy slave. (A) is not a good choice, because nothing is said in the reading about the beans being used as weapons to wage war. Since the text does not mention throwing beans into the sea for good luck, (B) is eliminated as a correct response. (C) cannot be right; since the Aztecs themselves make *chocolatl* from the cacao beans, it is not logical that they would use the same beans to poison their enemies.

101. **(B)** Choice (B) is the best answer. The first paragraph of the passage tells us that "cacao and its derivative, chocolate, can aid in digestion, stimulate blood flow to the heart, and help people with chest colds breathe better," all of which would come under the heading of "medicinal value" (*valor medicinal*). (A) is incorrect, since the information given in the text indicates that cacao became very popular in Europe, making the statement that it "was not very successful outside of Mexico" false. (C) is not the best response; the passage does not take up cacao's nutritional value. (D) is not a good choice; in the first sentence of the passage we are told that "cacao should not be confused with coconut (coco) or cocoa, the source of cocaine," so the assertion that cacao "resembles coconut and coco" cannot be right.

102. **(D)** The expression *soñar con* means "to dream about" and, in the context of the paragraph, implies a desire on Rafael's part. Consequently, the answer containing the verb *querer* is the most appropriate. Choice (A) would be wrong because *se hizo* means "became," but Rafael did not become a singer. In choice (B), *fingía* means "pretended," but the youth did not pretend he was a singer of popular music. Choice (C) is incorrect because *hacer falta* signifies "to need" (to be necessary), but López doesn't need money now that he has won the first prize in the Christmas lottery. In fact, he no longer has any financial problems, we are told. Note the use of the verb *tocar* in the first sentence of the paragraph. When it is preceded by an indirect object, as here, it may be translated as "to win something."

103. **(B)** The idiom *server de* signifies "to serve as." We know that Rafael serves as a substitute in a band because we are told that he worked with the band *solo cuando faltaba alguien* (only when someone was missing). Here the verb *faltar* has the special meaning of "to be absent." Rafael did not win a musical prize, as (A) says, but rather the Christmas lottery. Choice (C) would be incorrect because the word *pertinente* (relevant) has nothing to do with the subject. One might be tempted to choose it because of its similarity to the expression *pertenecer a* (to belong to). Choice (D) tells us that Rafael had his own group (*su propio conjunto*), but the expression *pertenecer a* again indicates that he merely belonged to the group, not that it was his own.

104. **(C)** To choose the correct answer, one must know that *ganó* is the past tense of *ganar* and that it means "(he, she) won." As we are told in the first sentence, *le ha tocado el gordo de la lotería de Navidad*, he has won the Christmas lottery. Therefore, he has won a lot of money, which corresponds to choice (C), *mucho dinero*. Note that *el gordo* is the name given to the grand prize in the yearly lottery drawn during Christmas time in Spain. Choice (A) would not be appropriate since there is no mention of a trip (*un viaje*) in the passage. Choice (B), *un conjunto musical*, refers to the band he plays in and has nothing to do with Rafael winning the lottery. Choice (D), *un tambor*, is just referring to the drum, and it is totally irrelevant to the question.

105. **(A)**   Getting the right answer here is dependent on knowing that *célebre* means "famous." The last sentence of the reading says that *no hay nadie que le desconozca*. The verb *desconocer* means "not to know or recognize." If there is no one who does not know Rafael, then he is famous. Notice that we have used the present subjunctive of the verb *desconocer*. This is necessary because the *que* refers back to a person whose identity is unknown (*nadie*). Whenever the relative pronoun *que* refers back to someone or something unknown or non-existent, the verb following the *que* appears in the subjunctive. Compare these two sentences: *No hay nadie que sepa más que tú* (There is no one who knows more than you); *Hay muchos que saben más que yo* (There are many who know more than I). In the first sentence, we use the subjunctive of *saber* because the relative pronoun refers back to the word *nadie*, a non-existent entity. In the second sentence we do not use the subjunctive, but the indicative of *saber* because the relative pronoun refers back to actual existing people, *muchos* (many). Choice (B) would be incorrect because of the verb *llorar* (to cry). Notice the particular use of *por qué* in choice (B). Here it means "motive" or "reason," but Rafael has little to cry about! To know that (C) is wrong, you must recognize the idiom *carecer de* + noun, which means "to be lacking (something)." It is used here in the present progressive tense with the auxiliary verb *seguir* (to continue), and means "continues to lack (need)" money. We know that this is untrue because Rafael has gotten rich from the lottery. Choice (D) uses the idiomatic expression *tener prisa* (to be in a hurry), which does not pertain to the situation.

106. **(D)**   *Reo* is a synonym for *ladrón* (thief). We know that after the hold-up at the branch office (*sucursal*) of the National Bank, the criminals escaped (*huyeron*) with an undetermined amount of money, *una cantidad de dinero todavía por determinar*. *Todavía por determinar* means "yet to be determined." The police surrounded (*rodearon*) the district, made a sweep of the area (*hicieron una redada*) and were successful in their search (*búsqueda*). In other words, they found the thieves. Crucial in choosing the right answer is the idiomatic expression *tener éxito (en)*, which has nothing to do with exits or leaving, but rather means "to succeed (in)" doing something.

107. **(D)**   The word *asalto* is a synonym of *atraco* (holdup). *Fue llevado a cabo* means "was carried out." Since the culprits were *una pareja campesina*, and *una pareja* means "a pair," *dos campesinos* is the correct answer. Choice (A) is incorrect because the crime took place in the afternoon, not the morning. (B) is not right since the crime occurred in the outskirts of the city (*las afueras*) and not downtown (*el centro.*) Choice (C) is incorrect since the police investigated the crime rather than being the ones to carry it out.

108. **(C)**   *Fue robado* means "was robbed," another way of conveying the idea of *hubo un atraco*. It is used here in the passive voice. *Ayer por la tarde* means "yesterday afternoon," and appears in the first sentence of the reading. Therefore, the bank was robbed yesterday afternoon. (C) is the correct response according to this first sentence. Choice (A) *cierra a las cinco de la tarde*, is incorrect, since there is no mention of the closing time of the bank in the reading. Choice (B) says the bank is located in the downtown area of the capital, which is incorrect, since the opposite is mentioned in the first sentence of the reading: …*situado en las afueras de la capital*. The expression *en las afueras* means "in the outskirts." Choice (D) is also incorrect since the actual size of the bank is never discussed in the passage. *Sucursal del Banco Nacional* means "a branch of the National Bank," which may or may not be the largest bank in the city.

109. **(C)**   The word *guardias* can mean "guards," but here it is used in a more general sense to signify "police." In answer (C), we have used the preterit tense of *saber*, which can often mean "found out," rather than simply "knew." We see at the end of the story that the police captured the *reos* (criminals) and identified them as a couple from the country. The police did not try to prevent a rebellion, as (A) indicates. The word *radicada* does not refer to "radical." We know that the two criminals were from the countryside, but the police did not have to follow them into the countryside, as (B) says. *Perseguir* means "to pursue" or sometimes "to persecute." We know that the police force was armed (*armada*). Therefore, choice (D) is wrong because it says that they arrived without *fusiles* (guns).

110. **(C)**   We are told in the story that the criminals were *enmascarados* (masked). Another way of saying this would be *disfrazados* (disguised), as in choice (C). Choice (A) does not mention that the criminals out of towners, but nowhere in the reading does it say that they are kids. Choice (B) is incorrect because *del extranjero* means "from abroad," in other words,

"foreigners." Choice (D) is also an inappropriate response because we know it is not the police (*la policía*) who robbed the bank.

111. **(C)**   We learn from the reading that the economic situation in Latin America is going from bad to worse (*va de mal en peor*) because of international debts (*deudas internacionales*) which many governments are unable to pay, the increase in the cost of living (*el aumento del costo de la vida*) and layoffs (*el paro forzoso*). Consequently, governments are lacking sufficient money (*a los gobiernos les fala suficiente dinero*), prices are rising (*Suben los precios*), and there is much unemployment (*desempleo*). Choosing the correct answer here can be aided by a clear understanding of certain other vocabulary and grammatical constructions: the difference between *subir* (to go up or rise) and *bajar* (to go down or fall), *bastante* (enough) and *demasiado* (too much). Notice also the use of the verbs *faltar* (to be lacking to) and *sobrar* (to be more than enough). Both of these verbs follow the pattern of *gustar*, i.e., they are normally used in only the third person singular or plural and are preceded by an indirect object pronoun. If the thing lacking is singular, then the verb will be singular; if it is plural, then the verb will be plural: *Nos falta tiempo* (We are lacking time); *Nos faltan amigos* (We are lacking friends). The same holds true for the verb *sobrar*: *Nos sobra tiempo* (We have more than enough time); *Nos sobran amigos* (We have more than enough friends).

112. **(A)** The delegates (*delegados*) to the international economic conference are concerned by the unstable situation on international stock markets (*la situación inestable de las bolsas internacionales*), the drop in the value of the dollar (*la bajada del valor del dólar*), and the lack of balance in international trade (*el desequilibrio de la balanza de pagos*). They seek to arrive at an agreement (*llegar a un acuerdo*) which will avoid possible financial collapse (*que evite un posible derrumbamiento*). Consequently, they are trying to stabilize (*estabilizar*) the international economy. The verb *evitar* means "to avoid." We have used it in the present tense of the subjunctive because the relative pronoun *que* refers back to an agreement (*acuerdo*) which is still in doubt, one which will perhaps be arrived at some time later during the conference. (B) is wrong because *apenas*, meaning "scarcely," would imply that the delegates barely realize (*se dan cuenta de*) the seriousness (*la seriedad*) of the problem. Because of the verb *negar* (*ie*), "to deny," in choice (C), the statement would be contradictory to what we know. The delegates are not meeting to deny the seriousness (*la gravedad*) of the problem, but rather to remedy it. Choice (D) is also wrong; the conferees are

not necessarily going to devalue or lower the value (*bajar*) of currency (*la moneda*). In fact, they have not yet decided what they must do.

113. **(B)** *Se entiende* is the reflexive form of the third person singular of the present tense of *entender* (*ie*), "to understand." Remember that this form of the reflexive can mean "one" does something. It is often used as a substitute for the true passive voice. Here it means "It is understood." Choice (A) tells us that the result (*el resultado*) will be effective (*eficaz*), but there is no certainty of that. Choice (C) says that the desired goal (*el fin deseado*) will be carried out (*se efectuará*): we have no assurance of that either. In (D) *propósito* means "purpose," and the future tense of *lograrse* signifies "will be accomplished," which is also a shaky assumption. In (B), the correct answer, *será necesario proceder con cuidado* means "it will be necessary to proceed with care." *Haber que* + infinitive, which appears in the third person singular of the future tense in the last sentence of the reading, means "to be necessary to," and is synonymous to *ser necesario*. The verb *obrar*, which appears in the same sentence, means "to work," and *con cautela* signifies "with caution," and represents the same idea as *con cuidado* (with care or carefully).

114. **(B)** In the middle of the reading it states that his uncle said to him, "Gil blas, ya no eres niño . . ." Therefore, the narrator must be Gil Blas. The other choices are his father, his uncle, and one of his professors.

115. **(A)** Choice (A) is the best answer. The second paragraph of the passage tells us that Gil Blas's uncle, Gil Pérez, taught him how to read. (B) is not a good choice, since according to the text Gil Blas already knew how to read when he went to Dr. Godínez's school. (C) is incorrect, because although the passage indicates that he is setting off for the University of Salamanca, it also tells us that his uncle taught him to read when he was very young. (D) is not the best choice; it was his uncle, not his parents, who taught him to read.

116. **(D)** Choice (D) is correct. According to the story, Gil Blas was leaving Oviedo to go to the University of Salamanca. (A) is not a good choice; Gil Blas could not leave Oviedo to go live with his uncle, because his uncle lived in Oviedo. (B) is incorrect, because Gil Blas was leaving Oviedo to go study at the University of Salamanca, not because he was planning to return to his hometown (Santillana). (C) is not correct, since Gil Blas was not leaving Oviedo because his parents threw him out of the house.

117. **(A)** Choice (A) is the best answer; it was his uncle, Gil Pérez, who told Gil Blas that he was sending him to the University of Salamanca, because he was intelligent and could become an important man. (B) is not the best answer, because the passage says nothing of Dr. Godínez suggesting that Gil Blas go to the university. (C) is not a good choice, since the text indicates that it was Gil Pérez's idea for his nephew to go to the university. (D) is not correct; we are told that Gil Blas liked the idea, but it originally came from his uncle, Gil Pérez.

118. **(B)** Choice (B) is the best answer; the narrator tells us that when he went to say goodbye to his parents, all they were able to give him were a hug and a lot of advice. (A) is not a good choice, since it was his uncle who gave him a mule and some money for the trip. (C) is not correct, since the passage never mentions anyone giving him "a black horse and a sword." (D) is incorrect, because nothing is ever said about "a new suit and several books."

119. **(C)** The correct answer is (C). In order to drive on public roads, you must register your vehicle with insurance. (B) is incorrect because it is not necessary to live in the state for 60 days before registering your vehicle, but you must do so within 60 days if you are a new resident. You must be at least 17 years of age, not less than 17 years of age in order to register (B). It is incorrect to say that you must have the vehicle titled and registered with "security" (*seguridad*) rather than *seguro* (insurance), as choice (D) states.

120. **(C)** The correct answer is (C). It is very important for the license plates to be visible and placed correctly. (A) is incorrect since both *enfrente* and *delantera* refer to the front of the vehicle, not the front and back. It is not necessary for the license plates to be visible by using "reflecting plates" (B). The reading states that although you have reflecting plates, they must also be illuminated in order to be seen at a distance of 50 feet. It is not necessary to replace your license plates when you buy a new vehicle since you may transfer them (D).

PRACTICE TEST 2

CLEP Spanish Language

Also available at the REA Study Center (*www.rea.com/studycenter*)

This practice test is also offered online at the REA Study Center. Since all CLEP exams are administered on computer, we recommend that you take the online version of the test to receive these added benefits:

- **Timed testing conditions** – Gauge how much time you can spend on each question.
- **Automatic scoring** – Find out how you did on the test, instantly.
- **On-screen detailed explanations of answers** – Learn not just the correct answer, but also why the other answer choices are incorrect.
- **Diagnostic score reports** – Pinpoint where you're strongest and where you need to focus your study.

PRACTICE TEST 2

SECTION I

Listening: Rejoinders

(Answer sheets appear in the back of the book.)

TIME: 30 Minutes
50 Questions

DIRECTIONS: For this section of the test, you will hear a number of conversations or parts of conversations. After each dialogue, you will hear four answer choices, identified as (A), (B), (C), and (D). When you have heard all four answer choices, choose the one that best completes or continues the conversation. Fill in the corresponding oval on your answer sheet. Neither the answer choices nor the conversations will be printed in your test booklet, so you must listen very carefully.

1.– 18. Mark your answers on your answer sheet.

SECTION II

Listening: Dialogues and Narratives

Directions: You will hear a series of selections, including narratives, news reports, announcements, and dialogues. A graphic or a picture accompanies each selection. Listen very carefully to each selection, as they are spoken only once. For each selection, one or more questions will be printed in your test booklet, each with four answer choices. The questions and answers will not be spoken. Choose the best answer to each question and fill in the corresponding oval on your answer sheet. You are given 12 seconds to answer each question.

Selección 1

19. Escoge la cosa que deciden no prestar.

    (A) la cámara
    (B) el videograbadora
    (C) el radio
    (D) el almuerzo

20. ¿Qué deciden hacer juntos los dos?

    (A) Van a sacar fotos.
    (B) Van a comer y ver una película.
    (C) Van a escuchar música.
    (D) Van a escribir un mapa.

Selección 2

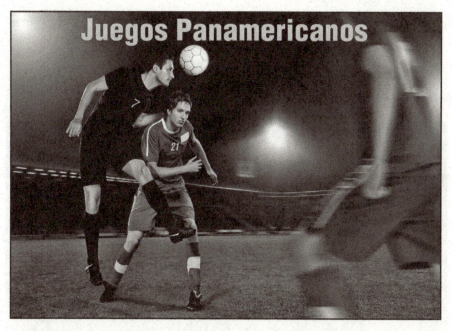

21. Indica el dibujo del deporte en el cual los dos hermanos venezolanos recibieron medallas distintas.

    (A) beísbol
    (B) fútbol
    (C) gimnasia
    (D) boxeo

22. Mira la tabla de abajo. Escoge la respuesta que tiene los números en el orden correcto para llenarla con el número de medallas de cada tipo que ganó Venezuela.

	Oro	Plata	Bronce	Total
Venezuela				

(A) 9, 32, 39, 80
(B) 2, 1, 1, 4
(C) 80, 9, 32, 39
(D) 9, 32, 9, 50

23. ¿Quiénes son los campeones de béisbol?

(A) Los venezolanos.
(B) Los dominicanos.
(C) Los Miramontes.
(D) Los mexicanos.

Selección 3

24. Escoge la línea que mejor indica la temperatura reciente en España.

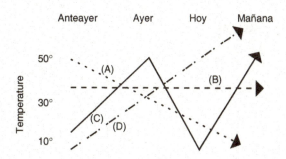

25. ¿Cuál es la temperatura máxima en España prevista para mañana?

(A) 25°
(B) 55°
(C) 85°
(D) 35°

Selección 4

26. ¿Quién escribió el cuento Lazarillo de Tormes?

   (A) Miguel de Cervantes.
   (B) Los religiosos de la Inquisición.
   (C) No se sabe.
   (D) Lazarillo de Tormes.

27. El protagonista es _____.

   (A) un amo
   (B) un pícaro
   (C) anónimo
   (D) la Inquisición

28. ¿Cuál es el orden correcto de lo que pasa con Lazarillo en la historia?

   (A) nacimiento, vida, muerte
   (B) años de servicio a los amos, matrimonio, muerte
   (C) nacimiento, años de servicio a los amos, matrimonio
   (D) nacimiento, matrimonio, la Inquisición

Selección número 5

Vuelo	Destino	Partida	Estado
595	El Paso	7:15	Retrasado
560	San Luis Potosí	7:15	
932	Guadalajara	7:45	A tiempo
755	Aguascalientes	8:00	A tiempo

29. Mira el horario de salidas de arriba. ¿Qué pertenece en el espacio oscuro (en gris)?

(A) Retrasado
(B) Cancelado
(C) A tiempo
(D) Abordando

30. ¿De dónde vienen los vuelos que van a llegar a tiempo?

(A) Michoacán y San Miguel
(B) Michoacán y El Paso
(C) San Luis Potosí y Guadalajara
(D) San Miguel y San Luis Potosí

31. ¿Dónde están las personas que están escuchando los anuncios?

(A) Michoacán
(B) un avión
(C) San Luis Potosí
(D) un aeropuerto

Selección número 6

32. ¿Con quién habla el hombre?

    (A) la propietaria de un café
    (B) una mujer en la tienda de bicicletas
    (C) una amiga de uno de sus amigos
    (D) la operadora de un periódico

33. ¿Qué quiere en cambio de la bicicleta?

    (A) una bicicleta nueva
    (B) una cita con la mujer
    (C) cualquier cosa que le guste
    (D) solamente dinero

34. Al final de la conversación, ¿qué pasa?

    (A) La mujer se enoja con el hombre.
    (B) La mujer quiere la bicicleta.
    (C) El aviso costó mucho.
    (D) Un perro muerde a la mujer.

35. ¿Qué va a obtener el hombre?

    (A) un periódico
    (B) un perro joven
    (C) un carro
    (D) una bicicleta

Selección número 7

36. ¿Qué comida se hace con esta receta?

   (A) Un taco
   (B) una ensalada de patatas
   (C) una tortilla de patatas
   (D) huevos fritos

37. ¿Cuál de estos ingredientes NO se necesita para cocinar esta receta?

   (A) huevos
   (B) tortillas de maíz
   (C) aceite
   (D) patatas

38. ¿Cómo se cocina esta receta?

    (A) en microondas

    (B) sobre la estufa

    (C) en el horno

    (D) a la parrilla

Selección número 8

39. ¿Dónde toma lugar esta conversación?

    (A) en el zoológico

    (B) en la tienda de mascotas

    (C) en el centro comercial

    (D) en la granja

40.– 43. Mira la tabla de abajo. Según lo que responde el hombre, escoge la mejor respuesta para llenar el espacio gris de cada número. Marca (A) si el número debe ser "sí." Marca (B) si debe ser "no."

Animal	¿Se come?	¿Se monta?	¿Se bebe su leche?	¿Se usa para hacer ropa o zapatos?
Cabra	sí	no	40.	sí
Oveja	Sí	41.	no	sí
Vaca	sí	no	Sí	42.
Caballo	43.	sí	no	no

Selección número 9

44. ¿Cuánto pagas si le compras la camisa a tu abuelo hoy? El precio normal es € 30.

(A) € 30
(B) € 60
(C) € 20
(D) € 15

45. ¿Cuánto costarán en total dos pares de zapatos esta semana? Cada par cuesta normalmente € 40.

(A) € 20
(B) € 60
(C) € 40
(D) € 80

46. Si tengo 15 años y me compro los pantalones (€ 35), la camiseta (€ 20), y los calcetines (€ 5), ¿cuánto pago hoy? Cada precio entre paréntesis es el precio normal.

(A) € 35
(B) € 20
(C) € 40
(D) € 60

47. ¿Cuál de estas frases será mejor para una letrera en el Corte Inglés esta semana?

  (A) La tienda se cierre esta semana- ¡Ahorra en todo!
  (B) ¡Ahorra! Descuentos para toda la familia esta semana.
  (C) Descuento en todo – 50%
  (D) ¡Compra hoy, paga mañana!

Selección número 10

48. ¿Cómo hablan las dos personas?

  (A) en persona en casa
  (B) por teléfono
  (C) en persona la oficina
  (D) a través de los abogados

49. Según lo que dice Marta, ¿qué había hecho María antes?

    (A) Trabajó con los abogados.

    (B) Llenó una solicitud de trabajo.

    (C) Pidió la ayuda de los abogados.

    (D) Entrevistó a Marta.

50. Mira el mensaje que le escribió el hijo a su mamá después de la conversación. Escoge la letra de la línea que tiene error.

    (A)   Mamá, llama a Marta González

    (B)   de las oficinas de Martínez y Solís

    (C)   después de las 5:30 hoy

    (D)   555-9452

This is the end of the audio section of Practice Test 2.
Please go to the Reading section on the next page.

SECTION III

Reading

TIME: 60 Minutes
70 Questions

Part A

DIRECTIONS: This section contains several incomplete statements, each having four completion choices. Select the most appropriate answer and fill in the corresponding oval on your answer sheet.

51. Las ovejas producen _____.

    (A) lana
    (B) seda
    (C) jamón
    (D) papas

52. Es _____ comer para vivir.

    (A) preciso
    (B) precioso
    (C) precario
    (D) precoz

53. Tú _____ antes de salir a la calle.

    (A) te viste
    (B) te vestiste
    (C) te pusiste
    (D) te pones

54. Todos vamos a _____ en el coche.

    (A) caber
    (B) empujar
    (C) empacar
    (D) dejar

55. Al fin de su discurso el general _____ que estaba dispuesto a morir por la patria.

    (A) sometió
    (B) sumó
    (C) agregó
    (D) encargó

56. Quisiera _____ al profesor Álvarez.

    (A) introduce
    (B) presentarte
    (C) conozco
    (D) saber

57. Hay un _____ en una cámara del piso cuarto.

    (A) incendio
    (B) huracán
    (C) nevada
    (D) fogata

58. La comida ha sido buenísima; vamos a dejarle una propina al _____.

    (A) cenicero
    (B) acero
    (C) camarero
    (D) bombero

59. ¿Por qué tienes _____ la pierna?

    (A) puesta
    (B) abierta
    (C) devuelta
    (D) rota

60. Se han apagado todas las luces. Estamos _____.

    (A) leyendo
    (B) a oscuras
    (C) a la luz
    (D) a tiempo

61. Anoche _____ a las doce pero no pude dormir.

    (A) soñé
    (B) me acosté
    (C) me desperté
    (D) me levanté

62. Enrique y Ángela se casaron el sábado. Esta semana fueron _____ .

    (A) a las estrellas
    (B) de luna de miel
    (C) de miel de abeja
    (D) de luna llena

63. Me cuesta trabajo captar la letra de esta _____ .

    (A) sinfonía
    (B) telegrama
    (C) baile
    (D) canción

64. No me siento bien; tengo un _____ .

    (A) reloj
    (B) enfermedad
    (C) resfriado
    (D) uña

65. El ruido de esa sirena _____ .

    (A) me tranquiliza
    (B) me molesta
    (C) es rojo
    (D) me da celos

Part B

DIRECTIONS: In each paragraph below, numbered blanks indicate that phrases or words have been purposely omitted. Four possible completion choices are provided for each blank space. Carefully read the paragraph and select the answer choice containing the word or phrase that is most suitable in the context of the paragraph. Fill in the corresponding oval on your answer sheet.

Según Yannover, no es posible efectuar cambios ni __(66)__ de los últimos __(67)__ tecnológicos si los __(68)__ nunca llegan. "Los mecanismos para conseguir dinero son eternos, puede pasar __(69)__ un año, y para __(70)__ tiempo ya se acabó el entusiasmo." Aunque no __(71)__ completamente justo comparar la biblioteca local con otras, vale la pena __(72)__ a __(73)__ Madrid, cuyo director tiene la dicha de manejar directamente un presupuesto anual de __(74)__ dólares.

66. (A) se aprovecha
    (B) se aprovechan
    (C) aprovecharse
    (D) se aproveche

67. (A) avances
    (B) aumentos
    (C) avanzados
    (D) adelantados

68. (A) fondos
    (B) fondillos
    (C) fondistas
    (D) folletos

69. (A) más que
    (B) más
    (C) más de
    (D) más de que

70. (A) eso
    (B) esa
    (C) ése
    (D) ese

71. (A) es
    (B) ser
    (C) será
    (D) sea

72. (A) echar un vistazo
    (B) echar un trago
    (C) echar un terno
    (D) echar un piropo

73. (A) al de
    (B) ella de
    (C) la de
    (D) el de

74. (A) millón de
    (B) millónes de
    (C) milliones de
    (D) millones de

Una tarde de lluvias primaverales, cuando viajaba sola hacia Barcelona __(75)__ un automóvil alquilado, María de la Luz Cervantes sufrió __(76)__ en el desierto de los Monegros. María de la Luz __(77)__ una mexicana de veintisiete años, bonita y seria, que años antes había tenido nombre como actriz de variedades. Estaba casada con un director de teatro, con __(78)__ iba a reunirse aquel día luego de __(79)__ a unos parientes en Zaragoza. Después de una hora de hacer señas __(80)__ a los automóviles y camiones que pasaban, el conductor de un autobús destartalado paró y __(81)__ ofreció ayuda.

75. (A) conducir
    (B) conducía
    (C) conduzca
    (D) conduciendo

76. (A) una avería
    (B) un colapso
    (C) una ruptura
    (D) una interrupción

77. (A) Era
    (B) Estaba
    (C) Fue
    (D) Estuvo

78. (A) que
    (B) quien
    (C) la que
    (D) quién

79. (A) visitando
    (B) visitara
    (C) visita
    (D) visitar

80. (A) desesperado
    (B) desesperadas
    (C) desesperada
    (D) desesperando

81. (A) Lo
    (B) Se
    (C) Le
    (D) La

Marcelo se sorprendió de que Alfredo Zambrano __(82)__ acompañado aquella mañana a Cristina, su esposa. __(83)__ en la mirada del hombre un __(84)__ de odio o __(85)__, algo que le avisara de que Alfredo estaba enterado de sus __(86)__ con ella. Pero fue en vano. La __(87)__ del empresario español, lejana, pasiva, no reflejaba nada que __(88)__ ser de cuidado.

82. (A) hubiera
    (B) había
    (C) haya
    (D) habría

83. (A) Busqué
    (B) Buscó
    (C) Observó
    (D) Veo

84. (A) artículo
    (B) sentido
    (C) indicio
    (D) sensorial

85. (A) amistad
    (B) deseo
    (C) curiosidad
    (D) enemistad

86. (A) hijos
    (B) relaciones
    (C) negocios
    (D) obligaciones

87. (A) estatura
    (B) emoción
    (C) mirada
    (D) vista

88. (A) pueda
    (B) podía
    (C) podría
    (D) pudiera

Part C

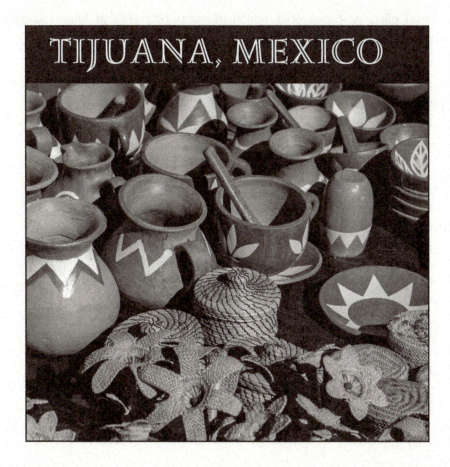

TIJUANA, MEXICO

Desde hace dos días la familia Rodríguez gozaba de la anticipación del viaje que iba a hacer a Tijuana. Los dos niños expresaban su entusiasmo no sólo con preguntas, sino también con la nerviosidad que demostraban incesantemente. La abuelita, aunque sentía la misma excitación, por ser mayor hacía todo lo posible para esconderla.[1] Siempre le gustaba ir a Tijuana.[2] Decían algunos que era ciudad fea, pero para ella era México.[3] Era ocasión de comprar tortillas, pan, jícama, vainilla, hierbas medicinales y lo más importante – estar en México donde todos hablaban español y ella no se sentía extranjera.[4] Los padres de los niños compartían los mismos sentimientos.

89. Calcula cuántos iban a Tijuana.

    (A) Dos
    (B) Tres
    (C) Cuatro
    (D) Cinco

90. En el párrafo, 4 oraciones tienen números pequeños al final. Escoge la oración que muestra que casi seguramente la abuelita era mexicana.

    (A) oración 1
    (B) oración 2
    (C) oración 3
    (D) oración 4

91. Una razón por la cual le gustaba Tijuana a la abuela era que _____.

    (A) era mayor
    (B) hablaban español allá
    (C) no vendían nada allá
    (D) era ciudad fea

92. A lo mejor le gustaba a la abuela _____.

    (A) salir de Tijuana
    (B) esconderse en Tijuana
    (C) poder gastar su dinero
    (D) hablar inglés

No sé cómo me enfermé. La comida sí era diferente, pero ha sido sabrosa y yo tenía un hambre atroz. Puede ser que haya comido demasiado. De todos modos esta mañana me atacó un retortijón de tripas insoportable que duró casi una hora. Apenas podía yo respirar por el dolor. Hablé con el gerente del hotel cuando pude para que me pusiera en contacto con un médico. Grande fue la sorpresa mía cuando me anunció sin emoción ninguna que aquí en este pueblo no había médico. Sólo había homeópata, pero era bueno y sabía curar. ¿Qué iba yo a hacer? Tenía que ir con él. Después de indicarle los síntomas, me dio ciertas hierbas indicándome cómo hacer el té que debiera tomar. Milagro de milagros. Después de tomar el té, comencé a sentirme mejor y en dos días estaba como nuevo.

93. ¿Dónde se encontraba la persona del cuento?

   (A) en una ciudad grande
   (B) en un hospital
   (C) en un pueblo chico
   (D) en su casa.

94. Indica dónde se siente los síntomas.

   (A) la cabeza
   (B) el estómago
   (C) la pierna
   (D) la nariz

95. El homeópata era _____.

   (A) bueno para curar
   (B) unas hierbas
   (C) el gerente del hotel
   (D) un hospital

96. La persona debiera hacer el té y _____.

   (A) las hierbas
   (B) aplicarlo al lugar del dolor
   (C) tomarlo
   (D) esperar dos días

97. Recobró la salud después de _____.

   (A) consultar con el médico
   (B) hacer un milagro
   (C) sufrir otros dolores
   (D) tomar el té

    Dicen que las playas de la Costa Brava son unas de las mejores del mundo.[1] Turistas de todas partes del mundo se dirigen a ésas durante todo el año, pero especialmente durante el verano.[2] Se oye un babel de lenguas y el español que se habla entre ellos representa docenas de acentos.[3] Naturalmente, el clima es muy agradable y los españoles son sumamente hospitalarios. Con razón España es el banco de gran parte de los turistas, especialmente los ingleses, los alemanes, los franceses y los suecos.[4]

98. En el párrafo, 4 oraciones tienen números pequeños al final. Escoge la oración que **NO** indica que hay personas de varios países que visitan Costa Brava.

    (A) oración 1
    (B) oración 2
    (C) oración 3
    (D) oración 4

99. Los españoles por naturaleza son _____.

    (A) tacaños
    (B) descorteses
    (C) médicos
    (D) amigables

100. La mayoría de los turistas vienen _____.

    (A) del norte de África
    (B) del oeste de Europa
    (C) de España misma
    (D) de Latinoamérica

Llovía a cántaros y era la medianoche. El tren seguía su trayectoria como de costumbre aunque <u>el ingeniero</u>[A] no podía ver nada, ni las vías. Era fuerte <u>el ojo ciclópico</u>[B] del <u>monstruo de hierro</u>[C], pero no servía de nada. Era tanta la lluvia que hasta goteaba por el techo de los coches. Unos pasajeros se mojaban, especialmente los que estaban dormidos. Otros, de menos fe en el ingeniero, miraban por las ventanas tratando de penetrar la oscuridad o se daban mirada de sospecha. El tren iba rápidamente, pero ahora comenzaba a caminar más despacio. Eso daba más razón de dudar a los preocupados que demostraban más inquietud como si anticiparan un desastre o algo semejante. Después de un rato no era tanta la velocidad del tren. De pronto el tren se paró Los pasajeros que dormían se despertaron y por todos los coches se oía el bullicio de comentarios y preguntas. Todos querían saber lo que pasaba.

–El ingeniero va delante del tren con su <u>linterna</u>D– dijo uno que se asomaba por una ventana.

Esto causó más excitación. Después de unos minutos corrían por todo el tren con estas noticias –¡El ingeniero ha descubierto que la mucha agua ha llevado gran parte de las vías! ¡El tren volverá atrás a la última estación!

101. ¿Por qué no podía ver bien el ingeniero?

    (A) por la oscuridad
    (B) por la lluvia
    (C) por el fuerte ojo
    (D) por su linterna

102. ¿Cuál de las palabras subrayadas indica el tren?

    (A) el ingeniero
    (B) el ojo ciclópico
    (C) monstruo de hierro
    (D) su linterna

103. Después de examinar las vías, el ingeniero _____.

    (A) decidió seguir adelante
    (B) mandó repararlas
    (C) decidió no mover el tren
    (D) decidió rogresar a la última parada

104. La mucha agua había _____.

    (A) ahogado a todos los pasajeros
    (B) llevado el tren de la vía
    (C) impedido el progreso del tren
    (D) apagado la luz

105. Algunos de los pasajeros _____.

    (A) estaban nerviosos
    (B) no pagaron el pasaje
    (C) tenían hambre y comenzaron a comer
    (D) bajaron del tren

106. El tren tenía_____.

    (A) unas ruedas rotas
    (B) una luz fuerte en frente
    (C) nada más un coche
    (D) solamente un pasajero

107. Los pasajeros no dormidos _____.

    (A) soñaban con los ángeles
    (B) caminaron al lado del tren
    (C) decidió no mover el tren
    (D) se sentían intranquilos

–No, no quiero confesarme. No sé por qué me tienen preso. No quiero que usted ni nadie me moleste. [1] Lo que sí quiero es vivir y no morir. No me nieguen la vida, es mía y no quiero que me la quiten. Si ustedes son cristianos, ¿por qué me la quieren quitar? Yo quiero vivir. Soy joven y tengo una novia que me quiere mucho, igual que mis padres. [2] Yo sé que usted me dirá que la muerte es la puerta para la vida eterna, pero ésta es la que me vale. No quiero dejar esta vida, ¿me entiende usted? La vida para mí es bella. [3] Si fuera cosa de morir en guerra, eso sería diferente. En ese caso uno moriría con respeto, luchando por una causa honrada y por principios. [4] Eso vale la pena, pero morir ante el paredón, ¡no! Eso no lo entiendo. No tiene sentido morir así. Hasta sería una vergüenza para mí, para la familia, para mi novia y para la humanidad. Es inhumano morir de esta forma.

108. ¿Dónde estará el joven?

    (A) con su novia
    (B) en la iglesia
    (C) en un cementerio
    (D) en la cárcel

109. ¿Quién vino a estar con él?

    (A) un sacerdote
    (B) su novia
    (C) toda su familia
    (D) un fantasma

110. (To answer question 110, choose the sentence from the reading selection that best answers the question.)

    Escoge y haz clic en la parte subrayada de la lectura que indica que van a matar al narrador.

    (A) Sentence 1
    (B) Sentence 2
    (C) Sentence 3
    (D) Sentence 4

111. ¿Dónde preferiría morir?

    (A) cerca de la novia
    (B) en el campo de batalla
    (C) en el hospital
    (D) con la familia

    Cuando el marinero se despertó, se encontraba solo y tirado en una playa extensa.

    –¿Sería isla? se decía. –¿Y dónde están los otros?

    [1] Él era el único sobreviviente del barco naufragado. [2] Él se acordaba de la tempestad violenta y la eminente destrucción del barco y luego esa ola inmensa que lo llevó al mar. [3] Con sus últimos esfuerzos pudo agarrar una tabla suelta. [4] Luego se había despertado adolorido y cansado, pero vivo y pudo ponerse de pie para mirar a su alrededor, buscando otro ser viviente–pero no había nadie. ¿Qué iba a hacer él? ¿Cómo podría vivir? ¿Qué comería? ¿Cómo podría protegerse de la intemperie? De repente se oyó un rugido fuerte. El náufrago quedó petrificado.

112. (To answer question 112, choose the sentence from the reading selection that best answers the question.)

    Escoge la frase subrayada de la lectura que indica la manera de la cual el marinero llegó a la isla. Marca la letra correspondiente al número después de la selección correcta.

    (A) Sentence 1
    (B) Sentence 2
    (C) Sentence 3
    (D) Sentence 4

113. Llegó a la playa_____.

    (A) cantando
    (B) nadando
    (C) flotando
    (D) andando

114. Le molestaba _____.

    (A) la soledad
    (B) el tráfico
    (C) la mucha arena
    (D) el sol caliente

115. Estaba preocupado por _____.

    (A) su familia
    (B) el tiempo
    (C) la ropa manchada
    (D) su situación física

116. ¿Cómo se sintió el marinero al final de la lectura?

    (A) tuvo miedo
    (B) emocionado
    (C) tranquilo
    (D) aliviado

En la actualidad, sigue pendiente el dilema del desarme, sobre todo entre los dos grandes poderes que poseen la mayoría de las armas. ¿Quién sabe si en algún tiempo lejano se planteará de firme la posibilidad de abolir este peligro para la vida? De vez en cuando han surgido propuestas para realizar este sueño pero hasta el momento escasos han sido los resultados.

Los partidarios del desarme opinan que el desarrollo de bombas de rendimiento cada vez más grande podría acarrearnos una catástrofe de dimensiones increíbles. Los informes más recientes vienen apoyando tal teoría. Por otra parte, hay los que están en contra del desarme, creyendo que el enemigo no es de fiar, a no ser que se permita la inspección, la cual presentaría tal vez inconvenientes insuperables para los dos lados. Según los proponentes del desarme, la inspección podría llevarse a cabo contando con una organización internacional como las Naciones Unidas.

Lo obvio es que tenemos que hacer algo a favor de la paz y la supervivencia de la humanidad a la cual pertenecemos todos, amigos y adversarios.

117. ¿Cuál de las siguientes respuestas es falsa?

    (A) Hay mucho desacuerdo en cuanto a la cuestión del desarme.
    (B) Es posible que en el porvenir se resuelva la cuestión del desarme.
    (C) De veras, ya se ha solucionado el problema de las armas.
    (D) Ya se han sugerido soluciones al problema del desarme.

118. Los que oponen al desarme _____.

    (A) son de otra parte
    (B) desconfían de la buena voluntad del adversario
    (C) están contra la supervivencia
    (D) apoyan la guerra

119. Los que favorecen el desarme _____.

    (A) rechazan la idea de la inspección internacional
    (B) temen abolir las armas
    (C) tienen confianza en el enemigo
    (D) están por la inspección internacional

120. Siempre va aumentando_____.

    (A) la escasez de propuestas
    (B) la realización de nuestras metas
    (C) la potencia de las bombas
    (D) el número de nuestros enemigos

PRACTICE TEST 2

Answer Key

Listening Comprehension

1.	(D)	14.	(C)	27.	(B)	40.	(A)
2.	(C)	15.	(C)	28.	(C)	41.	(B)
3.	(B)	16.	(C)	29.	(B)	42.	(A)
4.	(D)	17.	(B)	30.	(A)	43.	(B)
5.	(D)	18.	(A)	31.	(D)	44.	(D)
6.	(C)	19.	(C)	32.	(D)	45.	(C)
7.	(D)	20.	(B)	33.	(C)	46.	(C)
8.	(C)	21.	(D)	34.	(B)	47.	(B)
9.	(A)	22.	(A)	35.	(B)	48.	(B)
10.	(B)	23.	(B)	36.	(C)	49.	(B)
11.	(D)	24.	(B)	37.	(B)	50.	(C)
12.	(B)	25.	(D)	38.	(B)		
13.	(D)	26.	(C)	39.	(D)		

Reading

51.	(A)	69.	(C)	87.	(C)	105.	(A)
52.	(A)	70.	(D)	88.	(D)	106.	(B)
53.	(B)	71.	(D)	89.	(D)	107.	(D)
54.	(A)	72.	(A)	90.	(D)	108.	(D)
55.	(C)	73.	(C)	91.	(B)	109.	(A)
56.	(B)	74.	(D)	92.	(C)	110.	(D)
57.	(A)	75.	(D)	93.	(C)	111.	(B)
58.	(C)	76.	(A)	94.	(B)	112.	(C)
59.	(D)	77.	(A)	95.	(A)	113.	(C)
60.	(B)	78.	(B)	96.	(C)	114.	(A)
61.	(B)	79.	(D)	97.	(D)	115.	(D)
62.	(B)	80.	(B)	98.	(A)	116.	(A)
63.	(D)	81.	(C)	99.	(D)	117.	(C)
64.	(C)	82.	(A)	100.	(B)	118.	(B)
65.	(B)	83.	(B)	101.	(B)	119.	(D)
66.	(C)	84.	(C)	102.	(C)	120.	(C)
67.	(A)	85.	(D)	103.	(D)		
68.	(A)	86.	(B)	104.	(C)		

PRACTICE TEST 2

Detailed Explanations of Answers

Section I

1. **(D)** The correct answer is (D). Having money and going to the Greek Islands is the secret desire of the speaker. He doesn't have money, so going to a closer place is a good option (D). Therefore, the response of going there in a month is not logical (A). The response to ask for a loan if the person has limited funds is illogical. Maybe the Greek Islands are the most beautiful place on Earth, as (C) says, but the response is illogical, especially if you begin the sentence with "Better yet."

2. **(C)** The correct answer is (C). If you've spent the entire day on the internet, you haven't been in a physical place, but a virtual place, so it couldn't be hot (B). Also, not being home would be an impossible inference. It is not an open space outdoors, so (D) is incorrect. Therefore, (C), inquiring about having found interesting things on the internet, is the best response.

3. **(B)** The correct answer is (B). The speakers comment that they could ski if they had what they needed, inferring that they are in need of equipment, so "my brother's skis" is a good answer (B). A car is not required to ski (C), nor are beverages (A). "I can't leave home" (D) is not a logical response because it has nothing to do with the subject of having or not having equipment.

4. **(D)** The correct answer is (D). "This dog might bite you if you come closer." This dog is neither tame, docile, or friendly as (A) implies. To invite the dog owner to come closer to hug (B) is not a good idea unless you are trying to get bitten. To feed the dog if he bites you is not a logical response. (D) "This dog is well-trained indeed" is a logical response if the person believes that a well-trained protective dog should protect its owner by biting anyone who gets too physically close.

5. **(D)** The correct answer is (D), "I sigh each time you look at me." You might be in love, but not with a stomachache as (A) implies, and not with a problem in your eyes as (B) states. "It can't be my hairstyle that frightens and amazes you" (C) is not complementary. "The same happens to me" (D) would be a logical response.

6. **(C)** The correct answer is (C), "I will do it again if they call me." (*volver* + infinitive = to do something again). Asking for something from a place you are talking about is abrupt and not logical (A). The phone not working is never implied (B). The response that it seems like a good idea to do what you know how to do best is a logical reply (C). "It's always good to start something new" is an illogical response since it is not the beginning of something new, but a repetition of something already done.

7. **(D)** The correct answer is (D). The speaker invites Gabito to talk finally about something that has been eluded. The response that "One can't speak because he is mute" would not be possible if, in fact, the person were incapable of speaking (A). The response that "It's a lie" is not a logical response to a request, but rather to a statement (B). Music as the topic of the discussion is never implied (C). (D) is a logical response because it expresses interest, "Go ahead, I'm listening."

8. **(C)** The correct answer is (C) because among the ambiguities, it is possible to consider that there is something positive being said about the boss despite the speaker's opinion that he is unbearable. (A) is not possible because you cannot forget the unforgettable. (B) is not correct because you cannot infer from the sentence that the boss has no virtues at all. (D) is incorrect because even though the speaker's comment may suggest that there are positive aspects of his employment, the assumption that it is a comfortable place to work is presumptuous.

9. **(A)** The correct answer is (A). The speaker asks for directions to the hotel Miramar. The correct response is (A) "Yes, on the next street." "Don't stand in front of the hotel" (B) doesn't answer the question; nor does (C) "Yes, I'm a tourist." (D) "I can't accompany you there now" is illogical since only the directions were requested.

10. **(B)** The correct answer is (B). The speaker asks Margarita to do a favor. The most logical response is (B) "I'm sorry, but I'm exhausted." "Yes, I thank you very much" (A) is illogical since Margarita is the one who would be doing the favor and receiving the thanks. Nor would she say "You're welcome" (C) or "It would be unfortunate" (D) as a response to a request for a favor.

11. **(D)** The correct answer is (D). The speaker asks, "How long until the event begins?" The response of "five blocks" answers the question of distance, not time (A). It is not asking about the price of the ticket (B). And even though the word *falta* means "a sin," in this case, *hacer falta* refers

to the length of time remaining until the event begins. (D) is the correct response, "It should have already begun."

12. **(B)**   The correct answer is (B). The travel agent is making a reservation for two rooms during Holy Week. So, (A) asking for three weeks would not make sense, since the agent was referring to two rooms rather than two weeks. (B) asks for only one room, instead of two. (C) is wrong because the respondent confuses "reservation" with "reserve." (D) is an illogical response because there is no previous mention of an arrival date.

13. **(D)**   The correct answer is (D). The speaker suspects he has had a mysterious sickness since January and tells this to his doctor. The doctor would not make the assumption that the patient has only one month to live based solely on the patient's fears, (A). Nor would he say that the patient must take an aspirin and go away, (B). In (C) the question "Why are you so sure?" is a possible response, but there is a contradiction here. The doctor assumes that the patient is sure about the statement, but the patient expresses that he has only a vague suspicion. In (D) the doctor asks about the symptoms. This is closer to a doctor's logical response given the patient's statement.

14. **(C)**   The correct answer is (C). The buyer is asking for paper to write his family some letters. (A) assumes he is the one that has been written to. (B) asks about the color of the ink, but the speaker is buying paper. (C) is the correct response, "With lines or without?" since it refers to paper. (D) asks if they do it for the money, which is an illogical response.

15. **(C)**   The correct answer is (C). The speaker asks for verification of Luisa's birthday. (A) refers to the place of birth and (B) refers to her saint's day, which is distinct from a birthday. (D) refers to the day of the celebration, which is not necessarily the same day as her birthday. Therefore, (C) "my date of birth" is the only logical response to the question.

16. **(C)**   The correct answer is (C). The speaker is imagining what he would do if he had a motorcycle. (A), asking for postcards, is not related as is the question "Aren't you afraid of heights?" (B). The coast where the speaker wants to go cannot be above sea level. (C) is a logical response which expresses the respondent's belief that motorcycles are dangerous. (D) suggests what the speaker has already said by stating that it would be better if he went.

17. **(B)**   The correct answer is (B). The statement suggests that the spring air is dryer than that of autumn, but the summer climate is stifling. (A) autumn

cannot be more humid than summer nor can summer be drier than autumn (C). It would be erroneous to infer that winter is the most humid season. Therefore, the only logical statement to be inferred is that if spring is dry, then autumn is more humid than spring (D).

18. **(A)**   The correct answer is (A). (A) asks for a pen to sign the check. This would be a logical response to the speaker's request that the check can only be cashed with a signature on the back. (B) Not accepting those conditions is silly since a signature is always required. You are not told that you can't have the money, so there is no need to react desperately about the instructions (C). You are not asked to fill out a form, but rather to sign a check on the back side of the check (D).

Section II

19. **(C)**   The item that will not be lent is a radio (C) since the man says that he doesn't want to borrow it. He does borrow a still camera (*cámara fotográfica*) (A). There is no mention of a video camera (B). The lady says that if she is going to lend him her camera, she has to get the map from him and he has to take her to lunch (D), which he will buy for her, but not lend her. This is understood when she says, ". . . *me tienes que invitar a almorzar.*"

20. **(B)**   The man is the only one who wants to take pictures (A), which is why he asks for the camera. In the end, he agrees to (B) take her to lunch and also to the *cine* (movie theater), which is where they will watch a *película* (movie). He has expressed disinterest in listening to music (C) and she wants to him to lend (*prestar*) her a map, not write (*escribir*) one (D).

21. **(D)**   The question asks in which sport the 2 brothers (*hermanos*) won different (*distintas*) medals. Since baseball (A) and soccer (B) are team sports, anyone on those teams would receive the same medal. There was no mention of gymnastics (*gimnasia*), so (C) is incorrect. While talking about (D) boxing (*el boxeo*), the speaker mentioned that two *gemelos* (twins, and therefore brothers) won the gold and bronze medals.

22. **(A)**   When giving the medal count, the speaker says that Venezuela won a total of 80 (*ochenta*) medals and gives the breakdown as 9 gold (*nueve de oro*), 32 silver (*treinta y dos de plata*) and 39 bronze (*treinta y nueve de bronce*), so the correct order to fill in the table would be (A).

23. **(B)**   The question asks who the champions (*campeones*) of baseball were. Since Venezuela lost (*perdió*) in the championship (*el campeonato*), (A) is

incorrect. They lost to the Dominican Republic, whose natives are referred to as Dominicans (*dominicanos*), so (B) is the correct answer. (C) Miramontes is the last name of the twin boxers. Mexico (D) won the silver in soccer, but did not play in the baseball championship.

24. **(B)** The forecast for tomorrow says, ". . . *continúa el ambiente muy estable*," which translates as ". . . will remain stable." The rest of the forecast gives temperatures between 25 and 35 degrees Celsius, so the line most accurately depicting the trend would be line (B), which remains fairly steady and within the stated range. Line (A) shows a great decrease in temperature, while (D) shows a large increase, neither of which is indicated. Line (C) shows very erratic temperatures, which would contradict the term "stable."

25. **(D)** The highest (*máxima*) temperature mentioned in the forecast was 35 (*treinta y cinco*) degrees. 25 (*veinticinco*) was the lowest. 55 (*cincuenta y cinco*) and 85 (*ochenta y cinco*) were never mentioned.

26. **(C)** The speaker states that the author is *anónimo* (anonymous), which means that he or she is not known (*no se sabe*). Cervantes (A) is the author of several other works from Spain, including *El ingenioso hidalgo Don Quijote de la Mancha*, for which he is most famous. (B) refers to the religious leaders of the Inquisition, who are ridiculed in the book, but did not write it as far as anyone knows. Although the story is written from Lazarillo's point of view (*punto de vista*), he is a fictional character and therefore not the actual author.

27. **(B)** The *protagonista* (main character) is Lazarillo. Since the book is written from his point of view and is considered of the picaresque (*picaresco*) genre in which the *pícaro* (rogue, rascal) tells the story, the main character must be the *pícaro* (B). There are several masters (*amos*) throughout the story, but they are not the main character, so (A) would be incorrect. (C) *anónimo* is an unknown or anonymous person who, in this case, is the author, not a character. Since the Inquisition (D) is a period in Spanish history, it cannot be a character.

28. **(C)** The speaker states, "*Se cuenta de forma autobiográfica la vida desde su nacimiento hasta su matrimonio.*" This means that he tells the story of his own life from birth (*nacimiento*) until his marriage (*matrimonio*). He later refers to living as a servant to a series of masters (*sirviente a una serie de amos*) during the story, which would take place between the aforementioned events. Therefore, (C) shows the correct sequence of events.

Choices (A) and (B) both include *muerte (*death) as an event, but since the story ends with his marriage, he is still alive. While the Inquisition was in process throughout the story, it would not be an event occurring after his marriage as indicated in choice (D).

29. **(B)**   The airline employee is making announcements about expected arrivals (*llegadas*) and departures (*salidas*). She states, "... *el vuelo 560 con servicio a San Luis Potosí no va a poder salir hoy por problemas mecánicos*." This means that, due to mechanical problems, the indicated flight (*vuelo*) will not be able to leave and is, therefore, cancelled (*cancelado*). Since it will not leave at all, it cannot be (A) late, (C) on time, or (D) boarding.

30. **(A)**   The question asks the origin of the flights that will arrive on time (*llegar a tiempo*). Flights from Michoacán and San Miguel are reported to be arriving on time; therefore (A) is the correct answer. All of the other choices include destinations of departures (*partidas*) that are either late (El Paso – B) or cancelled (San Luis Potosí – C & D) rather than on-time arrivals.

31. **(D)**   Since the employee is announcing several arrivals and departures to and from various cities, she must be speaking in (D) an airport (*un aeropuerto*). If the listeners were already on (B) a plane (*un avión*), they would likely only hear about their own flight information. Because the cities in choices (A) and (C) are referred to as destinations or origins of the flights about which she is speaking, the listeners would have to be in a different city's airport.

32. **(D)**   The man calls to put an ad (*aviso*) in the daily newspaper (*diario*), so he is speaking to an operator at the newspaper (*periódico*) office. There is no mention of food, a café, or anyone's friend, so choice (A) the owner of a café and choice (C) a friend of one of his friends would both be incorrect. While the woman shows an interest in trading her puppy (*cachorro*) for the man's bicycle, she does not work at (B) a bike shop (*una tienda de bicicletas*).

33. **(C)**   While telling the woman what he would like his ad to say, the man suggests selling his bike for 100 (*cien*) pesos or trading it for any one of a list of items he may like. Therefore, choice (C), whatever thing he may like, would be the best answer. (D) says only (*solamente*) money. While money was one possibility, it was not the only one stated. He never mentioned wanting a new bike (A) nor did he request a date (*una cita*) with the woman.

34. **(B)** Near the end of the conversation, the woman suggests trading a Doberman puppy (*cachorro*) for the man's bike, so she must want the bike. The woman doesn't get angry (*se enoja*) with the man, as stated in (A). Nor does the dog bite (*muerde*) the woman (D). Choice (C) is incorrect since the man decides not to place the ad (*aviso*), therefore it did not cost a lot (*costó mucho*).

35. **(B)** Since the man decides to trade his bike for her Doberman puppy (*cachorro*), (B) is the correct choice. (C) *Carro* or *coche*, which both mean "car," sound similar to the word for puppy, but are distinct in meaning. He is trading his bike, rather than getting a new one, so (D) is not correct. (A) The *periódico* or *diario* (daily paper) is where he was going to place the ad.

36. **(C)** The recipe says to mix (*mezcla*) together and fry (*freír, fríe*) the ingredients. In (A) a taco, the ingredients are not cooked together. (B) potato salad has some of the same ingredients, but is not fried. (D) fried eggs are by themselves, separate from the other ingredients. (C) a potato omelet (*tortilla española/tortilla de patatas*) has all of the ingredients are mixed together before frying to a golden brown (*dorada*).

37. **(B)** The recipe makes a Spanish omelet (*tortilla española*), but does not include corn tortillas (*tortillas de maíz*), which are popular in Mexico and much of Latin America. The word *tortilla* is understood in Spain as "omelet" although it is a flat bread-like item made of flour or corn in most of the rest of the Spanish-speaking world. The recipe does include all of the other choices: (A) eggs, (C) oil, and (D) potatoes.

38. **(B)** The recipe says to fry (*freír, fríe*) the items in a *sartén* (frying pan), so choice (B*), sobre la estufa* (on the stovetop), is correct. One does not fry in a frying pan in a (A) *microondas* (microwave oven), in (C) *un horno* (an oven), or on a (D) *parrilla* (grill).

39. **(D)** Since all of the animals discussed are farm animals (*cabra* = goat, *oveja* = lamb, *vaca* = cow, and *caballo* = horse), they are most likely at a farm (D). There was no mention of animals likely to be encountered at (A) a zoo (*zoológico*) or (B) a pet store (*tienda de mascotas*). Animals are not frequently encountered at the mall or store, so choice (C) is incorrect.

40. **(A)** When discussing the *cabra* (goat), the man says, "*Produce leche para nosotros. . .*" which means that it produces milk for us. Since *se bebe su leche* indicates that one drinks its milk, the blank should be filled with (A) *sí*.

41. **(B)** When discussing the *oveja* (lamb), the man gives several uses, but never says that this animal can be ridden. "*Se monta*" means that people ride it, so the blank should be filled with (B) *no*.

42. **(A)** When discussing the *vaca* (cow), the man says, "*Mira tus tenis – el cuero de ellos es de la piel de vacas.*" This means that the leather that the boy's tennis shoes are made of comes from the skin of cows. Since "*¿Se usa para hacer ropa o zapatos?*" asks if it is used to make clothing or shoes, the blank should be filled with (A) *sí*.

43. **(B)** Indicating the *caballo* (horse), the boy asks if people eat (*se come*) that animal as well as the cow. The man responds that horses are ridden (*se montan*) but not eaten, so the blank should be filled with (B) *no*.

44. **(D)** Since your grandfather (*abuelo*) is a man and men's shirts (*camisas para hombres*) are 50% off (*se descuentan por cincuenta por ciento*), the answer should be 50% of the regular price (*precio normal*). 50% of € 30 is € 15, so (D) is the correct response. Note: € is the symbol for "euro," the monetary unit of Spain and several other European countries.

45. **(C)** The ad says that women's shoes (*zapatos para mujeres*) are buy one pair, get one free (*compra dos pares, pero sólo paga uno*). Since the regular price of each pair of shoes is € 40 and the second pair is free, the total cost would be only € 40, so the answer is (C).

46. **(C)** In the teen department (*para los adolescentes*), the ad states that you save € 10 for each € 30 in purchases (*ahorra diez euros para cada treinta en compras*). The pants (*pantalones*), t-shirt (*camiseta*), and socks (*calcetines*) that the 15-yr.-old is buying would normally total € 60 (35 + 20 + 5). Since this would constitute two 30-euro purchases, the savings would be two times € 10, or € 20. Normal price € 60 minus savings of € 20 would result in a total cost of € 40, so the answer is (C).

47. **(B)** The sign (*letrero*) should represent the information spoken. (A) indicates that the store will close this week (*se cierre esta semana*), which was not mentioned in the ad. (B) offers savings for clothing for the whole family. Since men's shirts (*camisas para hombres*), women's shoes (*zapatos para mujeres)* and teen and children's clothes (*ropa para adolescents y conjuntos para los niños*) were all mentioned as sale items, this would be the best phrase for the sign. (C) says that everything (*todo*) is 50% off, but that is only true of men's shirts. (D) translates as "buy today, pay tomorrow," but the ad never refers to a deferred payment plan.

48. **(B)** The question asks how the two are talking. Since the son (*hijo*) begins the conversation with *"Bueno,"* a common way to answer the phone in Mexico (similar to "hello" in the U.S.) and the woman requests to speak to someone else, it would be likely that the two were on the phone (B) rather than (A) & (C) in person (*en persona*). The lawyers (*abogados*) never spoke, so the people could not be conversing through (*a través de*) them as indicated in (D).

49. **(B)** Since Marta called to set up a job interview (*entrevista*) with María, she most likely filled out a job application, as indicated in (B). There is no indication that she previously worked with the lawyers (A) or asked them for help (C). She did not interview Marta, as stated in (D), but rather Marta wants to interview her.

50. **(C)** All of the information the son wrote on the message (*mensaje*) is correct except for line (C). He wrote that she should call *después de* (after) 5:30, but Marta said that she would only be in the office until (*hasta*) that time.

Section III - Part A

51. **(A)** *Ovejas* are "sheep." They do not produce *seda* (silk), *jamón* (ham), or *papas* (potatoes), but rather *lana* (wool). The word *"papas"* is used in South and Central America. In Spain, the word for "potatoes" is *patatas*.

52. **(A)** *Preciso* (necessary) is a synonym of *necesario*, which could also be used in this sentence. The three other possible choices, although they look or sound somewhat like *preciso*, are inapplicable here: *precioso* (precious, pretty), *precario* (precarious, dangerous), *precoz* (precocious). Clauses beginning with *"Es preciso . . ."* or *"Es necesario . . ."* are followed by the infinitive if they express a generalization, as is the case in our sentence. If, however, the idea referred to a specific person, we would then be required to use a subjunctive clause rather than simply the infinitive. For example, *"Es presciso que tú comas para vivir."* (It is necessary that you eat in order to live.)

53. **(B)** To make the right choice for this item you need to know the difference between *vestirse* (to get dressed) and *ponerse* (to put on an article of clothing). Since no item of apparel is mentioned, the two forms of *ponerse* cannot be used; we must say, *"Tú te vestiste"* (You got dressed). It could be easy to choose item (A) by mistake because it looks somewhat like several

forms of *vestirse*, but remember that *viste* is the second person singular of the preterit tense of *ver* (to see) and would make little sense here.

54. **(A)** The verb *caber* means "to fit." When we follow it by "*en*," as in our sentence, we mean "to fit into." *Empujar* (to push) and *empacar* (to pack) could be relevant to cars, but they would not be followed by "*en*." Rather, they would require that "*coche*" be a direct object instead of the object of a preposition. In these two cases, we would have to say, "*Todos vamos a empujar el coche*" (We are all going to push the car) or "*Todos vamos a empacar el coche*" (We are all going to pack the car). *Dejar* means "to leave," not in the sense of "to depart," but "to leave behind." It would also not be followed immediately by "*en*" and would require that "*coche*" be a direct object. For example: "*Vamos a dejar el coche aquí*"(We are going to leave the car here).

55. **(C)** The verb *agregar* means "to add," often in the sense of making an additional statement, which, of course, is what we mean in our sentence. Although *sumó* means "he added," it would not apply here because it is used only in a mathematical sense, as in "*Sumó la lista de números*" (He added the list of numbers). Neither *someter* (to subject or force to surrender) nor *encargar* (to entrust or to order goods) would make logical sense in our sentence.

56. **(B)** In our sentence, *Quisiera* is the imperfect subjunctive of the verb *querer*. This form is frequently used instead of *quiero*, for example, to express a courteous statement or request, for it is considered more polite. It is appropriate here because we are dealing with the formal situation in which someone is introducing one person to another. For introductions we use the verb *presentar*, not *introducir*. *Introduce* would not work here anyway because we need an infinitive following *Quisiera*. The *te*, which is attached to *presentar* in (B), is the second person singular direct object pronoun and means "you" (familiar). *Conozco* is also wrong because it is not an infinitive. For us to use *conocer* in the sentence we would have to say "*Quisiera conocer al Profesor Álvarez*" (I would like to know Professor Alvarez). This, however, would not refer to an introduction, but would instead simply state *my* desire to meet Professor Alvarez. In item (D), it is true that we have an infinitive, *saber*, but we cannot use it here, for this verb means "to know facts or information," not "to know or meet a person."

57. **(A)** In our sentence, *cámara* means "room," and *del piso cuarto* signifies "on the fourth floor." It is unlikely that there would be either a hurricane

(*huracán*) or a snow storm (*nevada*) at that location. *Fogata* means "bonfire," the kind we have outdoors at picnics. *Incendio* is a more general term for fire and is used to refer to buildings which are on fire. *Fuego*, a synonym for *incendio*, could also have been used in this case.

58. **(C)** *Propina* means "tip," the kind we leave for a waiter or waitress. The verb *dejar* signifies "to leave behind." One of the most common words for waiter is *camarero* (C). Possible synonyms are *mozo* and *mesero*, which are used in parts of South and Central America. Choice (A) is incorrect; *cenicero* means "ashtray." The word *acero*, in (B), means "steel." In (D), *bombero* is a fireman. We don't normally give him a tip. Notice the word *buenísima* in our sentence. The *-ísimo* ending may be attached to most adjectives to signify "very." Therefore, *buenísima* means "*muy buena*."

59. **(D)** Each of the possible answers is a feminine form of the past participle. When past participles are not preceded by some form of the verb *haber*, they function as adjectives and, therefore, agree in number and gender with the word they modify. In other words, we are looking for an adjective which can logically describe the word *pierna* (leg). The only sensible response here would be *rota* (broken). This is the irregular form of the past participle of the verb *romper*. The other possible answers would make little sense here: *puesta* (put on, placed), *abierta* (open), and *devuelta* (returned or given back) are not good adjectives to describe a leg. In Spanish, if we want to say, "Why is your leg broken?," we do not use the possessive adjective *tu*. Instead, by employing the verb *tener* in the second person singular, we know that we are referring to the subject *tú*. That person has his leg broken. Because of the verb *tener*, we can then use *la* instead of *tu* in front of *pierna*. In Spanish, when the meaning is clear, we use the definite article, rather than possessive adjective, with parts of the body and articles of clothing.

60. **(B)** The verb *apagar* means "to turn off," as with lights, etc. It is used in our sentence in the present perfect tense and in the reflexive form. Here it literally means "All the lights have turned themselves off," i.e., "All the lights have been turned off." Notice how Spanish can avoid the use of the true passive voice by substituting the reflexive form of the verb as long as the doer of the action is not mentioned. In the true passive voice our sentence would read as follows: "*Todas las luces han sido apagadas*." If all of the lights have been turned off, the implication is that we are "in the dark" (*a oscuras*). Choice (A) is not right because it would say that we are reading, which would be unlikely in the absence of light. *Estamos leyendo*

is the present progressive of the verb *leer*. This tense is arrived at by using some present tense form of *estar* and the *–ndo* form of the verb. Other progressive tenses may be created simply by changing the tense of *estar* in this construction. The progressive tenses are used to place *particular emphasis* on the fact that the action is (was, etc.) in progress at a given moment. If it is not necessary to give this special emphasis, then we use the simple tenses (present, imperfect, etc.). Choice (C) is wrong because *a la luz* (in the light) would be contrary to what we expect when the lights are extinguished. *A tiempo* (on time), in item (D), has no relation to the fact that the lights have been turned off.

61. **(B)** To answer this question correctly, it is necessary to pay particular attention to the second clause of our sentence. The word *pero* (but) is very important here. If you used choice (A), *soñé* (I dreamed), the sentence would be illogical because first you fall asleep, and then you dream, but the second clause says that you "failed to sleep." The preterit tense of *poder* in the affirmative form can mean "succeeded or managed to do something." If *poder* is used negatively in the preterit, as in our sentence, it means "failed" to do something. We hope you didn't confuse *soñar* (to dream) with *tener sueño* (to be sleepy). Choice (C), *me desperté* (I awakened), will not work, also because of the word *pero*. Item (D) is illogical. *Me levanté* means "I got up," and should not be confused with *me acosté* (I went to bed), the correct answer. Notice that in (B), (C), and (D) the verbs are reflexive because they all show actions which the subject does to itself.

62. **(B)** *De luna de miel* means "on their honeymoon," which is the only correct answer of the four choices because the first sentence tells us that "Enrique and Angela got married on Saturday." We place the preposition *de* in front of *luna de miel* when it is used with the verbs *ir* (to go) or *estar* (to be). This happens also with other expressions such as *ir de vacaciones* (to go on vacation) and *estar de vacaciones* (to be on vacation). Choice (A) means "to the stars," which is highly improbable. In (C), *miel de abeja* means "honey." In (D), *luna llena* signifies "full moon." Observe that in our sentence the verb *casarse* (to get married) is reflexive. The only time this would not be true is when, for example, a father says "I married off my daughter" (*Casé a mi hija*). Here, not only is the verb not reflexive, but also we must use a personal *a*, which precedes direct objects which refer to specific people. Remember that "to get married to" is *casarse*: *Enrique se casó* con *Angela* (Enrique married Angela).

63. **(D)** *Cuesta trabajo* is a synonym for *es difícil* (it is difficult). In any of the tenses, this expression is used only in the third person singular or third person plural, depending on the subject, which in this case is the infinitive *captar*. The pronoun *me* is an indirect object meaning "to me" or "for me." In other words, "*Me cuesta trabajo . . .*" means "It is difficult for me . . ." *Costar trabajo* follows the pattern of the verb *gustar*, which also is used only in the third person singular or plural and is also preceded by an indirect object pronoun. The verb *captar* means "to get" or "to catch," in the sense of "to hear clearly." The word *letra* here means "the words of a song." Consequently, *canción* (song) is the right response. Since a symphony (*sinfonía*), (A), and a dance (*baile*), (C), do not usually have words, these two choices are wrong. *Telegrama* will not fit in the sentence because it, like many words ending in *–ma, -pa,* and *–ta,* is masculine (*el telegrama, el mapa, el artista*). Also, telegrams are usually read, not heard.

64. **(C)** In this sentence, *me siento* comes from the verb *sentirse* (*ie, i*), which means "to feel." You should not confuse it with *sentarse* (*ie*) which means "to sit down." Remember that the first person singular of the present of these two verbs looks the same: *me siento*. It is only from the context that we can tell which of the two verbs we are dealing with. If the speaker says, "*No me siento bien*," followed by "*tengo un . . . ,*" we must look for an ailment to place in the blank. Consequently, (A), *reloj* (clock), and (D), *uña* (fingernail) are incorrect. Granted, *enfermedad* means "illness," but it will not fit in the sentence because it is feminine and the sentence gives us the masculine indefinite article *un*. Normally, words ending in *–a, -dad, -tad, -tud, -ión,* and *-ie* are feminine. The word *resfriado* means "cold," and fits logically and grammatically in the sentence.

65. **(B)** *Ruido* means "noise." Most people would agree that the sound of a siren tends to bother us. Therefore, we might expect to find some form of *molestar* (to bother or upset) in the answer. The pronoun *me* is a direct object of the verb *molesta* in this case. Choice (A) is wrong because it says the opposite of what we would normally anticipate, *me tranquiliza* (calms me). Choice (C) is wrong because *rojo* means "red" and noise does not have a color. *Me da celos* signifies "makes me jealous." Some form of the verb *dar* is often used in idiomatic expressions to convey the idea of "to make" in the sense of "to cause": *Los perros me dan miedo* (Dogs make me afraid, i.e., frighten me), etc.

Part B

66. **(C)**   *Aprovecharse* is correct. This infinitive along with the previous one, *efectuar*, are both linked to *es posible*. Since there is no change in subject (which would require a subjunctive verb), the infinitive is used. Since (A), (B), and (D) are all conjugated verb forms, they are incorrect.

67. **(A)**   *Avances* is correct. In this context, *avances* means "advances." (B) is a word indicating increase in price or value. (C) is the adjective form meaning "advanced." (D) is the plural adjective meaning "anticipated."

68. **(A)**   *Fondos* is correct. *Fondos* means "funds" (as in monetary). *Fondillos* (B) means the "seat of trousers." (C) means "innkeepers" and (D) means "brochures."

69. **(C)**   *Más de* is correct. In front of numbers, "more than" is expressed with *más de* rather than *más que*. This would make (A) incorrect since it is written with *que* and (B) also, since it is missing the equivalent of "than" completely. (D) uses both *de* and *que*, which is incorrect as well.

70. **(D)**   *Ese* is correct. The masculine singular demonstrative adjective is needed to modify the noun *tiempo*. (A) is neuter, (B) is the feminine adjective, and (C) is accented, which makes it the pronoun form of the demonstrative.

71. **(D)**   *Sea* is correct. In this adverbial clause beginning with the conjunction *aunque*, subjunctive is required since speculation and uncertainty are intimated. (A) is the present indicative, (B) is the infinitive, and (C) is the future tense.

72. **(A)**   *Echar un vistazo* is correct. (A) means "to glance at," which would imply looking at Madrid in the context of this reading. (B), which means "to take a drink," (C), which means "to swear," and (D), which means "to flatter" do not make sense in the context of this sentence.

73. **(C)**   *La de* is correct since it refers to the previously mentioned *biblioteca* and means "that of." It is not necessary to repeat the noun each time; the repetition of the article is all that is necessary. (B) means "she of" and makes no sense. (A) is the masculine article combined with *a*, but the feminine article is required here. (D) is simply the masculine article form.

74. **(D)**   *Millones de* is correct. The word for "million" in Spanish has two forms, singular and plural. Since it precedes a plural number (30), *millones* is required here. This would make choice (A) incorrect. Although choice

(B) is plural, the accent mark makes it misspelled. Choice (C) is also misspelled because there is no "i" in the Spanish ending.

75. **(D)** *Conduciendo* is correct. In translation, one would need the present participle for this verb form. Also, in Spanish, the verb form which commonly follows verbs of motion such as *viajaba* is the present participle. This would eliminate (A) the infinitive, (B) the imperfect tense, and (C) the present subjunctive.

76. **(A)** *Una avería* is correct since it refers to a breakdown of a motor. *Un colapso* (B) refers to a breakdown in one's health. Choice (C) refers to a breakdown in negotiations. (D) refers to an interruption in service.

77. **(A)** *Era* is correct. A form of *ser* is required since *mexicana* indicates nationality. This would eliminate choices (B) and (D) which come from *estar*. The imperfect is preferred since this indicates a characteristic which is ongoing. This would eliminate choice (C) which is the preterit of *ser*.

78. **(B)** *Quien* is correct. Expressing "whom" after a preposition in Spanish requires the use of *quien*. This would eliminate (A) which cannot be used to refer to persons after a preposition. (C) is the relative pronoun which would be used to refer to a feminine antecedent. (D) is accented and would be used as an interrogative.

79. **(D)** *Visitar* is correct. In Spanish, the only correct verb form after a preposition (*después de*) is the infinitive. Therefore, (A) the present participle, (B) the past subjunctive, and (C) the present indicative are incorrect.

80. **(B)** *Desesperadas* is correct. The past participle is being used here as an adjective and must agree with the noun *señas*. Therefore, choices (A) and (C) are incorrect because they have the wrong gender. (D) is the present participle, which is not used as an adjective.

81. **(C)** *Le* is the indirect object pronoun meaning, in this context, "to her." Since the "help" (*ayuda*) is being offered, it is the direct object, eliminating the need for a direct object pronoun such as (A) *lo* or (D) *la*. Choice (B) would be reflexive and the help is not being offered to the person doing the offering, so this would be wrong. *Se* could also be an indirect object pronoun meaning "to her," but only if it were followed by a direct object pronoun *lo, la, los* or *las*.

82. **(A)** *Hubiera* is correct. The subjunctive is required in the noun clause when the main clause states whishing or wanting, emotion, indirect

command, doubt or denial, or is an impersonal expression. The verb in the main clause is *sorprendió* (wondered at) and indicates doubt. The past subjunctive is required to follow the sequence established in the main clause, which is preterit. Therefore, (B) the imperfect, (C) the present subjunctive, and (D) the conditional tense are all incorrect.

83. **(B)** *Buscó* is correct. Because the subject is Marcelo and the action is completed, the third person singular of the preterit is needed. Therefore, (A) preterit (I looked for) and (D) present (I see) are incorrect. Although (C) is the appropriate person and tense, *observó* would not fit the context, since what was being looked for was not observed.

84. **(C)** *Indicio* is correct. The translation "he looked for in the man's glance a sign of hatred, etc." indicates that *indicio*, a sign or indication, is the proper choice. (A) means "item." (B) means "sense." (D) means "sensory." None of these words fit the context.

85. **(D)** *Enemistad* (hatred) is correct. The two nouns preceding this choice, *odio* (hatred) and *enfado* (anger) indicate negative qualities. Choices (A) *amistad* (friendship), (B) *deseo* (desire), and (C) *curiosidad* (curiosity) do not fit in this context.

86. **(B)** *Relaciones* is correct. Within the context of this paragraph and this particular sentence, the word for relationship is most logical. [Marcelo looked for in the man's glance a sign of hatred, anger, or something that would put him on guard that he (Alfredo) was aware of his "relationship" with her.] Therefore, (A) *hijos* (children), (C) *negocios* (business), and (D) *obligaciones* (obligations) are incorrect.

87. **(C)** *Mirada* is correct because the man's (A) height, (B) emotion, and (D) sight do not fit the context of the sentence.

88. **(D)** The subjunctive is required in an adjective clause with a negative antecedent (*nada*). To maintain proper tense sequence, the past subjunctive is needed (*reflejaba* is in the imperfect tense). Therefore, (A) the present subjunctive, (B) the imperfect, and (C) the conditional are all incorrect tenses.

Part C

89. **(D)**   Counting the people mentioned, we find five people were going to Tijuana – the parents (2), the grandmother (1), and the children (2).

90. **(D)**   Sentence 4 says that in Mexico she didn't feel like a foreigner (*no se sentía extranjera*), therefore, she is most likely Mexican.

91. **(B)**   She felt comfortable because they spoke Spanish there, not because she was older (A) or that the city was ugly (D). She bought several things there, so (C) would be incorrect. It says they didn't sell anything there.

92. **(C)**   The story indicates that the grandmother takes the opportunity to buy many things. It does not indicate that she likes to leave Tijuana (A) or hide there (B). She enjoyed being able to speak Spanish, but did not show a desire to speak English (D).

93. **(C)**   The story indicates that there is no doctor available, so he is not likely to be in a large city (A) or a hospital (B). Choice (D) is incorrect since the protagonist is speaking with the hotel manager. It is likely, however, that in a small town (C) there might not be a doctor available.

94. **(B)**   The text indicates the illness as *un retortijón de tripas*. This is a cramping in the "tripe," or intestines, which causes symptoms near the stomach. There is no indication of headache (A), leg pain (C) or sneezing/nose problems (D).

95. **(A)**   Since the person was cured quickly, the homeopath was good at curing (A). He is not the manager of the hotel (C) and, since he is a person, being herbs (B) or a hospital (D) would not make sense.

96. **(C)**   After making the tea, he should drink it (C). It would not make sense to apply tea to the sight of pain (B) or make the tea and do nothing but wait (D). Since the homeopath supplied the herbs (A), the patient would have no need to make them.

97. **(D)**   His health was recovered after drinking the tea. There was no indication that other pain came first (C). There was no doctor, so he did not consult one (A). Although he said that his recovery was a miracle, he did not perform a miracle (B), he simply drank tea.

98. **(A)**   Sentence 1 (A) says that the beaches of Costa Brava are some of the best in the world, but does not indicate anything about those who visit it. All other sentences make reference to people from other countries or that speak other languages visiting the beaches.

99. **(D)**   According to the reading, the Spanish people are naturally *hospitalarios* (hospitable), which is closest in meaning to (D) friendly. They are not stingy (A) or discourteous (B). Being naturally doctors (C) does not make sense.

100. **(B)**   The text lists the nationalities of the majority of the tourists, English, German, French, and Swedish (see sentence numbered 4). Since these are from western European countries, (B) is the correct answer.

101. **(B)**   The engineer couldn't see because it was raining heavily (*llovía a cántaros*). Although it was late at night, the darkness (A) was not the cause of him not seeing, because there was a light on the train, but it couldn't penetrate the heavy rain. The *fuerte ojo* (C) refers to the headlight of the train, which did not cause the difficulty in seeing. The *linterna* (D) did allow him to see when he got out of the train.

102. **(C)**   The entire train is referred to as a *monstruo de hierro* (iron monster). (A) is the engineer, (B) refers to the single headlight and (D) is the engineer's lantern.

103. **(D)**   The last line states that the train will return to the last station (*volverá atrás a la última estación)*. (D) says the same thing with different vocabulary.

104. **(C)**   Since the train was unable to proceed, its progress was impeded. Some passengers got wet, but none drowned (A). Some tracks (*vías*) were washed away, but the train was still on the tracks that were intact. There was no indication of the lights going out (D).

105. **(A)**   Some of the passengers demonstrated their uneasiness by anticipating some kind of disaster (*anticiparan un desastre*). There was no reference to (B) passengers not paying, (C) people getting hungry and eating, or (D) passengers getting off the train.

106. **(B)**   The cyclopic eye (*ojo ciclópico)* is a metaphor for a strong light in front. There were several passengers in different cars, so (D) and (C) are incorrect. There was no mention of broken wheels (A).

107. **(D)**   The passengers that were not asleep were uneasy and worried (*preocupados*). The other choices, (A) dreaming with the angels, (B) walked beside the train, and (C) decided not to move the train, were not indicated.

108. **(D)**   Even though the word *cárcel* (jail) is never mentioned, it is stated that he is *preso* (imprisoned). Although he was speaking to a Christian (*cristiano*) about his impending death (*muerte*), there is nothing to indicate

being in church (B) or in a cemetery (C). He talks about his girlfriend, but there is no indication that he is with her (A).

109. **(A)**   The protagonist states that he does not want to confess (*confesarme*) and goes on to beg for his life. It would seem likely that he is speaking with a priest who was sent to give him the Last Rites before execution. He talks about his family and girlfriend, but they are not with him. There is no indication of a ghost (D) in the reading.

110. **(D)**   The *paredón* is a firing squad, which means that the protagonist is going to be killed. The context of the story shows that he does not want his life to be taken, so even if the word for firing squad were unknown to the reader, it should be understood that it was a method of execution. Sentence 1 (A) simply says that he wants to live and not die, but doesn't indicate that they will kill him. Sentence 2 (B) indicates that they will tell him that death is the door to eternal life (*la muerte es la puerta para la vida eterna*), but does not indicate the manner of death. Sentence 3 (C) says, "If it were a matter of dying in war, that would be different." (*Si fuera cosa de morir en guerra, eso sería diferente.*) It does not indicate the actual manner of dying.

111. **(B)**   He stated that he could handle dying *en guerra* (at war), which would be most like dying on the battlefield. There was no mention of a hospital. (C) His girlfriend (A) and family (C) were only mentioned as reasons he should be spared from death.

112. **(C)**   Sentence 3 talks about finding "an available plank." (*una tabla suelta*) He could not arrive from the island the (A) shipwrecked boat, since it was destroyed (*eminente destrucción*) and carried out to sea (*llevó al mar*). (B) discusses the wave that carried the boat to sea. (D) describes him when he awoke, but the pain he experienced did not take him to the island.

113. **(C)**   He arrived floating on *una tabla suelta* (an available plank.) Since he was not conscious, he could not have been singing (A), swimming (B), or walking (D).

114. **(A)**   Upon awakening, he immediately started looking for other survivors and found that there wasn't anyone there (*buscando otro ser viviente – pero no había nadie*). This led to other fears, but not of traffic (B), sand (C), or the hot sun (D).

115. **(D)**   Questions regarding how he would live, what he would eat, and how he could protect himself indicate that he was most concerned about his physical needs, rather than (A) his family, (B) the weather, or (C) his stained clothing.

116. **(A)** After hearing a loud noise, the shipwreck victim was petrified (*El náufrago quedó petrificado*), or afraid. He was not excited (B), calm (C), or relieved (D).

117. **(C)** (C) means "In truth, the problem of arms has already been solved." This is obviously false, since the entire reading was about the dilemma of disarmament, as shown in the topic and first sentence (*sigue pendiente el dilema del desarme*). (A) means "there is much discord in regard to the matter of disarmament." This is true since the article speaks of the controversy between supporters (*partidarios*) and those who are against disarmament (*los que están en contra del desarme*). (B) is also true; "It is possible that in the future the problem of disarmament will be solved." (D) says that solutions have already been suggested, which is true since the reading stated, "*han surgido propuestas para realizar este sueño*" (proposals have arisen to realize this dream).

118. **(B)** Opponents of disarmament are "suspicious of" (*desconfían de*) the goodwill of the adversary. The same concept is indicated in the reading as "*no es de fiar*" (is not to be trusted). (A) implies that they are from elsewhere, which is not indicated. Choices (C) and (D) have no basis in fact. There is no mention made that those opposed to disarmament are against survival (C) or that they support war (D).

119. **(D)** Those in favor of disarmament want international inspection if it could be carried out (*si podría llevarse a cabo*) by an international organization like the United Nations. An important part of understanding this choice is knowing the idiom *estar por*, which means "to be in favor of." This would then make choice (A) incorrect because *rechazan* means "reject." (B) means that they fear abolishing arms, which is the opposite of being in favor of disarmament. (C) indicates that they have confidence in the enemy, which is not indicated in the reading.

120. **(C)** The potency of bombs is gradually increasing. In the first sentence of the second paragraph there is a reference to "the development of bombs with greater and greater force" (*el desarrollo de bombas de rendimiento cada vez más grande*). Choice (A) indicates a scarcity of proposals, the opposite of what was stated that "proposals have surged" (*han surgido propuestas*). The results are what have been lacking (*escasos han sido los resultados* – literally "few have been the"). This makes (B) also incorrect, as we have not met our goals. There is no mention of the number of enemies increasing (D).

CLEP Spanish Language
Test Transcripts

CLEP SPANISH TRANSCRIPTS

TEST 1

SECTION I

Listening: Rejoinders

Directions: You will hear short conversations or parts of conversations. You will then hear four responses, designated (A), (B), (C), and (D). After you hear the four responses, select the response that most logically continues or completes the conversation. Fill in the corresponding oval on your answer sheet. Neither the answer choices nor the conversations will be printed in your test booklet, so you must listen very carefully. You will have 10 seconds to choose your response before the next conversation begins.

Número 1. **MALE**   ¿Cómo está Ud. Señora Torres?

      FEMALE   (A) Más tarde a las nueve.
                  (B) Bastante cansada, gracias.
                  (C) Mañana temprano.
                  (D) Sí, gracias.

Número 2. **MALE**   ¿Cómo vino Pepe?

      FEMALE   (A) Él come con vino.
                  (B) El vino está delicioso.
                  (C) Vino en avión.
                  (D) Vino en verano.

Número 3. **MALE**   ¿Quién llamó anoche?

      FEMALE   (A) No sé quién llama.
                  (B) Yo te llamo luego.
                  (C) Vienes esta noche.
                  (D) Fue mi hermano Carlos.

Número 4. **FEMALE**   ¿Qué están poniendo dentro del recipiente?

        MALE   (A) Estoy poniendo unas fresas.

                          (B) Está muy mal puesto.

                          (C) Lo están llenando con agua.

                          (D) Estamos trabajando en la cocina.

Número 5. **MALE**   ¿Si sigo esta calle llego a la Casa Presidencial?

     FEMALE   (A) El presidente vive en esa casa.

                          (B) Pues sí, el presidente es un señor hecho y derecho.

                          (C) No señor, conduce al Paseo Colón.

                          (D) No señor, no siga diciendo esas cosas absurdas.

Número 6. **FEMALE**   Mozo, ¿cuánto le debemos?

        MALE   (A) Ahora mismo les ayudo con sus maletas.

                          (B) Deben marcharse en este momento.

                          (C) Enseguida les traigo la cuenta.

                          (D) Enseguida les traigo el menú de los postres.

Número 7. **MALE**   ¿Dónde trabaja tu prima Celeste?

     FEMALE   (A) Es profesora de español.

                          (B) Trabaja de ocho a dos.

                          (C) Es empleada en una escuela.

                          (D) Trabaja muy duro y le gusta mucho lo que hace.

Número 8. **FEMALE**   ¿Por qué compraste tantas manzanas?

        MALE   (A) Las compré en el supermercado ayer.

                          (B) Me gusta la mermelada de naranja.

                          (C) Voy a hacer una tarta deliciosa.

                          (D) Tengo demasiadas manzanas en casa.

Número 9. **MALE**   ¿Dónde se puede comprar cosméticos baratos?

     FEMALE   (A) Las puede encontrar en cualquier tienda.

                          (B) Se los encuentra muy fácil.

                          (C) Se los encuentra en cualquier farmacia o almacén.

                          (D) Se los puede comprar a un buen precio.

Número 10. **FEMALE** ¿Cuándo vamos a salir?

      MALE (A) Fuimos al supermercado ayer.
             (B) Son las cuatro en punto.
             (C) Siempre vamos al cine.
             (D) Saldremos en un momento.

Número 11. **FEMALE** Disculpe, ¿a qué hora sale el tren a Guanajuato?

      MALE (A) A las seis en punto.
             (B) En la estación.
             (C) Hacia el pueblo más cercano.
             (D) Llega temprano.

Número 12. **FEMALE** ¿Quién envió esta carta?

      MALE (A) En el correo.
             (B) En un sobre.
             (C) Mi novia.
             (D) Sin estampillas.

Número 13. **FEMALE** ¿Por qué corrían tan rápido?

      MALE (A) Porque estaban caminando.
             (B) Había un incendio.
             (C) Estaban paralizados de angustia.
             (D) No les gustaba la corrida.

Número 14. **FEMALE** Juan Carlos, ¿me alcanzas ese libro, por favor?

      MALE (A) No puedo, no tengo dinero.
             (B) No puedo, está muy caliente.
             (C) No puedo, está muy alto.
             (D) No puedo, es de física cuántica.

Número 15. **FEMALE** Ponte el suéter que hace mucho frío.

      MALE (A) El verano es muy largo.
             (B) No quiero. Es un día primaveral.
             (C) No lo haré, nieva demasiado.
             (D) Claro, voy a comprarlos.

Número 16. **MALE**   ¿Verdad que Julio es precioso?

           FEMALE   (A) Es después de agosto.
                           (B) Es demasiado caro.
                           (C) Sobre todo su carita.
                           (D) No, pero cuesta mucho.

Número 17. **MALE**   ¿Por qué no te dio la multa?

           FEMALE   (A) No tengo pierna rota.
                             (B) No voy de vacaciones.
                           (C) No me gusta comerla.
                           (D) Lloré y le pedí que me disculpara.

Número 18. **MALE**   ¿No vas a lavarte las manos?

           FEMALE   (A) Claro, pero necesito jabón.
                             (B) No, las manos están muy lejos.
                           (C) Sí, pero no las encuentro.
                           (D) No, no las quiero llevar.

This is the end of Test 1, Section I – Listening.
Continue with Test 1, Listening Section II.

SECTION II

Listening: Dialogues and Narratives

Directions: You will hear a series of dialogues, news reports, narratives, and announcements. Listen carefully, as each selection will only be spoken once. One or more questions with four possible answers are printed in your test booklet. They will not be spoken. After each selection has been read, choose the best answer choice for each question and fill in the corresponding oval on your answer sheet. You will be given 12 seconds to answer each question.

Selección número 1.

MALE:	– Señora, ¿ya salió el vuelo 517 para Bogotá?
FEMALE:	– Sí señor, acaba de partir.
MALE:	– ¡Qué lástima! ¿Y cuándo es el siguiente vuelo? Necesito llegar a Bogotá esta noche.
FEMALE:	– Lo siento mucho, señor, pero no hay vuelos nocturnos a Bogotá. El próximo sale a las cinco y media de la mañana y llega a Bogotá a las ocho.
MALE:	– ¿Hay cupo para uno en este vuelo?
FEMALE:	– Claro, señor. El pasaje es de 495 pesos. Es el vuelo número 914. Debe de llegar por lo menos una hora antes de la partida.
MALE:	– Vale. Muchísimas gracias.

NARRATOR: Ahora contesta las preguntas 19, 20, y 21.

Selección número 2.

FEMALE:	– Oye, Santiago, espérame. ¿Adónde vas con tanta prisa?
MALE:	– Me muero de la sed, Viviana. Después de un examen tan complicado, salgo volando para la cafetería. ¿Y tú?
FEMALE:	– Pues, te acompaño entonces. Yo quiero comer algo.

NARRATOR: Ahora contesta las preguntas 22 y 23.

Selección número 3.

MALE: – Nunca me acuerdo de los presidentes de México durante esa época. ¿Quién reinó primero, Manuel Ávila Camacho o Adolfo Ruíz Cortines?

FEMALE: – Claro que fue Ávila Camacho. Pero entre ellos sirvió de presidente Miguel Alemán Valdés.

MALE: – ¡Así es! Siempre pienso que fue Adolfo López Mateos, pero mi padre me dijo que votó por él cuando ganó en el año 1958. Y seis años después, votó por Gustavo Díaz Ordaz.

FEMALE: – Mi padre no votó por López Mateos. Prefirió el otro candidato popular, pero no me acuerdo de su nombre.

MALE: – Yo tampoco.

NARRATOR: Ahora contesta las preguntas 24, 25, y 26.

Selección número 4.

FEMALE: – Jaime, ¿qué te parecieron esos ensayos de la tarea? ¿Cómo crees que los hiciste?

MALE: – No estoy seguro, Alicia. Estudié con Pedro y Marta, repasé mis apuntes, releí los capítulos enteros, pero no alcancé a contestar todas las preguntas.

FEMALE: – Yo tampoco. No tuvimos suficiente tiempo para terminar, y estoy muy preocupada.

MALE: – ¿No crees que a lo mejor deberíamos ir a ver al profesor para pedirle más tiempo?

FEMALE: – Bueno, vamos a intentarlo, pero me parece que nos dirá que no.

MALE: – De todos modos debemos intentarlo… ¿quién sabe lo que pueda pasar? ¿De acuerdo?

FEMALE: – De acuerdo. Acudamos a sus horas de oficina mañana a las dos.

NARRATOR: Ahora contesta las preguntas 27, 28, y 29.

Selección número 5.

MALE: – ¿Qué le regalamos a Ricardo? ¡Tiene de todo!

FEMALE: – ¿Qué opinas de un autito a control remoto, Quique?

MALE:	–¡Tiene!
FEMALE:	– Pero uno lindo . . .
MALE:	– Tiene unos cuarenta.
FEMALE:	– Oh. Entonces algo de ropa, una camiseta con la cara de alguno de sus artistas preferidos.
MALE:	– Tiene, y todas autografiadas.
FEMALE:	– Oh. Bueno, entonces yo le hago una torta con mis propias manos.
MALE:	– Eso está bien, ¿pero yo qué puedo hacer, Maribel?
FEMALE:	– Lo que quieras, pero no le cantes, por favor.

NARRATOR: Ahora contesta las preguntas 30 y 31.

Selección número 6.

MALE:	– Bueno, hijos, su mamá y yo tenemos mucho que hacer antes de las acaciones. Necesitamos su ayuda en algunas cosas. Primero, es necesario que los dos le traigan a mamá su ropa limpia para que ella pueda poner todo en el equipaje. Mimi, no olvides tu traje de baño este año. Pepe, recuerda que sólo vamos a estar en Costa Rica una semana. No traigas demasiado o mamá va a tener que llamar a dos taxis para llevarnos al hotel cuando lleguemos. Mimi, llama por favor al aeropuerto para ver si todo va bien y vamos a poder salir a tiempo. Yo tengo que usar la computadora para enviarle el número de la tarjeta de crédito a la aerolínea. Me parece que esto es todo.
FEMALE:	– Ay, Papi, ¿todavía no has comprado los boletos? Espero que haya cupos para nosotros.

NARRATOR: Ahora contesta las preguntas 32 hasta 35.

Selección número 7.

MALE:	– Hola, cariño.
FEMALE:	– Hola, tesoro. Acabo de salir de la farmacia con Miguelito. Estaré en casa en media hora.
MALE:	– ¿Qué pasó?
FEMALE:	– El niño tenía fiebre muy alta, tenía dolor de garganta y no podía tragar.

MALE:	– ¡Pobrecito! ¿Y qué hiciste?
FEMALE:	– Llamé al consultorio del Dr. Ponce. La enfermera me dijo que debería llevarlo a ver al médico lo antes posible. Me dio una cita inmediatamente.
MALE:	– ¿Y lo examinó el doctor?
FEMALE:	– Sí, le recetó un antibiótico y me dijo que le diera dos píldoras el primer día, y luego una tres veces al día por diez días. Quiero que Miguelito se quede en cama y beba muchos líquidos hasta que se mejore. También creo que una sopita de pollo liviana le hará bien.
MALE:	– Y ahora, ¿cómo se siente? ¿Todavía tiene fiebre?
FEMALE:	– Igual que antes, el pobrecito. Espero que se mejore pronto.
NARRATOR:	Ahora contesta las preguntas 36, 37 y 38.

Selección número 8.

MALE:	Ushuaia, la capital de Tierra del Fuego, es la ciudad ubicada más al sur que cualquier otra ciudad del mundo. Fundada en 1770 en el sur argentino, fue el primer puesto de evangelización de los indígenas, pero fue devastada por la tuberculosis. Luego fue una parada de aventureros y busca fortunas. Más tarde, su fama se oscureció por la existencia de una prisión para reincidentes levantada a fines del siglo pasado. Pero hoy la prisión es una base naval y la ciudad es un centro de pesca, turismo, y fabricación de tecnología.
NARRATOR:	Ahora contesta las preguntas 39 y 40.

Selección número 9.

FEMALE:	– Me preguntan por qué no quiero vengarme de la gente que realizó esos actos de violencia que nos conmocionaron el fin de semana pasado. Muchos han sido víctimas de estos abusos de violencia callejera a los que no estamos acostumbrados y lo tomamos casi con indiferencia, y esto me asusta. Y cuando por fin despertamos, tenemos sed de sangre. No, no, no. No es que no crea que estos seres violentos no merezcan justicia. Pero creo que no está en nuestras manos hacernos cargo de ejercer su justicia. Yo no he de utilizar violencia

para atacar la violencia. Así habría triunfado una manera de pensar y de vivir que no es la que queremos para nuestra vida. Es la que nos propone esta gente. Utilizar sobre ellos la misma vara sería un error, sería darles el triunfo, cederles el trono, concederles que sus leyes sean las nuestras. Y no lo son. Yo digo que hemos de luchar hombro a hombro contra estos hechos desafortunados, pero con la fuerza de la convicción y la paz.

NARRATOR: Ahora contesta las preguntas 41, 42 y 43.

Selección número 10.

MALE: – ¿Quieres ir a comer conmigo esta noche?

FEMALE: – Sí, me encantaría. ¿Adónde quieres ir?

MALE: – Pues, hay un restaurante vegetariano nuevo que se llama La Esperanza. ¿Qué

FEMALE: piensas?– No sé qué quiero comer. Me gustaría poder beber sangría o una cerveza. ¿Se sirven allí?

MALE: – Creo que no. Tampoco se sirven en El Palenque, pero sí en Sabor de México y Girasol.

FEMALE: – Uno de estos estaría bien, entonces. Después de comer, siempre me gusta algo dulce, como pastel, helado, o churros con chocolate.

MALE: – Entonces, no vamos a Girasol, porque no tienen postres. Debemos ir a Sabor de México porque es famoso por su pastel de tres leches. ¡Es maravilloso!

FEMALE: – Pero allí van muchas familias con sus hijos, ¿no? ¿No prefieres comer en un lugar más privado?

MALE: – No me importa mucho un poco de ruido. Los precios son muy buenos y tienen algo para todos. Podemos pasar tiempo solos después en un café al aire libre y tomar café con leche.

FEMALE: – Está bien. Te encuentro en Sabor de México a las ocho, entonces.

MALE: – Bueno, te veo pronto.

NARRATOR: Ahora contesta las preguntas 44 hasta 48.

Selección número 11.

MALE: Probables lluvias ligeras hacia el anochecer, con descenso de la temperatura. Un aire frío del sur se dirige al noreste con alta velocidad y podría sorprendernos con un inesperado invierno primaveral. La sensación térmica debido al viento hará que registremos una temperatura inédita para esta época del año.

NARRATOR: Ahora contesta las preguntas 49 y 50.

CLEP SPANISH TRANSCRIPTS

TEST 2

SECTION I

Listening: Rejoinders

Directions: You will hear short conversations or parts of conversations. You will then hear four responses, designated (A), (B), (C), and (D). After you hear the four responses, select the response that most logically continues or completes the conversation. Fill in the corresponding oval on your answer sheet. Neither the answer choices nor the conversations will be printed in your test booklet, so you must listen very carefully. You will have 10 seconds to choose your response before the next conversation begins.

Número 1. **FEMALE** Si tuviera dinero, viajaría a las islas griegas.

　　　　MALE (A) Bueno, te veo allá el mes que viene.
　　　　　　　　(B) Bien, ¿me puedes prestar para comprar una televisión, entonces?
　　　　　　　　(C) Mejor, no hay lugar más hermoso en la tierra.
　　　　　　　　(D) Entonces, confórmate con un lugar más cercano.

Número 2. **FEMALE** ¡Me pasé el día en el internet!

　　　　MALE (A) ¿Hacía calor?
　　　　　　　　(B) Con razón no te encontré en tu casa.
　　　　　　　　(C) ¿Encontraste algo interesante?
　　　　　　　　(D) Yo odio el aire libre.

Número 3. **FEMALE** Podremos esquiar si llevan con qué hacerlo.

　　　　MALE (A) Bien, yo llevo las bebidas.
　　　　　　　　(B) Bien, tengo los esquíes de mi hermano.
　　　　　　　　(C) Bien, yo tengo automóvil.
　　　　　　　　(D) Bien, no puedo salir de casa.

Número 4. **FEMALE** Este perro te mordería si tú te me acercaras.

    MALE (A) ¡Ay, que mansito perrito!
        (B) Bueno, entonces abrázame.
        (C) Le daríamos de comer si sucediera.
        (D) ¡Qué bien enseñado está!

Número 5. **FEMALE** Cada vez que me miras no puedo evitar suspirar.

    MALE (A) Tengo pastillas para la acidez estomacal, si quieres.
        (B) Es que tengo una basurilla en el ojo.
        (C) Es que me asombra tu peinado.
        (D) A mí me pasa lo mismo.

Número 6. **MALE** Volveré a hacerlo si me llaman desde España.

    FEMALE (A) Tráeme algo típico de allá.
        (B) Pero el teléfono no funciona, entonces.
        (C) Me parece bien, pues es lo que sabes hacer.
        (D) Siempre es bueno comenzar con algo nuevo.

Número 7. **FEMALE** Gabito, debemos hablar de cierto tema.

    MALE (A) Imposible, soy mudo.
        (B) Mentira, mentira.
        (C) Siempre estoy listo para hablar de música.
        (D) Muy bien, te escucho, comienza tú.

Número 8. **MALE** Si mi jefe no fuera tan insoportable sería incomparable; pero de todas maneras es, sin duda, inolvidable.

    FEMALE (A) Mejor, así no te acuerdas más de él.
        (B) Es bueno saber que no tiene ninguna virtud.
        (C) Es bueno saber que tiene algo bueno a pesar de todo.
        (D) Es una fortuna trabajar en un sitio tan cómodo.

Número 9. **FEMALE** ¿Puede decirme dónde queda el Hotel Miramar?

    MALE (A) Sí, está en la próxima calle.
        (B) Ah no, no pare Ud. enfrente del hotel.
        (C) Sí, soy turista.
        (D) No te puedo acompañar ahora.

Número 10. FEMALE ¿Me puedes hacer un favor, Mario?

      MALE   (A) Sí, te lo agradezco mucho.
                 (B) Lo siento, pero estoy agotado.
                 (C) No hay de qué.
                 (D) Sí, sería una desgracia para mí.

Número 11. FEMALE ¿Podría usted decirme cuánto falta para el evento?

      MALE   (A) Faltan cinco cuadras.
                 (B) Con ocho pesos más, tendrá la cantidad completa.
                 (C) Me lo impide el pecado.
                 (D) Ya debió haber comenzado, señorita.

Número 12. FEMALE Le reservo dos habitaciones de lujo hasta Semana Santa.

      MALE   (A) No, mejor tres semanas.
                 (B) No, por favor, sólo una.
                 (C) Dígame lo que tenga que decir sin reservas.
                 (D) Esa fecha de arribo no me conviene.

Número 13. FEMALE Doctor, me parece, por lo que sospecho vagamente, tener síntomas de una enfermedad muy rara desde enero.

      MALE   (A) Tiene usted un mes de vida.
                 (B) Tome una aspirina y vuelva en un mes.
                 (C) ¿Por qué está tan segura?
                 (D) ¿Podrá Ud. decirme cuáles son esos síntomas?

Número 14. FEMALE Buenas tardes, quisiera papel para escribirle cartas a mi familia. . .

      MALE   (A) ¿Y le dan buenas noticias?
                 (B) ¿Tinta azul o tinta negra?
                 (C) ¿Con rayas o sin rayas?
                 (D) ¿Lo hacen por dinero?

Número 15. FEMALE Luis, el 5 de octubre es tu cumpleaños, ¿verdad?

      MALE   (A) Sí, es mi lugar de nacimiento.
                 (B) Sí, es mi santo.
                 (C) Sí, es mi fecha de nacimiento.
                 (D) Sí, es la fecha de la celebración.

Número 16. **MALE**   Si me comprara una moto, iría a visitar a mis parientes en la costa.

        FEMALE   (A) Adiós, ¡manda postales!
                    (B) ¿No le tienes miedo a las alturas?
                    (C) Yo gastaría ese dinero en otra cosa menos peligrosa.
                    (D) Y si tú vas, mejor.

Número 17. **MALE**   El aire de primavera es más seco que el de otoño, pero en verano el clima es agobiante.

        FEMALE   (A) Entonces el otoño es más húmedo que el verano.
                    (B) Entonces el otoño es más húmedo que la primavera.
                    (C) Entonces el verano es más seco que el otoño.
                    (D) Entonces el invierno es la estación más húmeda.

Número 18. **MALE**   Usted puede cobrar este cheque si firma al dorso del mismo.

        FEMALE   (A) Muy bien, ¿me presta un bolígrafo?
                    (B) ¡De ninguna manera aceptaré estas condiciones!
                    (C) ¡Pero señor, no necesito ese dinero!
                    (D) Muy bien, deme el formulario y lo firmo de inmediato.

This is the end of Test 2, Section I – Listening.
Continue with Test 2, Listening Section II.

SECTION II

Listening: Dialogues and Narratives

Directions: You will hear a series of dialogues, news reports, narratives, and announcements. Listen carefully, as each selection will only be spoken once. One or more questions with four possible answers are printed in your test booklet. They will not be spoken. After each selection has been read, choose the best answer choice for each question and fill in the corresponding oval on your answer sheet. You will be given 12 seconds to answer each question.

Selección número 1.

FEMALE:	– ¿Me prestas tu mapa?
MALE:	– Si tú me prestas tu cámara fotográfica.
FEMALE:	– Caramba, no suelo prestar mi cámara fotográfica, pero puedo prestarte mi radio a cambio de tu mapa.
MALE:	– No quiero tu radio. Quiero sacar fotos y no puedo con una radio.
FEMALE:	– Bueno, ¿me prestas el mapa?
MALE:	– ¿Me prestas la cámara?
FEMALE:	– Bien, te presto la cámara pero además del mapa me tienes que invitar a almorzar.
MALE:	– Muy bien. Encantado. ¿Qué te parece si vamos al cine también?
FEMALE:	– Me parece bien, pero dame el mapa así sabemos dónde ir.
NARRATOR:	Ahora contesta las preguntas 19 y 20.

Selección número 2.

MALE: Los Juegos Panamericanos de este año han sido fantásticos para el equipo venezolano. Todos los atletas se entrenaron fuertemente y jugaron con entusiasmo. En el campeonato contra México, el equipo nacional de fútbol le ganó en los últimos segundos con un gol increíble. Aunque no ganó el equipo de béisbol, recibió la medalla de plata cuando perdió el campeonato contra La República Dominicana. En el boxeo, Pedro Miramontes recibió la medalla de bronce y su gemelo Pablo ganó la de oro. En total, los venezolanos ganaron 80 medallas, 9 de oro, 32 de plata, y 39 de bronce. Debemos aplaudir a estos atletas tan dedicados y estar orgullosos de lo que lograron en nombre de nuestro país.

NARRATOR: Ahora contesta las preguntas 21, 22 y 23.

Selección número 3.

FEMALE: La previsión para mañana en España es que continúa el ambiente muy estable. El viento del noroeste impide que las temperaturas se disparen en el norte. Las máximas diurnas volverán a rondar los 25-30° C en el norte peninsular. Las temperaturas diurnas volverán a superar los 30° C en el interior de Andalucía. Incluso en algunos puntos se pueden alcanzar valores cercanos a 35° C. Esta situación se mantendrá durante la mayor parte de la semana.

NARRATOR: Ahora contesta las preguntas 24 y 25.

Selección número 4.

FEMALE: El cuento Lazarillo de Tormes toma lugar en España en el siglo 15. El autor es anónimo, pero la historia está escrita en primera persona, desde el punto de vista del protagonista, Lazarillo. Se cuenta de forma autobiográfica la vida desde su nacimiento hasta su matrimonio. El cuento se considera una de las primeras del género picaresco porque nos habla el personaje del pícaro, o sea persona que vive por sus mañas, engañando a la gente para vivir. Durante el cuento, Lazarillo vive como sirviente a una serie de amos. Algunos le tratan mal, otros no tan horriblemente, pero Lazarillo aprende algo de cada amo que le sirve bien en la vida. El tono de su historia es realista, moralizante, y bastante irónico. A través del cuento, el autor muestra los vicios y actitudes hipócritas de los religiosos y políticos de la época de la Inquisición en España. A lo mejor es por eso que el autor queda anónimo.

NARRATOR: Ahora contesta las preguntas 26, 27 y 28.

Selección número 5.

FEMALE: Atención pasajeros del vuelo 595 a El Paso. Vamos a salir con un retraso de casi 30 minutos para esperar al piloto que llega retrasado desde Cancún. Favor de escuchar todos los anuncios para no perder su vuelo. Otros anuncios – los vuelos 610 desde Michoacán y 430 desde San Miguel van a llegar a tiempo. Desafortunadamente, el vuelo 560 con servicio a San Luis Potosí no va a poder salir hoy por problemas mecánicos. Los pasajeros de este vuelo deben ir al contador de la aerolínea para hablar con un agente.

NARRATOR: Ahora contesta las preguntas 29, 30, y 31.

Selección número 6.

MALE: – Quisiera poner un aviso en su diario.

FEMALE: – ¿En qué rubro?

MALE: – Ventas o Canjes.

FEMALE: – ¿Qué ofrece?

MALE: – Vendo o cajeo una bicicleta de cinco velocidades, negra, con todos los accesorios impecables.

FEMALE: – ¿Y qué querría Ud. a cambio?

MALE: – 100 pesos o bien, podría cambiarla por muchas cosas, veamos, un televisor mediano, clases de natación, ropa, discos compactos si son de músicos que me gusten, libros interesantes, -pero muchos-, ehhhhh.

FEMALE: – Este aviso le va a costar caro.

MALE: – Oh, perdone usted. Ponga que canjeo por cosas que me interesen.

FEMALE: – Bien, ¿le interesa un cachorro de doberman?

MALE: – ¿Cómo dice?

FEMALE: – Sí, me interesa a mí su bicicleta y mi perra tuvo cachorros. Son de pura raza.

MALE: – Me interesa, sí. Entonces, no ponga el aviso. ¿Cuándo puedo ir a ver al cachorrito?

NARRATOR: Ahora contesta las preguntas 32 hasta 35.

Selección número 7.

MALE: Para hacer una tortilla española, primero hay que freír cuatro patatas y una cebolla (en pedazos) en aceite. Cuando estén cocinadas completamente, mézclalas con cuatro huevos revueltos (crudos) y un poco de sal. Regresa la mezcla al sartén y fría unos 5 minutos. Pon un plato sobre el sartén y revuélvelo todo para que la tortilla esté en el plato. Desliza la tortilla otra vez al sartén para freír el otro lado. Fríe hasta que los dos lados estén dorados. Sirve caliente o a temperatura ambiente. ¡Buen provecho!

NARRATOR: Ahora contesta las preguntas 36, 37, y 38.

Selección número 8.

CHILD: – ¿Qué es esto?

MAN: – Es una cabra. Produce leche para nosotros y se puede comer su carne. A las cabras les encanta comer todo Mira, ¡está tratando de comer mi camisa!

CHILD: – ¿Esto es una cabra también?

MAN: – No, es una oveja. La afeitamos para hacer lana para las telas y la ropa. Su carne es deliciosa asada a la parrilla.

CHILD: – Y este animal grande, ¿qué es?

MAN: – Es una vaca. Su leche es la más común que compramos para beber. De la vaca viene el bistec y la hamburguesa. Mira tus tenis – el cuero de ellos es de la piel de vacas.

CHILD: – ¿Se come aquel animal también?

MAN: – No, ése es un caballo. ¡¡Los caballos se montan, pero no se comen!!

NARRATOR: Ahora contesta las preguntas 39 hasta 43.

Selección número 9.

MALE: Esta semana en el Corte Inglés ofrecemos una gran venta en cada sección de la tienda. Todas las camisas para hombres se descuentan por 50%. Y para las mujeres – ¡compra dos pares de zapatos, pero paga sólo uno! Para los adolescentes, ahorra diez euros para cada treinta en compras. Los conjuntos para niños están todos en liquidación también. ¡Ven hoy y compra algo para todos!

NARRATOR: Ahora contesta las preguntas 44 hasta 47.

Selección número 10.

MALE: – Bueno.

FEMALE: – ¿Está María Ramos, por favor?

MALE: – ¿De parte de quién?

FEMALE: – Yo soy Marta González. La llamo desde las oficinas de los abogados Martínez y Solís.

MALE: – Un momento, por favor. Pues, lo siento, pero acaba de salir. Soy su hijo. ¿Le puedo dar un mensaje?

FEMALE: – Claro que sí, gracias. La llamo porque se solicitó la puesta de secretaria legal con nosotros. Me gustaría hacer una cita con ella para una entrevista. Me puede volver a llamar al 555-9452 lo más pronto posible. Estaré en la oficina hasta las cinco y media hoy.

MALE: – Muchísimas gracias. Le daré el mensaje en seguida cuando regresa.

FEMALE: – Gracias, adiós.

NARRATOR: Ahora contesta las preguntas 48, 49, y 50.

PRACTICE TEST 1

Answer Sheet

1. Ⓐ Ⓑ Ⓒ Ⓓ	27. Ⓐ Ⓑ Ⓒ Ⓓ	53. Ⓐ Ⓑ Ⓒ Ⓓ
2. Ⓐ Ⓑ Ⓒ Ⓓ	28. Ⓐ Ⓑ Ⓒ Ⓓ	54. Ⓐ Ⓑ Ⓒ Ⓓ
3. Ⓐ Ⓑ Ⓒ Ⓓ	29. Ⓐ Ⓑ Ⓒ Ⓓ	55. Ⓐ Ⓑ Ⓒ Ⓓ
4. Ⓐ Ⓑ Ⓒ Ⓓ	30. Ⓐ Ⓑ Ⓒ Ⓓ	56. Ⓐ Ⓑ Ⓒ Ⓓ
5. Ⓐ Ⓑ Ⓒ Ⓓ	31. Ⓐ Ⓑ Ⓒ Ⓓ	57. Ⓐ Ⓑ Ⓒ Ⓓ
6. Ⓐ Ⓑ Ⓒ Ⓓ	32. Ⓐ Ⓑ Ⓒ Ⓓ	58. Ⓐ Ⓑ Ⓒ Ⓓ
7. Ⓐ Ⓑ Ⓒ Ⓓ	33. Ⓐ Ⓑ Ⓒ Ⓓ	59. Ⓐ Ⓑ Ⓒ Ⓓ
8. Ⓐ Ⓑ Ⓒ Ⓓ	34. Ⓐ Ⓑ Ⓒ Ⓓ	60. Ⓐ Ⓑ Ⓒ Ⓓ
9. Ⓐ Ⓑ Ⓒ Ⓓ	35. Ⓐ Ⓑ Ⓒ Ⓓ	61. Ⓐ Ⓑ Ⓒ Ⓓ
10. Ⓐ Ⓑ Ⓒ Ⓓ	36. Ⓐ Ⓑ Ⓒ Ⓓ	62. Ⓐ Ⓑ Ⓒ Ⓓ
11. Ⓐ Ⓑ Ⓒ Ⓓ	37. Ⓐ Ⓑ Ⓒ Ⓓ	63. Ⓐ Ⓑ Ⓒ Ⓓ
12. Ⓐ Ⓑ Ⓒ Ⓓ	38. Ⓐ Ⓑ Ⓒ Ⓓ	64. Ⓐ Ⓑ Ⓒ Ⓓ
13. Ⓐ Ⓑ Ⓒ Ⓓ	39. Ⓐ Ⓑ Ⓒ Ⓓ	65. Ⓐ Ⓑ Ⓒ Ⓓ
14. Ⓐ Ⓑ Ⓒ Ⓓ	40. Ⓐ Ⓑ Ⓒ Ⓓ	66. Ⓐ Ⓑ Ⓒ Ⓓ
15. Ⓐ Ⓑ Ⓒ Ⓓ	41. Ⓐ Ⓑ Ⓒ Ⓓ	67. Ⓐ Ⓑ Ⓒ Ⓓ
16. Ⓐ Ⓑ Ⓒ Ⓓ	42. Ⓐ Ⓑ Ⓒ Ⓓ	68. Ⓐ Ⓑ Ⓒ Ⓓ
17. Ⓐ Ⓑ Ⓒ Ⓓ	43. Ⓐ Ⓑ Ⓒ Ⓓ	69. Ⓐ Ⓑ Ⓒ Ⓓ
18. Ⓐ Ⓑ Ⓒ Ⓓ	44. Ⓐ Ⓑ Ⓒ Ⓓ	70. Ⓐ Ⓑ Ⓒ Ⓓ
19. Ⓐ Ⓑ Ⓒ Ⓓ	45. Ⓐ Ⓑ Ⓒ Ⓓ	71. Ⓐ Ⓑ Ⓒ Ⓓ
20. Ⓐ Ⓑ Ⓒ Ⓓ	46. Ⓐ Ⓑ Ⓒ Ⓓ	72. Ⓐ Ⓑ Ⓒ Ⓓ
21. Ⓐ Ⓑ Ⓒ Ⓓ	47. Ⓐ Ⓑ Ⓒ Ⓓ	73. Ⓐ Ⓑ Ⓒ Ⓓ
22. Ⓐ Ⓑ Ⓒ Ⓓ	48. Ⓐ Ⓑ Ⓒ Ⓓ	74. Ⓐ Ⓑ Ⓒ Ⓓ
23. Ⓐ Ⓑ Ⓒ Ⓓ	49. Ⓐ Ⓑ Ⓒ Ⓓ	75. Ⓐ Ⓑ Ⓒ Ⓓ
24. Ⓐ Ⓑ Ⓒ Ⓓ	50. Ⓐ Ⓑ Ⓒ Ⓓ	76. Ⓐ Ⓑ Ⓒ Ⓓ
25. Ⓐ Ⓑ Ⓒ Ⓓ	51. Ⓐ Ⓑ Ⓒ Ⓓ	77. Ⓐ Ⓑ Ⓒ Ⓓ
26. Ⓐ Ⓑ Ⓒ Ⓓ	52. Ⓐ Ⓑ Ⓒ Ⓓ	78. Ⓐ Ⓑ Ⓒ Ⓓ

(Continued)

PRACTICE TEST 1

Answer Sheet

79. Ⓐ Ⓑ Ⓒ Ⓓ	93. Ⓐ Ⓑ Ⓒ Ⓓ	107. Ⓐ Ⓑ Ⓒ Ⓓ
80. Ⓐ Ⓑ Ⓒ Ⓓ	94. Ⓐ Ⓑ Ⓒ Ⓓ	108. Ⓐ Ⓑ Ⓒ Ⓓ
81. Ⓐ Ⓑ Ⓒ Ⓓ	95. Ⓐ Ⓑ Ⓒ Ⓓ	109. Ⓐ Ⓑ Ⓒ Ⓓ
82. Ⓐ Ⓑ Ⓒ Ⓓ	96. Ⓐ Ⓑ Ⓒ Ⓓ	110. Ⓐ Ⓑ Ⓒ Ⓓ
83. Ⓐ Ⓑ Ⓒ Ⓓ	97. Ⓐ Ⓑ Ⓒ Ⓓ	111. Ⓐ Ⓑ Ⓒ Ⓓ
84. Ⓐ Ⓑ Ⓒ Ⓓ	98. Ⓐ Ⓑ Ⓒ Ⓓ	112. Ⓐ Ⓑ Ⓒ Ⓓ
85. Ⓐ Ⓑ Ⓒ Ⓓ	99. Ⓐ Ⓑ Ⓒ Ⓓ	113. Ⓐ Ⓑ Ⓒ Ⓓ
86. Ⓐ Ⓑ Ⓒ Ⓓ	100. Ⓐ Ⓑ Ⓒ Ⓓ	114. Ⓐ Ⓑ Ⓒ Ⓓ
87. Ⓐ Ⓑ Ⓒ Ⓓ	101. Ⓐ Ⓑ Ⓒ Ⓓ	115. Ⓐ Ⓑ Ⓒ Ⓓ
88. Ⓐ Ⓑ Ⓒ Ⓓ	102. Ⓐ Ⓑ Ⓒ Ⓓ	116. Ⓐ Ⓑ Ⓒ Ⓓ
89. Ⓐ Ⓑ Ⓒ Ⓓ	103. Ⓐ Ⓑ Ⓒ Ⓓ	117. Ⓐ Ⓑ Ⓒ Ⓓ
90. Ⓐ Ⓑ Ⓒ Ⓓ	104. Ⓐ Ⓑ Ⓒ Ⓓ	118. Ⓐ Ⓑ Ⓒ Ⓓ
91. Ⓐ Ⓑ Ⓒ Ⓓ	105. Ⓐ Ⓑ Ⓒ Ⓓ	119. Ⓐ Ⓑ Ⓒ Ⓓ
92. Ⓐ Ⓑ Ⓒ Ⓓ	106. Ⓐ Ⓑ Ⓒ Ⓓ	120. Ⓐ Ⓑ Ⓒ Ⓓ

PRACTICE TEST 2

Answer Sheet

1. Ⓐ Ⓑ Ⓒ Ⓓ	27. Ⓐ Ⓑ Ⓒ Ⓓ	53. Ⓐ Ⓑ Ⓒ Ⓓ
2. Ⓐ Ⓑ Ⓒ Ⓓ	28. Ⓐ Ⓑ Ⓒ Ⓓ	54. Ⓐ Ⓑ Ⓒ Ⓓ
3. Ⓐ Ⓑ Ⓒ Ⓓ	29. Ⓐ Ⓑ Ⓒ Ⓓ	55. Ⓐ Ⓑ Ⓒ Ⓓ
4. Ⓐ Ⓑ Ⓒ Ⓓ	30. Ⓐ Ⓑ Ⓒ Ⓓ	56. Ⓐ Ⓑ Ⓒ Ⓓ
5. Ⓐ Ⓑ Ⓒ Ⓓ	31. Ⓐ Ⓑ Ⓒ Ⓓ	57. Ⓐ Ⓑ Ⓒ Ⓓ
6. Ⓐ Ⓑ Ⓒ Ⓓ	32. Ⓐ Ⓑ Ⓒ Ⓓ	58. Ⓐ Ⓑ Ⓒ Ⓓ
7. Ⓐ Ⓑ Ⓒ Ⓓ	33. Ⓐ Ⓑ Ⓒ Ⓓ	59. Ⓐ Ⓑ Ⓒ Ⓓ
8. Ⓐ Ⓑ Ⓒ Ⓓ	34. Ⓐ Ⓑ Ⓒ Ⓓ	60. Ⓐ Ⓑ Ⓒ Ⓓ
9. Ⓐ Ⓑ Ⓒ Ⓓ	35. Ⓐ Ⓑ Ⓒ Ⓓ	61. Ⓐ Ⓑ Ⓒ Ⓓ
10. Ⓐ Ⓑ Ⓒ Ⓓ	36. Ⓐ Ⓑ Ⓒ Ⓓ	62. Ⓐ Ⓑ Ⓒ Ⓓ
11. Ⓐ Ⓑ Ⓒ Ⓓ	37. Ⓐ Ⓑ Ⓒ Ⓓ	63. Ⓐ Ⓑ Ⓒ Ⓓ
12. Ⓐ Ⓑ Ⓒ Ⓓ	38. Ⓐ Ⓑ Ⓒ Ⓓ	64. Ⓐ Ⓑ Ⓒ Ⓓ
13. Ⓐ Ⓑ Ⓒ Ⓓ	39. Ⓐ Ⓑ Ⓒ Ⓓ	65. Ⓐ Ⓑ Ⓒ Ⓓ
14. Ⓐ Ⓑ Ⓒ Ⓓ	40. Ⓐ Ⓑ Ⓒ Ⓓ	66. Ⓐ Ⓑ Ⓒ Ⓓ
15. Ⓐ Ⓑ Ⓒ Ⓓ	41. Ⓐ Ⓑ Ⓒ Ⓓ	67. Ⓐ Ⓑ Ⓒ Ⓓ
16. Ⓐ Ⓑ Ⓒ Ⓓ	42. Ⓐ Ⓑ Ⓒ Ⓓ	68. Ⓐ Ⓑ Ⓒ Ⓓ
17. Ⓐ Ⓑ Ⓒ Ⓓ	43. Ⓐ Ⓑ Ⓒ Ⓓ	69. Ⓐ Ⓑ Ⓒ Ⓓ
18. Ⓐ Ⓑ Ⓒ Ⓓ	44. Ⓐ Ⓑ Ⓒ Ⓓ	70. Ⓐ Ⓑ Ⓒ Ⓓ
19. Ⓐ Ⓑ Ⓒ Ⓓ	45. Ⓐ Ⓑ Ⓒ Ⓓ	71. Ⓐ Ⓑ Ⓒ Ⓓ
20. Ⓐ Ⓑ Ⓒ Ⓓ	46. Ⓐ Ⓑ Ⓒ Ⓓ	72. Ⓐ Ⓑ Ⓒ Ⓓ
21. Ⓐ Ⓑ Ⓒ Ⓓ	47. Ⓐ Ⓑ Ⓒ Ⓓ	73. Ⓐ Ⓑ Ⓒ Ⓓ
22. Ⓐ Ⓑ Ⓒ Ⓓ	48. Ⓐ Ⓑ Ⓒ Ⓓ	74. Ⓐ Ⓑ Ⓒ Ⓓ
23. Ⓐ Ⓑ Ⓒ Ⓓ	49. Ⓐ Ⓑ Ⓒ Ⓓ	75. Ⓐ Ⓑ Ⓒ Ⓓ
24. Ⓐ Ⓑ Ⓒ Ⓓ	50. Ⓐ Ⓑ Ⓒ Ⓓ	76. Ⓐ Ⓑ Ⓒ Ⓓ
25. Ⓐ Ⓑ Ⓒ Ⓓ	51. Ⓐ Ⓑ Ⓒ Ⓓ	77. Ⓐ Ⓑ Ⓒ Ⓓ
26. Ⓐ Ⓑ Ⓒ Ⓓ	52. Ⓐ Ⓑ Ⓒ Ⓓ	78. Ⓐ Ⓑ Ⓒ Ⓓ

(Continued)

PRACTICE TEST 2

Answer Sheet

79. Ⓐ Ⓑ Ⓒ Ⓓ	93. Ⓐ Ⓑ Ⓒ Ⓓ	107. Ⓐ Ⓑ Ⓒ Ⓓ
80. Ⓐ Ⓑ Ⓒ Ⓓ	94. Ⓐ Ⓑ Ⓒ Ⓓ	108. Ⓐ Ⓑ Ⓒ Ⓓ
81. Ⓐ Ⓑ Ⓒ Ⓓ	95. Ⓐ Ⓑ Ⓒ Ⓓ	109. Ⓐ Ⓑ Ⓒ Ⓓ
82. Ⓐ Ⓑ Ⓒ Ⓓ	96. Ⓐ Ⓑ Ⓒ Ⓓ	110. Ⓐ Ⓑ Ⓒ Ⓓ
83. Ⓐ Ⓑ Ⓒ Ⓓ	97. Ⓐ Ⓑ Ⓒ Ⓓ	111. Ⓐ Ⓑ Ⓒ Ⓓ
84. Ⓐ Ⓑ Ⓒ Ⓓ	98. Ⓐ Ⓑ Ⓒ Ⓓ	112. Ⓐ Ⓑ Ⓒ Ⓓ
85. Ⓐ Ⓑ Ⓒ Ⓓ	99. Ⓐ Ⓑ Ⓒ Ⓓ	113. Ⓐ Ⓑ Ⓒ Ⓓ
86. Ⓐ Ⓑ Ⓒ Ⓓ	100. Ⓐ Ⓑ Ⓒ Ⓓ	114. Ⓐ Ⓑ Ⓒ Ⓓ
87. Ⓐ Ⓑ Ⓒ Ⓓ	101. Ⓐ Ⓑ Ⓒ Ⓓ	115. Ⓐ Ⓑ Ⓒ Ⓓ
88. Ⓐ Ⓑ Ⓒ Ⓓ	102. Ⓐ Ⓑ Ⓒ Ⓓ	116. Ⓐ Ⓑ Ⓒ Ⓓ
89. Ⓐ Ⓑ Ⓒ Ⓓ	103. Ⓐ Ⓑ Ⓒ Ⓓ	117. Ⓐ Ⓑ Ⓒ Ⓓ
90. Ⓐ Ⓑ Ⓒ Ⓓ	104. Ⓐ Ⓑ Ⓒ Ⓓ	118. Ⓐ Ⓑ Ⓒ Ⓓ
91. Ⓐ Ⓑ Ⓒ Ⓓ	105. Ⓐ Ⓑ Ⓒ Ⓓ	119. Ⓐ Ⓑ Ⓒ Ⓓ
92. Ⓐ Ⓑ Ⓒ Ⓓ	106. Ⓐ Ⓑ Ⓒ Ⓓ	120. Ⓐ Ⓑ Ⓒ Ⓓ

Notes

Notes

Notes

Notes